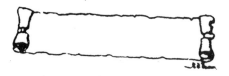

SHE SAID *WHAT?*

SHE SAID *WHAT?*

Interviews with
Women Newspaper Columnists

MARIA BRADEN

THE UNIVERSITY PRESS OF KENTUCKY

Copyright © 1993 by Maria Braden

Published by The University Press of Kentucky

Scholarly publisher for the Commonwealth,
serving Bellarmine College, Berea College, Centre
College of Kentucky, Eastern Kentucky University,
The Filson Club, Georgetown College, Kentucky
Historical Society, Kentucky State University,
Morehead State University, Murray State University,
Northern Kentucky University, Transylvania University,
University of Kentucky, University of Louisville,
and Western Kentucky University.

Editorial and Sales Offices: Lexington, Kentucky 40508-4008

Library of Congress Cataloging-in-Publication Data

Braden, Maria, 1946-
    She said what? : interviews with women newspaper columnists /
Maria Braden.
        p.   cm.
    Includes bibliographical references.
    ISBN 0-8131-1819-0 (alk. paper)
    1. Women journalists—United States—Interviews. 2. Journalism—
United States—History. 3. Women—United States—History.
I. Title.
PN4872.B73   1993
070′.92′273—dc20   92-36460

This book is printed on recycled acid-free paper meeting
the requirements of the American National Standard
for Permanence of Paper for Printed Library Materials.

CONTENTS

To MIA and JOE

PREFACE

When I told Anna Quindlen I was writing a book about women syndicated columnists, she laughed. "All three of us?" she asked. "That's going to be a pretty short book." There's truth in Quindlen's facetious response. Historically, newspapers have tended to represent male points of view. Even today, when more women are writing columns than ever before, Quindlen is the only regular woman columnist on the op-ed page of the *New York Times,* one of the nation's most influential newspapers.

Women columnists traditionally wrote about home and family concerns, and their writing was relegated to the women's pages. About 20 years ago, as the women's movement took hold, women's sections were transformed, and traditional limitations on women's writing began to dissolve. Women now write about politics, government, finance, health and/or international affairs in addition to family matters and personal concerns. Some women columnists have stretched the boundaries of the form by creating columns that combine personal and political issues. The women represented in these pages are vastly different in background, voice, style, and subject matter.

Because I teach journalism at a large state university, I regularly encounter students who tell me they'd like to be columnists. They're not interested in spending time learning how to report and write news; they want to be free to express their opinions in their writing. I respond that reporting and newswriting skills underpin column writing, but they figure I'm paid to tell them that. So I asked successful women columnists to tell their own stories. I talked to them about how they got their first shot at writing a column, where they get the nerve to tell the world what they think, how they generate ideas, and what it's like to write a column over and over again on deadline. In order to focus the book, I decided to limit it to a cross-section of nationally syndicated or nationally distributed columnists, which necessitated leaving out some wonderful local and regional columnists. I did profile two local columnists so that the work of African-American women would be represented.

I want to thank the women included in this collection for sandwiching interviews into their busy schedules. I am grateful for their time, their energy, and their candid answers to my questions. Some invited me into their homes, while others met me in their offices or at private clubs or restaurants. Erma Bombeck deserves special thanks for entrusting me with her life and holding the tape recorder when time constraints required us to do part of the interview in a moving car.

I also want to thank the columnists' assistants who helped arrange meetings and secure copies of the columns reprinted in this book: Norma Born, Bombeck's assistant; Celia Lees-Lowe for Ellen Goodman; Liz Faulk for Molly Ivins; Tina Toll for Mary McGrory; Elizabeth Cohen for Anna Quindlen; and Lynn Kane for Jane Bryant Quinn. Thanks also to Vince Davis, director of the University of Kentucky Patterson School of Diplomacy; Carl West, editor of the *Frankfort* (Kentucky) *State Journal*; and Cindy Williams of United Media for their help in arranging interviews.

Editors at newspapers around the country offered suggestions on whom to include and gave me a sense of what these women's voices mean to the national dialogue. I am grateful to them and regret that I could not include all the columnists whose work they praised. Some were regional or local favorites and were not included because they were not nationally distributed. In some cases, a better known columnist writing on the same general topic was chosen.

My thanks to David Hendin at Pharos Books, who read part of this manuscript in its early stages; to my parents, Lachy and Bill Braden, for their support and encouragement; to Scoobie Ryan and Lynne Anderson and the other friends who said the right things at the right times; and to Pat Matthews, whose humor and common sense got me back on track so many times. Thanks also to my friends and teachers, James Baker Hall and Medford Moreland, who nourished my spirit throughout this endeavor and freed me to write. And thanks to my family for their patience and understanding.

INTRODUCTION

Dorothy Thompson strode into Madison Square Garden on the evening of February 20, 1939, where thousands of people had gathered to oppose American military involvement in European problems. She took a seat in the press section at the front of the hall and listened as a speaker accused the Jews of trying to drag America into the war. Then Thompson, a passionate opponent of fascism, did something that stopped the show: She laughed, a loud whoop of derisive laughter. It caused an uproar. Amid angry cries of "Throw her out," Thompson left under police escort—but not before she had made her point. The woman who called herself a "warrior of the spirit" had a singular weapon with which to attack Hitler's regime— her syndicated newspaper column. As the Madison Square Garden story illustrates so well, Thompson's column empowered her to challenge Nazi supporters on their own turf.

Writing a column has long been one of the most coveted assignments in print journalism. Columnists enjoy fame, independence, and a special relationship with readers. Frequently they are given the kinds of perks enjoyed by management, such as a private office and a secretary. In a field where objectivity is akin to the Holy Grail, newspaper columnists are free to express opinion. Unfettered by the need to be objective or fair, columnists can be scathing in their criticism, unabashed in their praise, funny or poignant, arrogant or intensely personal. In fact, columnists earn their followings by the very boldness of their remarks, by carving out a niche for their opinions.

Reporters must suffer the tyranny of editors, but columnists have a free hand. Reporters know their copy inevitably will be trimmed to fit a changing news hole, but columnists write to a predetermined length. Reporters must fight to preserve the integrity of their writing, but columnists are spared heavy editing because their styles are considered unique.

A newspaper column is like an essay—free to explore any topic. But some essayists speak of columns with disdain; Wilfred Sheed, for one, has called columns "the fast food of literature." They do, however, tend to attract large and devoted followings. Columnists are the celebrities of the newspaper world. Because columns are featured in the same place in a newspaper, usually with a drawing or picture of the author alongside the name, columnists have a visibility unknown to other print journalists.

Syndicated columnists enjoy even wider recognition. Their words are distributed nationally and reach hundreds of thousands, sometimes millions, of readers. In addition to commanding a regular forum in newspapers, syndicated columnists travel and lecture extensively. Many are panelists on current affairs talk shows; some are regulars on prime-time network news programs. Collections of their columns and other works, including fiction, generally sell well. Many regularly hit the best-seller lists.

"In one small way, the lowly columnist is like an artist," political columnist George Will has written. "What distinguishes a good artist is a way of seeing. What made Van Gogh a genius was his distinctive way of seeing sunflowers. What distinguishes a valuable columnist is a distinctive way of seeing the social landscape. It is an ability to see what everybody sees, but not in quite the way that everybody sees it."

Newspaper columns have been an American institution since Colonial days, but for two centuries most of the pundits have been male. In revolutionary times, newspapers were primarily opinion sheets, and writers such as Benjamin Franklin, Thomas Paine, and James Madison used the column as a tool with which to mold and define the politics and culture of the country. By the beginning of the nineteenth century, more than 360 newspapers were being published in this country; they provided a forum for political commentary and an outlet for humor writing. Some of the great American writers of the 1800s, including Walt Whitman, Mark Twain, Ambrose Bierce, and Joel Chandler Harris, used the newspaper column as a way of reaching mass audiences.

There have always been women in the newspaper business, as printers in colonial times, then as publishers and reporters during the nineteenth century. Because there were so few women, their names stand out in the history of journalism. By contrast, women columnists wrote mainly about home and hearth, gardening, gossip, and other topics society deemed acceptable for women, and their names have been forgotten.

The first female columnist to break through those boundaries was Fanny Fern, a nineteenth-century novelist who wrote satirical columns on literary, political, and social issues. Fern, who was born in 1811 as Sarah Payson in Portland, Maine, commented on such issues as women's rights, marriage, prostitution, and prison conditions, and wrote about the Civil War. Fern was in many ways out of place in nineteenth-century America, a time when women were urged to be gentle, "feminine," and submissive, according to Fern's biographer, Joyce Warren. Although critics have dismissed Fern as a sentimental moralist—"the grandmother of all sob sisters"—Warren says that criticism is off base. Fern's traditional sentimental pieces may have been what gave her the respectable reputation she needed in order to publish other, sharply satirical columns, Warren contends. Fern was paid $100 per column when she began writing for the *New York Ledger* in 1856 and was the highest paid newspaper writer of her time. She died in 1872 after writing a regular column for sixteen years.

But Fern was an exception. The newspaper column was becoming an entrenched part of American culture, but women's voices were still confined to the women's pages. As Elizabeth Janeway has written, at the turn of the century, "women were kept in place by the continual suggestion that women weren't worth arguing with."

By the 1920s, the column was "the most sophisticated of the minor arts in America," wrote the distinguished critic Gilbert Seldes. Column writing was "a decent art, except for occasional lapses into the usual journalistic disrespect for privacy," he added. Seldes was writing about an era when some of the great columnists used humor to drive home their points. Writers such as H.L. Mencken, Will Rogers, and Heywood Broun were among those who helped popularize the form.

The 1920s also saw the debut of a special page for commentary, called the "op-ed page" for its placement opposite the editorial page. The idea for the op-ed page is generally credited to Herbert Bayard Swope, editor of the *New York Evening World*, who recognized the value of opinion in hooking and retaining readers. Today the op-ed page is a fixture at most American newspapers, providing a highly visible showcase for opinion writers. But despite the increasing popularity of newspaper columns, women continued to write columns mainly for the women's pages of newspapers well into the twentieth century.

The exceptions are notable. In the 1930s and 40s, some syndicated women columnists became so popular that their names were synonymous with what they wrote. Hedda Hopper and Louella Parsons, for example, were the acknowledged queens of Hollywood gossip, claiming a combined readership of some seventy-five million. They were so well known that even today most people can identify them by their first names alone. The story is told that Hedda would point to her Beverly Hills home and gleefully say, "There's the house that fear built."

Emily Post was the doyenne of good behavior, starting a column on etiquette after the huge success of her encyclopedic *Etiquette: The Blue Book of Social Usage*. She debunked contrived mannerisms that pass for refinement, favoring principles of kindness, courtesy, and good taste. "Manners are made up of trivialities of deportment which can easily be learned if one does not happen to know them," she wrote in the introduction to the first edition of her book. "Manner is personality—the outward manifestation of one's innate character and attitude toward life. . . . Etiquette must, if it is to be more than trifling use, include ethics as well as manners. Certainly what one is, is of far greater importance than what one appears to be." After doing a three-times-a-week radio broadcast for several years and writing for several women's magazines, Mrs. Post began a daily newspaper column distributed by the Bell Syndicate throughout the English-speaking world.

During that time, Elizabeth Meriwether Gilmer, writing as Dorothy Dix, was the matriarch of the so called "advice to the lovelorn" columnists. Dix's syndicated column dealt with the problems and changing social and ethical standards of several generations, spanning fifty-five years and reaching an estimated sixty million readers. The column ran until her death in 1951. Dix was straightforward and even-handed in the advice she dished out, as likely to skewer women as men for their foibles. Although Dix's columns reflect the morals and standards of another era, they are still entertaining because of her timeless subject matter and her wit.

In a column on how to treat a husband, for example, Dix observed that women in general fail to strike just the right note in their attitude toward their husbands. The reader assumes that Dix is about to lecture women, but instead she offers this tongue-in-cheek observation: "Sometimes they treat them better than they deserve. Sometimes worse, but seldom do they treat the men just as the men would like to be treated. Perhaps the real reason that women fail in this most important particular is because they make the mistake of treating a husband as if he were a rational human being, and the same sort of an individual inside the home circle as he is outside of it."

In the mid-1950s, after Dix died, Esther Pauline Lederer began writing the "Ann Landers" advice column. Lederer's twin sister followed suit within a few months, initiating the "Dear Abby" column under the pen name of Abigail Van Buren. Their success was immediate and sustained: "Ann" and "Abby" are still among the most widely syndicated columnists in the world, receiving several thousand letters from readers in any given week.

Another long-running syndicated column during the first half of the twentieth century was written by First Lady Eleanor Roosevelt, whose *My Day* spanned thirty years and was read by millions. Written initially as a sort of journal or daily diary, the column provided glimpses of her life in the White House, later evolving into essay-style commentary on social issues. Her credo seems embodied in a 1945 column: "Young or old, in order to be useful, we must stand for the things we feel are right, and we must work for those things wherever we find ourselves."

Roosevelt's column addressed a number of controversial topics, such as the role of women in society. She urged almost fifty years ago, for example, that laws discriminating against women be removed from the statute books. And her columns often show a certain prescience, such as a 1958 piece in which she spoke of the potentially adverse effect of television: "If the use of leisure time is confined to looking at TV for a few extra hours every day, we will deteriorate as a people," she warned. In spite of its vast readership and the range of serious topics the column addressed, its importance was downplayed by the president. Roosevelt told reporters his wife "simply writes in a daily diary."

Women columnists had long been accepted if they wrote gossip or advice, and Roosevelt's acceptance and popularity as a columnist stemmed primarily from her position in the White House. Despite the continuing popularity and apparent influence of these kinds of columns, their placement on the women's pages, which are less prestigious and targeted to a different audience than the op-ed page, signaled their second-class status. Newspapers continued to be fundamentally male institutions, employing mainly men, shaped by masculine views and responding to male interests. That's why Dorothy Thompson's emergence as a nationally syndicated political columnist in the 1930s was so significant.

Thompson and her contemporary, Anne O'Hare McCormick,

were women writing about government and politics, traditionally masculine areas. Thompson, born in 1893, became a foreign correspondent for the *Philadelphia Ledger* in the 1920s, and then started a column for the *New York Herald Tribune* in 1936, later moving to the *New York Post*. McCormick was the *New York Times*'s first foreign affairs columnist, the first woman appointed to the *Times* editorial board, and the first woman to win a Pulitzer Prize in journalism, in 1937. Her three-times-a-week column, "In Europe" (later retitled "Abroad"), alternated with Arthur Krock's *In the Nation*. McCormick was said to have a "masculine mind," meant as praise for her clear thinking and logical, objective approach to news. But she was also credited with having an extraordinary ability to get along with people, to be on intimate terms with important people.

A tribute to McCormick appearing in the *Times* after her death in 1954 said she understood politics and diplomacy, "but for her they were not the whole truth, and no abstraction was ever the whole truth. The whole truth lay in people." One memorable column that illustrates that quality was written in 1945 in the aftermath of World War II. McCormick wrote about women in the devastated European countryside using their brooms to sweep the debris of war from their thresholds—a symbolic gesture of readiness to rebuild their lives.

Sylvia Porter also broke new ground for women, cracking the financial pages in the 1930s with her personal finance column in the *New York Post*. Although Porter joined the staff full time in 1942, the paper continued to byline her work "S.F. Porter" until management was certain the public had accepted her. Porter's three-times-a-week column on finance and consumer issues was later syndicated, running in more than 350 newspapers throughout the world and reaching an estimated forty million readers. She also wrote a monthly column for the *Ladies' Home Journal* and was the author of several books on money and taxes. She died in 1991.

In the mid-1940s, Doris Fleeson began writing a vivid syndicated political column in Washington that ran for thirty-four years, containing graphic portrayals of national politics. "We belonged to the who the hell reads the second paragraph school," she once said. *Washington Post* columnist Mary McGrory, who admired Fleeson, describes her as "well in advance of the women's liberation movement, a militant feminist." McGrory also says Fleeson was "the only one of either sex to approach national affairs like a police reporter." President John F. Kennedy quipped once that he would "rather be

Krocked than Fleesonized," a reference to the less pugnacious *New York Times* national affairs columnist.

The intrepid war correspondent Marguerite Higgins turned to column writing in the early 1960s after carving out a reputation for thorough reporting. In her syndicated column for the Long Island newspaper *Newsday,* Higgins took a strong pro-administration stance in the early days of the Vietnam war. She died in 1966, at age forty-five, after contracting a tropical disease on her tenth trip to Vietnam.

Other women were also writing columns for a national audience, but not necessarily for mainstream newspapers. Their journalistic homes were magazines and the alternative press, which traditionally have been more welcoming to women. Dorothy Day, for example, a founder of the *Catholic Worker,* wrote a column for that monthly paper from 1933 until her death in 1980, pricking the conscience of church leaders and hammering away at the themes of pacifism and community building with which she identified so strongly.

The power of Day's column derived from her ability to focus on people in order to illuminate larger issues, and from the way she wove personal details into her writing. The poignant column she wrote on the electrocution of Ethel and Julius Rosenberg in 1952, for example, begins with the sweetness of summer smells, her own bathing of a child, and the reflection that Ethel "must have been thinking with all the yearning of her heart of her own soon-to-be-orphaned children."

Janet Flanner, whose dispatches from Europe were a regular feature in the *New Yorker* magazine from 1925 to 1975, chronicled events, profiled famous people, and wrote commentaries on art, film, theater, music—and whatever else captured her attention. Her essays, published as "Letters from Paris," were signed "Genet." Flanner's gift was the sureness of her instinct, said *New Yorker* editor William Shawn. "Her mind was an exquisite mechanism, awhirr with wit, warmed by reserves of passion."

Even by the mid-1960s, column writing was still very much male turf, as Shana Alexander recognized when she undertook a column called "The Feminine Eye" for *Life* magazine in 1964. "Such a thing— a woman writing regularly as a woman—had never happened at our magazine," she later wrote. "My hands shook. Twenty years a professional reporter, I was about to make my debut as myself, to say for the first time what I felt personally about events." Alexander said the column's name was chosen "because it seemed important then for readers to know that the writer whose opinions, crotchets and glees would hereafter appear on that page was female. Women's liberation was not invented yet." Alexander's columns ran the gamut from witty reflections on hair and fashion to a series of elegant pieces on the meaning of the 1968 presidential candidacy of Eugene McCarthy. "'Poets,' said Shelley long ago, 'are the unacknowledged legislators of the world.' Today we have a legislator who is an unacknowledged poet," Alexander wrote of McCarthy. "There is novelty in the idea of a poet-President, but no incompatibility, for McCarthy's political strength and his verse flow from the same richness of mind."

Women began entering journalism in significant numbers during the late 1960s and early 1970s, but even then many were still assigned soft features or the society beat. Those who gained a toehold in newspaper column writing during the 1960s and later came to national prominence included Mary McGrory, now a *Washington Post* political columnist, and humor columnist Erma Bombeck. After working as a reporter for the *Washington Star*, McGrory began her column in 1960, blending political commentary with essays on literature and other topics. Bombeck began writing her humor column for the *Dayton Journal-Herald* in 1965, a fixture now carried by more than 900 newspapers.

But perhaps more typical of those years is what happened to two women who have since become nationally syndicated columnists, Jane Bryant Quinn and Ellen Goodman. Both applied for writing jobs at a news magazine in New York in the mid-1960s, but were told they could be hired only as researchers or mail clerks because the writing jobs went to men. In an ironic twist, Quinn now writes a regular column for the same magazine and her office is located there.

By the 1970s, newspapers had begun to change. Reflecting the influence of the women's liberation movement, women's pages were being phased out by many newspapers and replaced with genderless feature sections with names like "Accent," "Style," and "View." Some syndicated women columnists, such as Landers and Bombeck, survived the changeover, but many local columns addressing traditional home and hearth concerns of women went by the board. Nobody seemed quite sure what should take their place. Society was changing, and so were many women's lives, as more began combining careers with raising families.

Among those who filled the void were Goodman, creating her personal/political column for the *Boston Globe*; Quinn, who started a personal finance column for the *Washington Post*; Judith Martin, who undertook her witty column on society and politics, "Miss Manners," for the *Post,* and Jane Brody, who began writing a personal health column for the *New York Times.* In another significant development, the *Times* introduced the weekly "Hers" column in 1977. A.M. Rosenthal, who had just taken over as executive editor, wanted a column different from traditional women's columns. "I didn't think of it as a column *for* women," he said. "I thought of it as a column *by* women."

Rosenthal says the idea came to him at a party where feminists were discussing the new *Times* "Living" section that he had started. "I was so taken with their approach," he says, "I thought one thing I could do in response to this openness was to start a column giving women writers a crack at expressing themselves—not once, but six or seven (columns) in a row." Rosenthal says the column gave *Times* readers "the opportunity to *meet* a lot of writers—not just read them—and second, it gave a hell of a lot of writers the chance to display themselves in the daily paper. A lot got their start there." The long running fixture, which moved from the news columns to the Sunday magazine in 1988, has been an eclectic mix of commentary on global and personal issues. Authorship has rotated among women writers not on the *Times* staff. The tone of the essays is sometimes funny, often serious; the approach reportorial, whimsical, nostalgic, or speculative. The many voices reflected in the "Hers" essays suggest the difficulty of defining what it is that constitutes a "woman's voice."

Columns written by women are diverse in topic and style. Quinn is an authority on personal finance, for example; Brody is knowledgeable about health matters, and Bombeck has been called the "Socrates of the Ironing Board." Goodman and Anna Quindlen of the *New York Times* both write columns that could be characterized as personal/political, yet their approach is very different. Despite the differences between women columnists, one fact stands out: women's voices often contrast significantly with those of men.

Georgetown University linguistics professor Deborah Tannen says women are different in the way they communicate and in the way they react to information. In her book *You Just Don't Understand: Women and Men in Conversation,* Tannen says the difference between men's and women's styles of conversation amounts to "cross-cultural communication." Although her book is about talking rather than writing and reading, Tannen's theory is useful in thinking about all kinds of communication, including newspaper columns.

Recent studies have shown that newspaper coverage *by* women is low, and coverage *of* women is even lower. Because men have controlled the nation's news organizations for so long, men also have defined what is newsworthy. Newspapers, of course, reflect the larger society. "As long as men—white men—hold most of the keys to power throughout our society, it will be their pictures we see most often on Page One, their comments we read most often in stories, their voices we hear most often from the editorial pages," said the late Janet Chusmir, former executive editor of the *Miami Herald*.

"Women need to hear voices they can identify with," says Robert Fertik, co-publisher of *Women's Voice,* a news magazine he is starting for women. "They want to hear people who sound like them, who believe in the things they do, who care about the same issues and approach them from a similar, though not monolithic, point of view." Fertik says the mainstream media have ignored women's rights issues, and newspapers have tended to look at issues that concern women, such as war and peace, "strictly from a man's point of view." Women columnists can bring up different issues and provide a fresh perspective. "Women columnists have the opportunity to articulate things that women feel very strongly," Fertik says. "The downside is that each is a token."

In San Diego, the publisher of *Women's Times* started the monthly paper for women because, she says, "I felt very strongly that there weren't enough women's voices" represented in the mainstream media. Because male principles have dominated society, "the world is tilted out of balance," says publisher Mary Ellen Hamilton. "In our small way, we're trying to right that balance."

Men and women have different interests and concerns, says Scott McGehee, chair of a task force set up by the Knight-Ridder newspaper chain to find ways to win back women newspaper readers. "We are not different, of course, in intelligence or ability or energy or most of our news and information interests. We do continue to lead somewhat different lives, whether or not it's right or fair," McGehee says. "Women still have the lioness's share of responsibility for child care and home care and care of aging parents. Women still face different treatment and obstacles in the workplace. Women have gender-specific health concerns. Women say they are more pressed for time than men say they are. Women in groups talk with each other about subjects that don't come up—or don't come up the same way—in groups of women and men."

McGehee, a former features editor at three newspapers and general manager of the *Lexington* (Kentucky) *Herald-Leader,* once believed that anything that was "just for women" was devalued. She has since changed her mind. Her thinking is reflected across the country by editors trying to find ways to recapture women readers. Several have inaugurated special sections or pages targeting women; others have become more conscious of the need to incorporate news useful and interesting to women throughout the paper.

Susan Miller, vice president/editorial for Scripps Howard Newspapers, who has done extensive research on women's lifestyles and reading habits, thinks newspapers must include more content relevant to women employed outside the home and to their families, and must do it every day. Columns play a role in this. Women columnists bring a perspective to newspapers that is important to the national dialogue, lending substance to the abstract ideal of the newspaper as a forum for divergent ideas and opinions.

"Women do have different perspectives," says Mary Ann Lindley, a general interest columnist and former National Society of Newspaper Columnists president. Columns written by women are important because ideas and issues "are being run through a woman's set of values and perspectives on society," she says.

Women's voices contribute to what CBS news correspondent Mike Wallace has called "the vitality, the variety, the yeasty and never ending debate from which we grow and think and flourish, without Big Brother peering over our shoulder." Women bring a different perspective to the news, National Public Radio correspondent Susan Stamberg has said, adding that she hopes women will have the confidence to retain that female view, "and not feel they have to do the news just like a man does."

The spirit of the First Amendment demands an energetic and free exchange of information and opinion; the omission of women's voices diminishes the fruitfulness of that exchange. Newspapers need more female and minority columnists and more diverse views, said newspaper editors on a 1988 panel on how to become syndicated, even though smaller news holes at most papers have made it tougher than ever to enter syndication.

Newspaper columns obviously play a part in the national dialogue, but it is difficult to evaluate their impact. The number of letters and telephone calls in response to a column is one gauge. Columnists' name recognition is another. Whether a columnist influences the national or the local political agenda is not always a criterion. Some columnists do seek to persuade and to influence events. But many others shun the idea of telling their readers what to do. Some are more interested in sharing with their readers the thought processes that led them to a particular conclusion; they want to encourage readers to think for themselves.

More than providing a new set of facts and opinions, a newspaper "will open a new set of your own questions," political columnist David Broder writes in *Behind the Front Page*. "A good newspaper has both immediacy and perspective that foster the discussion and judgment so essential to the dialogue of democracy."

John Fischer, a former author of "The Easy Chair" column in *Harper's* magazine, once said the function of a column "is to help readers arrive at conclusions of their own. . . . Whether they agree with the columnist's interpretation doesn't matter much. . . . Here, I believe is the chief justification for any column, in newspaper or magazine. It offers the reader a chance to become familiar enough with a given point of view so that he can use it to work out his own intellectual bearings."

Columnists should play a number of roles: As the "humanizers of the newspaper," as humorists, and as explainers, says Mary Ann Lindley. Columns help people sort out the information that saturates them daily. "Columnists can infuse the facts and information with meaning and put them in perspective," she says. "I think it's a real gift that newspapers can give their readers. That's what we can do that radio and tv can't."

Conservative political columnist George Will has characterized columns as "optional delights." The normal newspaper reader may feel he has a civic duty to keep up with the principal national and local news stories, but reading a column is a habit based on familiarity with a writer's mind and personality. "It is not a habit people are apt to acquire unless it is pleasurable," Will says. "What most readers want from a columnist is the pleasure of his company."

The late Walter Lippmann said columnists can help readers think through events and issues: "In some field of interest, we make it our business to find out what is going on under the surface and beyond the horizon, to infer, to deduce, to imagine, and to guess what is going on inside, what this meant yesterday, and what it could mean tomorrow. In this we do what every sovereign citizen is supposed to do, but has not the time or interest to do for himself."

Of course, the role of newspapers was different in the 1930s and 40s, when Lippmann was among the best known columnists of the day. It was an era when small boys ran through the streets at night shouting "Extra" when a great event had occurred. Newspapers were the first to deliver the news. That changed with the invention of radio and television and growth of the electronic media.

As the public came to rely on radio and television for the first report of events, newspapers began to emphasize the why and how of events more than the who and what. Newspaper columnists have played an important role in that trend toward explanation of the news. And although newspaper readership has declined, syndicated columnists continue to be widely read. Their individual influence on public opinion may not be direct, but they exert an indirect influence that helps shape public discussion.

Retired *New York Times* political columnist James Reston describes the power of columnists as "tangential," not direct. "If a columnist makes a very good case that, say George Bush should do more to change the priorities of the country from foreign policy to domestic policy, if we hammer at this long enough, the Congress then picks it up. So that our power may be to begin the debate, but it's not a real power—it's the power to initiate thought, to change the question."

Closely linked with the question of influence or impact is the importance of having a female byline and photo or drawing of a woman author in a place reserved for commentary on the op-ed page or elsewhere in the paper. By 1980, researchers had documented a bleak composite picture of women's representation in the mass media. Magazine articles and advertisements showed few women working; there were far fewer women characters than men in television programs, and television commercials were more likely to show women working inside the home and men working outside it. As late as 1987, the American Women in Radio and Television organization didn't give its annual award to ads that feature women positively; it found none.

So it's clear that putting a column by a woman on the same page as columns written by men has symbolic value. It says the woman's opinion matters, that she's worth listening to and worth taking seriously. "The problem with newspapers is that they have symbolically annihilated women," says Jean Gaddy Wilson, director of New Directions for News. "They've dismissed, trivialized and demeaned them in their coverage."

The paucity of women's voices in American newspapers until recent years is well illustrated by a 1967 column in the *Los Angeles Times,* which in subsequent years has been among the most progressive papers in the country in covering the women's movement. The column explained how *Times* editors were attempting to balance fifteen syndicated political columnists to represent liberal, moderate, and conservative views. However politically balanced the *Times* op-ed page may have been, it was off-balance in a fundamental way: Not one of the syndicated columnists was a woman. Things have changed, of course, at the *Los Angeles Times* and elsewhere, as more women have entered journalism. But the prestigious op-ed page of the *New York Times* provides another powerful reminder of how slowly change occurs: In 1992, all but one of the regular *Times* columnists were men.

And many women columnists still have a hard time gaining credibility with male readers. Lindley, who writes a general interest column for the *Tallahassee* (Florida) *Democrat,* says she encounters an "almost instinctive reaction by some readers that 'she's a girl—what can she possibly tell us?'" Worse than angry responses to her columns are those that are "sweetly condescending," she says. And that reaction is not limited to the conservative southern city where she works. At the National Society of Newspaper Columnists annual meetings, attended mainly by men, "Even the other columnists would say, 'You must write women's columns.' Even my own kind!" she says with exasperation.

While many columns by women are positioned in newspaper feature sections, an increasing number of women are represented on the op-ed page and other traditionally male pages, such as business, finance, and science. Thompson was one of the first to recognize the value of having her commentary appear on the page dominated by Lippmann, a powerful political guru, when she agreed to write "On the Record" for the *New York Herald Tribune* in 1936: She asked that it alternate with Lippmann's "Today and Tomorrow" on the front page of the second section. Lippmann welcomed the addition of Thompson's voice. "I like enormously having you as a neighbor," he wrote her, "but have you any idea of what a term of hard labor you have committed yourself to?"

American newspapers were becoming blander and more homogenized in the 1930s, and the concept of objective reporting had taken hold in newsrooms, making for a more responsible but more sedate press. Against that graying backdrop, Thompson's column was vivid, its force flowing from the way she expressed deeply felt emotion, from her thorough reporting, and from her penetrating analysis. By 1940, her column was syndicated in 150 newspapers, with an estimated seven million readers.

Her infusion of emotion into her political commentary was new, and different from the pattern followed by many male political pundits. She was said by contemporaries to write in a white heat. "Dorothy Thompson is not afraid of admitting that, like the rest of the human race, she is subject to emotion. She gets mad. She pleads; she denounces," said a critic reviewing a collection of her pieces. "And the result is that where the intellectualized columns of her colleagues fade when pressed between the leaves of a book, these columns still ring."

Obviously, not all columns written by women echo Thompson's style—a blend of insightfulness and passion. But Thompson's writing is a starting point in seeking common threads in the many-voiced patchwork of columns by women. Virginia Woolf knew how difficult it was to characterize a woman's voice, when she said a woman's writing cannot help being feminine: "At its best it is most feminine. The only difficulty lies in defining what we mean by feminine."

The *New York Times* "Hers" columns, written by many different women, have been praised as "intimate" and "caring"—two qualities that repeatedly surface in descriptions of columns by women. Jane Brody's personal health columns, for example, are packed with medical facts but inviting to readers. Trained as a biochemist, Brody is thorough and tenacious in her reporting of science. Yet she has been said to have a "woman's way" of writing, meaning she empathizes with and reaches out to her readers. It is this quality, as much as her thoroughness and the lucidity of her prose, that has earned her a wide following. Brody herself has said her ability to empathize with others was probably a major factor in her getting a column.

Joyce Maynard's columns about her family were intimate and intensely personal, a quality recognized by readers who wrote and told her they drank their morning coffee with her: Her writing made her as close to them as a neighbor sitting at the kitchen table. The intimate quality of Maynard's writing came from the honesty with which she shared her life with readers. Other women columnists have shared intimate moments with their readers—personal events in their own lives. Political columnist Mona Charen, for example, stepped away from commentary on government and social issues to tell her readers about her inability to conceive a child and her decision to adopt. Even hard-boiled political columnist Mary McGrory reveals a tender side in her columns about animals, especially dogs.

The capacity for intimacy and caring is not exclusively female, of course, but may have a higher priority for some women columnists. The way in which some are able to connect with women readers seems to reflect what psychologist Carol Gilligan has written in her book *In a Different Voice:* that women are more likely than men to define themselves in terms of their interdependence and ability to care.

Some columnists, regardless of gender, seek to persuade through intellectual prowess, while others take an ideological approach and browbeat their readers. Still others have an emotional linkage with readers. The capacity to be passionate or outraged is shared by both sexes, but generally speaking women have been encouraged more than men to communicate their feelings, and that seems reflected in some columns written by women.

Washington Post columnist Colman McCarthy, a man who writes passionately about issues, quoted Saul Bellow in pointing up the main fault of the American media: "Here we write well when we expose frauds and hypocrites. We are great at counting warts and blemishes and weighing feet of clay. In expressing love, we belong among the undeveloped countries." Even though passionately written columns are powerful precisely because of their emotional impact on readers, some regard them as inferior to so-called intellectual columns. The *New York Times*'s Anna Quindlen, for example, is sensitive about how others perceive her emotional approach. She would like her writing to be more cerebral, but says that's not her style.

Another common thread cited by several women columnists is that columns by women often validate the way other women feel and think. That suggests fundamental differences between male and female readers, a fact confirmed by readers' letters. Goodman's readers often tell her, for example, "You wrote just what I was thinking." Quindlen's say her columns reflect what is going on in their lives. Maynard became accustomed to readers telling her that their lives were just like hers. And Bombeck's column has flourished precisely because she is able to distill with humor a universality in the way women react to experiences.

Women are shaped by class, race, nationality, and history, and also by uniquely female experiences within the culture as a whole. Feminist scholar Elaine Showalter calls that collective female experience "the binding force of women's culture." Although their styles and the topics they write about are diverse, women columnists reflect shared experiences that may differ from those of men. Women columnists are likely to have a vested interest in and a direct personal connection to subjects such as abortion or child care. They are wife, mother, and/or daughter. Their perspective is shaped by family responsibilities; many have had to balance caring for children with work outside the home, and they know firsthand the feeling of being pulled in different directions. They may have encountered discrimination in the workplace, or felt challenged to prove themselves in a field dominated by men.

The most visible evidence of that "collective experience" is seen in some of the examples women choose to illustrate points—examples their male colleagues may ignore or overlook. When conservative political columnist Charen wanted to bring the effect of liberalism home to her readers in a column, she used the metaphor of how badly liberal men treat women. Quindlen, on the other end of the political spectrum, has examined the effect of governmental budget-cutting by focusing on how such cuts affect programs that assist unmarried mothers or help children learn to read. McGrory brought the public school quality issue home to readers by spending a long day sitting in Chelsea, Massachusetts, elementary school classrooms, trying to assess the takeover of that community's public school system by Boston University.

Georgetown socio-linguist Tannen suggests that a woman's way of making sense of the world is a more private endeavor than that of men, involving observing and integrating personal experience and drawing connections to the experiences of others. All columnists draw on their personal experience, of course. But the *New York Times* op-ed page provides an illustration of the differences that Tannen noted. Quindlen, the only regular woman contributor, writes a column that moves from the personal to the political; it is usually constructed around a personal anecdote, and Quindlen employs detailed personal observations to establish support for her opinion on a larger issue. In contrast, the other regular political columnists—all men—tend to buttress their statements of opinion with fact and logic and the statements of other "experts."

While their topics and approach to what they write differ, women syndicated columnists do share certain attributes. They are risk takers, venturing into a highly competitive and rapidly shifting field. Despite the self confidence they may exude, several had doubts about writing a column but were willing to take financial and emotional risks that their writing would succeed in a high-pressure arena. Quinn was learning how to be a manager when she was asked to write a financial column by the *Washington Post*; she wasn't sure she wanted to gamble on it, but did. Merlene Davis, one of the few black women columnists in the country, remembers being terrified at the responsibility that column writing entailed but took the plunge anyway.

Women syndicated columnists tend to value independence. Many work without the security of a home paper, relying on their wits and writing skills to keep their audience. Political columnists Charen and Georgie Anne Geyer, for example, both make a living from column writing without the backup security of a home paper. Tenacity is another attribute. Many of these women experienced discrimination early in their journalistic careers, yet held on until they became established. Outspokenness is another obvious attribute. Readers have empowered them to be bold. Women columnists have broken long-standing taboos that kept women from speaking out on controversial subjects.

All must walk the tightrope between being consistent, a quality that binds readers to a column, and being predictable, which turns them off. The ideal that columnists strive for is to provide a recognizable perspective—a "voice"—through which events and ideas are filtered, and a freshness of expression and insight that rewards readers for their loyalty. Not every column hits the mark, but syndicate deadlines require that they be sent out regardless. All writers vest themselves in their writing, making themselves vulnerable to criticism, but columnists put themselves on the line because they're asking for reaction, trying to provoke a response.

The negative feedback columnists sometimes receive requires them to develop thick skins and to be able to deal with conflict. Their name and/or picture over the column make them easy targets. They may relish their freedom to speak out and enjoy being at center stage, but all have had to learn to insulate themselves against criticism. Some of the mail is ugly, like the racist missives received by Davis or Dorothy Gilliam, a black *Washington Post* columnist. Or like the hate-filled letter Charen received in response to her column on adopting a child, which said God obviously knew what he was doing when he made her infertile. Or the letter from a reader who attacked not only Molly Ivins's politics but the way she looks.

Not all the mail is negative, but the response can be overwhelming. Some columnists receive several hundred letters a week, some as many as several thousand. It's an indication of the influence they have, but also a reminder of the responsibility that writing a column entails. Financial columnist Quinn, for example, says the hardest thing about writing her column is knowing that people will act on what she says. Even when the mail is supportive or comes from readers seeking help or advice, it imposes a burden on columnists. They must decide whether the letters have to be read, much less answered.

Health columnist Brody, who often receives requests for medical advice, understands her readers' desperation, but in most cases can't respond outside her column. So much mail comes to the office that she brings it home in shopping bags and stashes it in a closet. Others have worked out a way to respond personally to readers. Many compromise by sending a postcard rather than a letter, acknowledging a reader's comments.

Although it can be overwhelming, the feedback from readers does have a positive side, both refreshing and empowering women columnists. Davis, for example, says that writing a column put her, for the first time, on an equal footing with her white, male editors because she knew she had thousands of readers behind her. Quindlen's following allows her to say what she wants, enabling her to criticize even her own newspaper, as she did when the *Times* published the accuser's name in the William Kennedy Smith rape case.

Women columnists share the ability to write with authority under deadline, but many who enjoy a secure place today say they found it difficult to be taken seriously when they started in journalism. McGrory remembers being shunted aside by politicians who preferred talking with male reporters. Quinn edited a financial newsletter before starting her column, but was not permitted to use her first name on the masthead because it would have revealed that the editor was a woman. Gilliam confronted discrimination daily as a black woman journalist in the 1960s. And even in the 1980s, when Quindlen started writing a column, she was kidded about her expressions of outrage. She said the emotion that packs her writing was likely to be put down with a comment like, "Anna's just got PMS" (premenstrual syndrome).

Although relatively few women columnists are syndicated, an increasing number of local newspaper columnists are women. Young female journalists can now look at a newspaper and see column writing as a realistic goal. Even though they paved the way for other women, some successful syndicated columnists wish they had gone further. Quinn, for example, says she and Sylvia Porter demonstrated that women can write competently about personal finance. But she wishes she had proved through her column that women also can write lucidly about broader financial topics, such as economic policy and the Federal Reserve.

The generally accepted assumption is that one out of three columns can be a throwaway, but some women feel pressured to make every column sing. Some are driven by the knowledge that they are highly visible role models for younger women, although not all like to think of themselves that way. Political columnist Geyer, for example, says it's superficial to think in terms of role models, because young women must discover their own strengths and find their own opportunities. Gilliam doesn't think of herself as a role model, but she's aware that her name is legend among young minority journalists.

In the mid-1970s, a journalist like Goodman could find no models for the eclectic personal/political column she wanted to write. Ironically, Goodman's column has now become so entrenched in the culture that younger female columnists are often compared with her. In fact, women columnists are frequently compared with one another, an indication of just how new or different they seem. Goodman was labeled the "thinking woman's Erma Bombeck" by *Time* magazine. She wrote to Bombeck to apologize, but Bombeck understood; she wrote back and told Goodman what publicists had emblazoned on her first book: "Jean Kerr, look to your daisies." Merlene Davis, in turn, has been called the "black Erma Bombeck," and Mona Charen was dubbed "the conservative Ellen Goodman" by *National Review* editor William F. Buckley, Jr. "I wrote to him to say there must have been a long line of women through history who have only been compared to each other," Goodman observed, adding dryly, "Jane Austen was probably known as the country Mary Wollstonecraft."

Thousands of columns are syndicated in the United States on every conceivable subject, from saving the earth to death and dying. The freedom to write at home, the independence, the ability to say what they want, the opportunity to be heard by a mass audience—all contribute to the lure of column writing. It is lucrative, however, only for the most widely syndicated columnists, such as Bombeck, Landers, and Goodman. But for many others, the financial reward is not always as great as the satisfaction of having a forum and a regular audience.

The price newspapers pay for syndicated columns is based on circulation and varies with the size of the newspaper. Small newspapers pay far less than large metropolitan newspapers for the same column. Columnists get a percentage of what the syndicate takes in. So the number of newspaper clients buying a column is not in itself an indication of how much a columnist earns. Maynard, for example, was syndicated in close to fifty newspapers and made about $18,000 a year writing her once-a-week column. Charen earned just $8,000 the first year of writing her column, before it caught on and was purchased by several major metropolitan newspapers.

Work environment is another symbol of columnists' autonomy and independence. Unlike reporters, whose desks crowd the vast field of a newsroom, syndicated columnists who work for local newspapers often have their own offices, and many have assistants to help deal with mail and scheduling. Dorothy Thompson led the way, asking for an office, a secretary, two months' annual vacation, and "a guarantee of freedom to write as I please, provided that I remain within the canons of good taste and within the libel laws."

Other syndicated columnists, especially those without a base paper who deal directly with a syndicate, are able to work at home, thanks to computer hookups and fax machines. Some started out in a newsroom but, like Judith Martin, became so successful they severed ties with a paper and work at home. Geyer works out of an improvised office in her dining room in Washington, for example, while Maynard's computer is set up in a room off her living room.

For those with small children, working at home can be both a blessing and a curse. Quindlen has an upstairs study and full-time sitter for times when the children are home from school; Charen deliberately chose to work at home, in part to be with her infant son, but she acknowledges that some days are quieter than others.

The women portrayed in this collection of profiles are all nationally syndicated or nationally distributed newspaper columnists, with two exceptions. Gilliam, a metro columnist for the *Washington Post,* and Davis, a lifestyle columnist for the *Lexington Herald-Leader,* were chosen to represent some of the work being done by African-American women columnists.

A diversity of subjects and writing styles is represented here. The names of some of the women I chose to interview are well known; others are gaining a national reputation. All have written columns for at least five years and some for more than twenty-five years. All but Joyce Maynard are still writing. Maynard, who ended her column after seven years, is included because her story says much about the relationship between a columnist and her readers.

New columns are introduced weekly, often capitalizing on trends such as cleaning up the environment or how to choose healthful foods. At least three different nationally syndicated columns deal with the problems and pleasures of being single. Others are unique, like Sara Ingram's column on death and dying, "Mortal Matters." Only women who write essay-style columns were considered for inclusion. This book looks at how those columnists got started, where they get ideas for columns, and what their writing processes are like. Other columnists who follow a question and answer format, such as Ann Landers, Heloise, or Dr. Joyce Brothers, were not considered for this collection. Judith Martin was selected because, in addition to answering readers' queries in "Miss Manners," she also writes a weekly essay on the art of living gracefully.

The following chapters are based on interviews with each of the columnists, background research, and conversations with people who know them or their work. Some columnists were interviewed in their homes, some in their offices, others in restaurants, clubs, or hotels in cities they were visiting for conferences or lectures or to promote their books. Where information was obtained exclusively from one source, it has been attributed in the copy. Other sources are listed in the bibliography. The chapters are arranged in roughly chronological fashion according to the decade when each columnist began writing or syndicating her column.

The range and variety of these women's columns underscores the rich diversity that women's voices bring to newspapers. They have contributed different perspectives and new ways of seeing and interpreting life. Collectively, they might be described by a phrase the *New York Times* used to sum up the scope of Dorothy Thompson's column: "She gave herself her own assignment, which was no less than the whole human situation."

SHE SAID *WHAT?*

MARY McGRORY

Mary McGrory is known as an astute observer of the Washington political scene, a sharp-tongued critic of Republican administrations, defender of the English language. But her first love will always be dog stories. "I will drop anything to read a dog story. I love dogs, I love to read about them. I like dog rescues. I like eccentric dogs," McGrory says. "I just find they never fail you."

Dog stories were the assignments no one else wanted when McGrory started out in journalism as secretary to the book editor of the old *Boston Herald.* So she took them on, along with book reviews. Now a nationally syndicated columnist at the *Washington Post,* McGrory's reputation is built on political commentary, but some of her most readable columns continue to be about canines.

In fact, the woman whose political columns landed her on President Richard Nixon's enemies list says that the largest response to any of her columns has been to the ones about animals, not politics. "The all-time response getters were squirrels. People are very worked up about squirrels because they get into bird feeders," she says. "Washington is a big bird feeding town."

She also has been surprised by the "overwhelming response" to columns about nineteenth-century novelist Jane Austen and her columns about adoption, which she calls a "radioactive issue." Writing three times a week, McGrory says she can't be fussy about choosing topics. "If something strikes you, you tend to go with it. You don't examine it from every angle." Sometimes ideas come from headlines, sometimes from observing the way politicians act. "I am beset by PR people," she adds. "I get press releases, telephone calls, and faxes." Her column is syndicated by Universal Press Syndicate.

McGrory's speech is laced with expressions like "beset," a remnant of her rigorous early education at Girls Latin School in Boston, which she describes as being like the Marine Corps. Later she studied English at Boston's Emmanuel College, and she's never lost her passion for literature. Volumes of poetry are tucked in alongside the political books in her *Washington Post* office.

Her father had been a Latin scholar and two aunts were school teachers, so it was understood that McGrory would go on to college. But in order to get a job with a publishing house, she went to secretarial school and studied shorthand. "I thought I would like to be in publishing in sort of a general way without understanding what that meant," she says. "I was fairly bookish so it was logical."

Journalism was also a possibility, but only because McGrory had read *Jane Arden,* a popular comic strip in the 1930s and 40s. Jane Arden was depicted as a single woman in her twenties who was a reporter, detective, and war correspondent rolled into one. "She was a folk heroine," McGrory says. "I thought I'd like to do that without knowing anything about it, without having the faintest idea." There were few other role models for women interested in journalism. McGrory worked as a secretary for a couple of years at Houghton-Mifflin, then joined the now-defunct *Boston Herald.*

Although she had learned from the experience of women in her family that women could be competent professionals, it took time for her to rise in a male-dominated profession. After working for the *Herald* for several years, McGrory was offered a job by United Press wire service. She was told she would be a columnist, she says, but first she was to be a reporter. "I said, 'What's the point of that? That's like a dog walking on its hind legs. It's quite remarkable that he can do it, but what does it prove? How does it advance things? So maybe I could learn to do it, and then you would want me to go back and do what I'm doing now.'" Instead, McGrory joined the *Washington Star.*

She says she wanted to write the "with" stories—sidebars that explore interesting angles of a main story or profile people involved in the news. "I didn't care where it was in the papers," she says. She learned to write the kind of prose that readers would respond to. When *Star* owner Newbold Noyes sent McGrory to cover the controversial 1954 Army-McCarthy hearings, he told her to write the story the way she would a letter to her favorite aunt, McGrory recalls. "It happened I had a favorite aunt to whom I did write. [Aunt Sarah] was old and not well and lonely, so I used to write to her."

In 1960 her editors at the *Star* asked her to start a column. She remains grateful for the support and encouragement she received. "I had to clean out papers a while back and I found handwritten notes from the editor. It was a wonderful climate in which to develop and grow," she says. "You had all the encouragement imaginable—not just for what you wrote, but they would tell you what they wished you would write. I got so many column ideas."

McGrory's writing is still much like a lively letter to her aunt. "I try to keep the reader in mind. I don't write for my sources, because I really don't have any," she says. "Well, I've got 500 up there [on Capitol Hill]," she adds after a pause, "but I don't work for the State Department, where the undersecretary will not speak to you for six months if you get the wrong nuance. I don't worry about that really. I've got nothing to lose, which is very, very liberating.

"The kind of thing I write does not endear me to anybody, really. They forgive me on the Hill because they've got so much on their minds and they're not all that proud," she says. "But downtown does not forgive." In fact, McGrory was ostracized by the Reagan administration to the point where she wasn't recognized at a presidential press conference during Reagan's entire eight-year term in office. Elsewhere, she is generally accepted, even by the Republicans. "I think they expect me to be extremely hard-nosed and loud and obnoxious," she says, "and the fact that I don't raise my voice or anything seems to impress them favorably."

In person, McGrory is softspoken, and her voice still carries a hint of her New England childhood. She enjoys telling a good story, especially a funny one, and she doesn't mind laughing at herself. In print, by contrast, she can heat up the page. "When Mary McGrory gets pissed off, she is more pissed off than anyone," says *New York Times* columnist Anna Quindlen. "I expect [her column] to catch fire around the edges."

One of McGrory's trademarks is that she's always on the scene, preferring to observe for herself rather than accept secondhand information. "I wouldn't trust anyone else. That's very important, because something would strike me that wouldn't strike anyone else. And you like to see their demeanor, the whites of their eyes," she says. "I hope I give [readers] a sense of people, and the sort of currents and cross currents, and the characters as they relate to the issues."

McGrory tells a story about the Brontë sisters to explain what she tries to do in her columns: "Emily Brontë was much questioned about why she didn't go about in society—she never went anywhere. She said, 'Why should I? My sister Charlotte brings it all home to me.' That's my job," McGrory says, "bringing it home to you. I think I've gotten away from it a little bit, what it was like in the room, how they looked, what you thought they meant—flustered or happy or righteous. That's what I'm trying to do. It's a freedom but it's a pressure too to try to do it just as well as you can."

She is something of an outsider, perferring not to run with the pack of Washington journalists. "I don't move in the circles that all go together and watch each other," she says, but adds that it puts her at a disadvantage because she doesn't get any "inside dope." McGrory says she rationalizes this by telling herself all she would be getting is the party line—which she can figure out from what administration officials say in public.

For years McGrory felt the added pressure to do well because she was one of a handful of women in the male-dominated Washington press corps. She acknowledges that prejudice existed but says it wasn't all bad. On the negative side, she remembers being relegated to the balcony of the National Press Club to cover luncheon speeches. "Some fat lobbyist [was] lighting his cigar and having his second cup of coffee at the table while I was up there," she recalls, "and I resented that." Male clubbiness made the life of a female journalist pretty lonely.

But she enjoyed the perks of being female in an era when even members of the press corps were chivalrous. "The fact is that being one of four women among ninety-five men traveling is by far not the worst thing that can happen to you," she says. "I never carried anything. They carried my typewriter, they carried my notes, gave up their seat on bus, the best room, and they would take you aside and tell you how glad they were that you had come, because they were getting sloppy, dirty, and profane."

McGrory calls World War II the great breakthrough for women journalists. Newsrooms were depopulated, so they had to hire women. She is matter-of-fact in her assessment of working conditions for women, saying she has not dwelled on the discrimination. "It's extremely hard work and you don't have a chance to think about these things much," she says.

She tells a story that epitomizes the way it was for her: "One morning, Senator John Stennis, chairman of the Armed Services Committee, emerged from a closed-door session. I ran over with my notebook and asked what happened. 'Oh, little lady,' Stennis said in his southern drawl, 'I don't think I want to go through all that now.' Then Roger Mudd at NBC took him by the arm and they went down to an open mike." McGrory says Mudd's success in capturing Stennis for an interview was partly because Mudd was a television correspondent and partly because he was male.

"It's very difficult to get yourself taken seriously [as a woman]," she says. "They think you're related to the candidate, or that you're head of the Westchester volunteers, or whatever. It doesn't make much difference. It did bother me but not to the extent it did some people." What made her madder than being passed over because she was a woman was being excluded from reporting pools because she was a columnist. McGrory considers herself a reporter first. A reporter with an unmistakable point of view.

Her steady liberal voice has been assailed by critics as too predictable. She is well aware of the criticism, saying, "That's the administration line about me." McGrory tells a story about the time Office of Management and Budget director Richard Darman told her at a party that she had no influence. "I said, 'Probably not.' He said, 'Oh, I enjoy reading it, I wouldn't miss it, but you have no influence whatever, you're just too predictable. Everybody knows what you're going to say.' I said, 'You're probably right.'" McGrory shrugs. "I've known him a long time."

McGrory tells the next part of her story with great relish. "As God is my witness, Ann Compton of ABC, one of the nicest women in this business, just happened to come bubbling up at that moment. She said, 'Oh, Mary, I want to thank you. Because of your story I wasn't just on the evening news, I was the lead story.'" McGrory chuckles, remembering Darman's expression. "I said to her, 'By the way, what was your lead?' She said, 'Oh I just took what you wrote and put it on the air.' So they read me, but kind of under the desk. And that's the line—she's so predictable, nobody reads her, don't bother."

The winner of a Pulitzer Prize for political commentary in 1975, McGrory doesn't feel constrained to be consistent in her political commentary. "To be always liberal, always progressive? Not if the liberals are wrong. Who would tell me what to write? Who would I look to for the party line?" she asks. "Democrats do dumb things like the Persian Gulf resolution, so I say so in the Sunday paper. [House Majority Leader] George Mitchell will glare at me—that's his problem."

McGrory has been reporting on politics for close to forty years, and she says there's nothing else she wants to do. "It's a laborious life, but it's not bad. I don't know that I have to do it, but that's what I do, is keep on doing it." Although some of her columns have been fiery, she doesn't look at her job as a mission. "You do the best you can. It's never good enough, but you try," she says. "It's always wrong to be self-important. You're always going to fall over your feet when you do that. I like to tell people what goes on, and occasionally what I think should go on, and I feel an obligation to expose the pompous and self-important." Her motto: "I've got to write it, you don't have to read it."

The Funeral Had That Special Kennedy Touch . . .

Of John Fitzgerald Kennedy's funeral it can be said he would have liked it.

It had that decorum and dash that were in his special style. It was both splendid and spontaneous. It was full of children and princes, of gardeners and governors.

Everyone measured up to New Frontier standards.

A million people lined every inch of his last journey. Enough heads of state filed into St. Matthew's Cathedral to change the shape of the world.

The weather was superb, as crisp and clear as one of his own instructions.

His wife's gallantry became a legend. His two children behaved like Kennedys. His 3-year-old son saluted his coffin. His 6-year-old daughter comforted her mother. Looking up and seeing tears, she reached over and gave her mother's hand a consoling squeeze.

The procession from the White House would have delighted him. It was a marvelous eye-filling jumble of the mighty and the obscure, all walking behind his wife and his two brothers.

There was no cadence or order, but the presence of Gen. de Gaulle alone in the ragged line of march was enough to give it grandeur. He stalked splendidly up Connecticut Avenue, more or less beside Queen Frederika of Greece and King Baudouin of Belgium.

The sounds of the day were smashingly appropriate. The tolling of the bells gave way to the skirling of the Black Watch Pipers whose lament blended with the organ music inside the Cathedral.

At the graveside there was the thunder of jets overhead, a 21-gun salute, taps, and finally the strains of the Navy hymn, "Eternal Father Strong to Save."

He would have seen every politician he ever knew, two ex-Presidents, Truman and Eisenhower, and a foe or two. Gov. Wallace of Alabama had trouble finding a place to sit in the Cathedral.

His old friend, Cardinal Cushing of Boston, who married him, baptized his children and prayed over him in the icy air of his Inaugural, said a low mass. At the final prayers, after the last blessing, he suddenly added, "Dear Jack."

There was no eulogy. Instead, Bishop Philip M. Hannan mounted the pulpit and read passages from the President's speeches and evoked him so vividly that tears splashed on the red carpets and the benches of the Cathedral. Nobody cried out, nobody broke down.

And the Bishop read a passage the President had often noted in the Scriptures: "There is a time to be born and a time to die." He made no reference to the fact that no one had thought last Friday was a time for John Fitzgerald Kennedy to die—a martyr's death—in Dallas. The President himself had spent no time in trying to express the inexpressible. Excess was alien to his nature.

The funeral cortege stretched for miles. An old campaigner would have loved the crowd. Children sat on the curbstones. Old ladies wrapped their furs around them.

The site of the grave, at the top of one slope, commands all of Washington. Prince Philip used his sword as a walking stick to negotiate the incline.

His brother, Robert, his face a study in desolation, stood beside the President's widow. The children of the fabulous family were all around.

Jacqueline Kennedy received the flag from his coffin, bent over and with a torch lit a flame that is to burn forever on his grave—against the day that anyone might forget that her husband had been a President and a martyr.

It was a day of such endless fitness, with so much pathos and panoply, so much grief nobly borne that it may extinguish that unseemly hour in Dallas, where all that was alien to him—savagery, violence, irrationality—struck down the 35th President of the United States.

[*November 26, 1963*]

[Copyright © 1963 by Mary McGrory.]

Ingrate Flowers and Drunken Squirrels

Once again, I have had confirmation of my theory that if man doesn't put you in your place, nature will. I have been the subject of two major open-air putdowns this summer. In one case, I got above myself. In the other, as usual, I was confounded by squirrels.

I started off the planting season in my small spread with delusions of grandeur. It happens to everyone who puts things in the ground. Study the faces of people leaving Johnson's parking lot on Saturday morning, bearing a cardboard box as if it were the Holy Grail, their faces alight with dreams of glory. You may see a couple of spindly plants. They are looking at tomatoes the color of Krakatoa's fire; they can taste the tomato sauce, their neighbor's envy. You think they are carrying petunias, larkspur, the gaudy zinnia. You are wrong. They are holding in their hands a garden of the type Percy Granger wrote music to. They see a riot of blossoms, they smell the perfumed air.

This year, I had a fateful encounter with the dianthus, the flower that looks and smells like a small carnation and is also called a pink. They go to my head. I don't know how many I had bought before I came out of my trance at Johnson's. It was a new life, horticulturally speaking, for me.

No more the humble, long-suffering impatiens, the uncomplaining, ever-blooming, sun-or-shade, if-you-forget-to-water-me-it's-okay plant that has saved so many gardeners from a blossomless summer. The pink, the cerise, the delicate flame-color, the fringed, the exquisite dianthus would take its place.

They looked lovely in June. I was miffed when a neighbor came by and said in a tone that suggested that I had forgotten my roots, "No impatiens?" "No," I said, I suppose a mite smugly, "not this year."

I admired her loyalty, of course, but I pitied her for not seeing the little Versailles that was unfolding at her feet.

But now it is July, and the dianthus, having done their stuff, are resting. They have gone to green stalks. The only blooming in sight is being done by—who else?—an impatiens. I put out, strictly for auld lang syne, a last year's relic that had obligingly wintered over inside. It is foaming with orange blossoms. It has even put out a few striped blooms. It is a reproach to the exhausted dianthus, a reproach to me.

Meanwhile, there is high drama in the basil patch. It is my one relia-ble crop. It makes me feel like a farm-er. I am insufferable about my pesto.

One morning I went out, and there were cut-outs on the leaves. They were not exactly shredded, but I was put in mind of Fawn and Ollie.

"Slugs," said the organic gardener, who gave me the plants. "Put a saucer of beer in the middle of the patch. The slugs will climb in and drown. They will die blissfully happy."

How humane, I thought. How environmentally sound.

I poured out the Coors in two foil tins and placed them in the ground.

The next morning, the tins were flung on the grass, one of them upside down. They were empty. I suspected a late-night orgy.

Obviously, lightweight containers that could be carried off by the customers would not do. I got hold of a heavy terra cotta saucer, filled it to the brim, dug a little space for it, and waited.

By this time I knew who I was dealing with: the squirrels who are still trying to get even for the bird-feeder they can't crack. They can do everything else, like the urban guerillas they are. They transplant bulbs. They moved all my daffodils down the hill so I can't see them. A reader wrote that a squirrel tried to gnaw down his house in Chicago when he stopped putting peanuts on the window sill.

But I hadn't known they drank. How could I not have known? They have all our vices. Avarice, greed—take over, eat everthing in sight. Where do you think Michael Milken learned about getting it all?

Next morning, the saucer was still in place, but empty. So was a box of raisins I had dumbly left out. But there were no slugs in sight, dead or alive. No squirrels with big heads and unsteady feet either. They had gone underground, which is what they do after a big job.

A friend from Georgia offered a rural recipe. Eat the contents of half a canteloupe. Line the rind with salt. Place in garden. I did all that. The next morning the melon was gone.

The squirrels may have sold the husk to a susceptible raccoon as a quonset hut. Who knows?

My guess is that the slugs hired the squirrels as consultants, and that I now am like so many people in Washington—fighting an unseen enemy that has unlimited resources and no conscience. I can go on putting out melons and beer until the squirrels get so fat they can't function. Or else I can face the fact that the only thing I can grow is impatiens and learn to love Franco-American spaghetti.

[*July 9, 1989*]

Thomas Walks in Scalia's Shoes

People thought that Clarence Thomas might not be much of a protector of the powerless—he had pretty much erased his past as a poor black and rejected the legal remedies proffered by the government. But he has exceeded dreadful expectations. In a disgusting dissent in the case of the beating of a shackled, manacled prisoner he shows he doesn't subscribe even to a bedrock tenet of human decency: Don't kick a man when he's down.

His Senate confirmation hearings cost the country a great deal, due to the explosive allegations by Anita Hill. If he continues to reason the way he did in *Hudson v. McMillian* for the next 30 years or so, his tenure will cost even more. The outstanding mediocrity of his mind was evident in the little we were given about his record. The distortions and the denials of his personal life and the fatuous declarations of self-reliance boded ill for justice. But the hair-splitting pitilessness of his dissent is a new dimension.

At the confirmation hearings, he had an opportunity to explain why he wanted the job for which George Bush perjuriously claimed he was the best qualified. When Sen. Herbert H. Kohl (D-Wis.) asked him the question, he was ready. From his window at the U.S. Circuit Court of Appeals here, he could see criminal defendants being bused to court. He thought he could have been one of them, he said.

"So you feel you have the same fate, or could have. . . . So I walk in their shoes, and I could bring something different to the court."

But judging from the dissenting opinion in the case of a prisoner being beaten by prison guards—under the observing eye of a supervisor who merely cautioned the perpetrators "not to have too much fun"—he's going to bring the same old constitutional crankiness that is the principal contribution of Justice Antonin Scalia.

Scalia, a brilliant and compelling extremist on the limits of the

Constitution, raised most of the points in oral argument that Thomas folded into their joint dissent in the case. The plight of handcuffed, shackled prisoners being kicked and beaten by guards moved such sticklers for the protection of authority as Chief Justice William H. Rehnquist and Justice Byron White to find for the prisoner, Keith J. Hudson, and to find his torturers' conduct a violation of Eighth Amendment sanctions against "cruel and unusual punishment." Justice Sandra Day O'Connor, hardly a radical, wrote the majority opinion.

But rookie Thomas, standing with Scalia, brushed aside individual rights in favor of a handkerchief-sized interpretation of the Constitution. Never mind the rights of the prisoner. The federal Constitution must not be stretched to cover matters that can be handled by the state. The injuries inflicted on Hudson were not "significant" enough to warrant invoking the Constitution, a document that should be whisked into the vault when ordinary citizens come seeking redress.

Thomas makes some specious arguments about the uncongenial state of prisons at the time of the Founding Fathers. Prisons are meant to be harsh and unwelcoming. That's part of the punishment. But to go from there and say that the Constitution does not prevent guards from kicking and punching a handcuffed and manacled prisoner is too long a trip for the strictest constructionist. Americans have little sympathy for prisoners—Keith Hudson was doing 15 years for armed robbery—

and generally think convicts get what they deserve.

To follow Thomas's reasoning, we would make our prison system a school for sadism, where guards can manhandle a prisoner at will as long as they don't meet the Scalia-Thomas test for "serious injury." With prison population at an all-time high and recidivism at a truly appalling rate, it would seem wiser to emphasize rehabilitation and education in our jails. But that's the kind of soft-headed thinking that conservatives frown on.

Hudson suffered minor bruises and swelling of his face, mouth and lip and a crack in his dental plate, and that just wasn't enough for Scalia and Thomas.

Says Sen. Arlen Specter (R-Pa.), one of Thomas's most vociferous defenders at the awful confirmation hearings, "I think he needs to mature a little."

Alvin J. Bronstein, the American Civil Liberties Union lawyer who was Hudson's court-appointed attorney, says the bad news is that Thomas has come on as Scalia's puppet. Worse news, of course, is that he reached his conclusions on his own.

Either way, it is a distressing debut for a man who was born an underdog and has forgotten all about what it was like. Far from identifying with the poor defendants who were on the bus that he saw from his window, Thomas seems more like the bus driver.

[*February 27, 1992*]

ERMA BOMBECK

Some have waited in line more than an hour to ask Erma Bombeck to autograph her latest book. Even after six hours of nonstop signing at a book fair, Bombeck is zinging one-liners at her readers like sparks from a forge. Her laugh, a heh-heh-heh like a creaky hinge on a gate, bubbles up over the murmur of other voices. Three hours remain until closing, and all 750 of her books on hand have already been sold; but people are still waiting in line to meet her, so she signs her name on slips of paper.

"You get a lot of people coming out to see you and see how many wrinkles you really have, and whether you really are 120 years old," says Bombeck, who has been writing her syndicated humor column for more than a quarter of a century. "I'm seeing a second generation coming in—you know, the ones who say, 'I thought you wrote fiction before; my mother used to put it on the refrigerator.' Now it's beginning to come together for them and they're fans."

Fans include men as well as women, and many want to tell her about a column with special meaning for them. Usually it's one that's down to earth, simple, funny, and true: one that clicked with the reader. Ellen Goodman once wrote that Bombeck's columns "strike a responsive truth . . . made less desperate because it is universal."

Bombeck doesn't always remember writing the column a reader is enthralled with because the subject is frequently so commonplace. That's her gift. "I can take small topics. I don't have to discuss the impact of World War II. I can take something really tiny and go with it," she says. "Those are the best kind, those are the fun kind. The columns that get the best response in terms of laughter are those little, mundane things like 'I can't throw away a spice.'"

Columnists are like leeches, she says. "We attach ourselves to something and say here's another viewpoint for you. How do you like this? How does this play for you? All we do is sort of dissect it and go round again, and never come up with anything really new. That's what columnists are all about. We play off everything else."

Bombeck fishes for laughs with the quick punch delivery of a vaudeville comedienne, and has successfully adapted that technique to her newspaper column. "I've only got 450 words. I've got to tell you at the beginning what this is all about," she says. "I've got to get in and out and leave you with a laugh." Even after twenty-six years, maintaining the focus and "voice" of the column is hard work. "The focus has always been a problem for me," Bombeck says. "I feel very passionate about a lot of things—politics, issues—and I have to fight all the time to keep my focus . . . [on] these little mundane things, these little snatches."

The voice of her column has been consistent over the years, grounded in her middle-class midwestern childhood and life as a homemaker and mother. "I think the whole world knows I'm pretty moralistic, pretty square about things. I'm not Anita Bryant or anything," she says, laughing at herself, "but I think that's the humor of it all. I think people would be very amazed if I were to do a column on condoms or something—they'd absolutely be in a state of shock." Unable to resist pitching for a laugh at her own expense, she adds, "They know that I know about condoms. They know that. Surely they must know that I live in the twenty-first century."

Her goal is to connect with readers, but to do that she writes for herself, not for some imagined reader. "I still write for me, because if you start anticipating or aiming at a certain group, then you're in deep trouble, because you don't know that group very well," she says. "At some point you're going to get caught. There's going to be a dichotomy. You're going to ride one side of the fence here, and one over here."

Bombeck's humor works precisely because she so frequently uses herself as the fall guy—much the way Robert Benchley, her idol as a humorist, did. She tries never to be funny at her readers' expense. "My job is real simple. It's just to take something everyone relates to and put it in perspective, and put some distance between it, and say this is really pretty funny," she says. "You're going to laugh at this. Trust me. We can do this because look what happened to me. I can use myself as a foil because I don't write rotten mail to myself."

Because column writing is so personal, readers develop a close relationship with the columnist. "You make it personal—you give away a piece of yourself with every column you do," Bombeck says. In her column she portrays herself as a woman who has lived a life much like theirs, who validates the ordinary happenings of their everyday life, and who consistently sees the bright side. "After years of reading someone, you feel you know them pretty well," Bombeck says. "And they build up this relationship with you through your column and if they see a story on the front page about [a pregnant] Demi Moore appearing with nothing but a wedding ring on, they say, 'Oh, I wonder what Erma's going to do with that one. I bet she's going to come down on her.'"

Regular readers usually know ahead of time what a columnist will say about things, and believe they know what the columnist's life is like because they may have read some details of her life. But Bombeck says she doesn't tell readers everything. "I tell them what I want them to know and I tell them what's amusing. I don't tell them the sad parts of my life." When she came back from her sister's funeral, for example, she wrote a column, but said nothing about the death. "I don't want to tell [readers] about that yet," she says. "At some point maybe I will, after I've lived with it for a while and maybe it has some meaning for somebody, but people don't care about that. Not really."

Readers want to laugh, and Bombeck tries to give the brighter side of life. "That's what I want to be known for," she says. "I don't want to get in a position of being so personal they feel sorry for you and they're not laughing with you, they're sort of commiserating with you—you never want to get to that point." In some respects Bombeck is just the way she sounds in her column, amused by life. But she's also very private. "I'm not the column. I'm not that same person in the column, and people want to believe that I am like that," she says. "To some degree I am, but to a lot of degrees I'm not—not at all."

Her wit spills over in the one-liners that pepper her conversation; she clearly enjoys the way she is able to entertain people. Her ability to make people laugh relies on their expectation that she will be funny, she says, though that may not be the way she feels at that moment. "That is not me. I'm doing what I'm supposed to do. That's why I'm there," she says. "They don't want to know about my life, they don't want to know what deep thoughts I'm having. I mean, get real. They want to laugh. So you go out and do your routine."

Bombeck gave up regular television appearances because they required too much time away from home, and she has cut back on public engagements. But she still packs the house whenever she lectures, and she loves to hear an audience laugh. "You can't imagine the wonderful feeling of walking into a room, and people start to smile," she says. "There's no other reason to smile except they know that you're going to smile back; that's what you're noted for."

Laughter is her index of whether she's doing a good job. "For an hour, these people have forgotten about all their problems—and we all have them," she says. "They're in this darkened theater, and [their problems] mean nothing to them any more. They're going to have a good time and that's it. That's what I work at. When I go home, I've got my own set of problems and so do they."

It is the sense of connecting with people, of making people laugh, that has sustained Bombeck. "You can't imagine what it's like to say something and get a laugh out of somebody," she says, "I mean, this is an emotion people don't part with easily." Her technique is to "set up a situation and it just sort of lays there, it's not hilariously funny. What makes it funny is what you're going to bring to it. Your imagination is going to take it a step further, much more than I could do. You're going to take it places where I've never even been before." Humor is ineffable. "You don't just sit there and measure it out," she says. "Humor is a spontaneous, wonderful bit of an outburst that just comes. It's unbridled, it's unplanned, it's full of surprises. It's just magic."

But it takes an enormous amount of work to make the column appear effortless to readers. Bombeck tells aspiring writers that she lists "rewrite" as her occupation on her driver's license. "That's what I do for a living. It's not wonderful," she says. "It's supposed to sound like something that came off the top of my head as I was folding the laundry, and I thought, 'Oh God, I just want to say this.' That's not true at all.

"To loosen something up and not make it sound like an English textbook takes a lot of work and a lot of rewriting. And after a while you get your own way of saying things, and that is called style," she says. "You just keep writing and writing and rewriting and rewriting."

To be effective, a writer has to describe things. "You have to make them see a situation," she says. "OK, you're in the kitchen, and you set up a scene where you're getting a large knife out of the knife rack and your husband looks at you and says, 'You're going to cut off your arm with that.' And you look at him dryly and say, 'You've just ruined my surprise.' You're getting a picture of those two standing there and he's driving you nuts. Men are always saying that—'You're going to cut your finger off. You're doing this to torture me . . .'"

She composes on a typewriter, without notes, saying it buys her time to think, and that she wouldn't know how to use a computer anyway. "While I'm x-ing stuff out, I'm thinking about what I want to do with it," she says. "I do every bit of revising. I mother that right along. I don't have notes to go on. I'm just pulling it out of the air." She revises the column until she's satisfied. Although she seems gregarious, she is a solitary writer and never reads her columns aloud. No one in her family reads her columns before they're done.

Ideas for columns come from everywhere, but mostly from her daily experience. She doesn't keep a file of ideas, preferring to let a column sprout from a chance encounter or a line she hears. Some ideas don't pan out. "You get an idea and you think there ought to be something here and you slave over it," she said. "After about two days I figure, Erma, there ain't nothin' there—get rid of it. You're forcing this and it won't play."

Not every column is a gem, she readily admits. "When you write on deadline like we do, you've got to understand. . . . I've got three columns that have got to go out on Monday, as sure as that week's going to roll around." Bombeck faxes them to Universal Press Syndicate in Kansas City, which distributes them to more than 700 newspapers. "You go with what you've got," she says. "You have to. You have to compromise with yourself at some point and say this is the best that I can do."

Her appeal seems universal. Bombeck's columns run in small dailies in midwestern communities like Ada, Oklahoma, and big city papers like the *New York Daily News*. "I like it because it's funny and I can relate to some of the things she has to say," said Brenda Tollett, *Ada Evening News* lifestyle editor. "It's a little bit of enjoyment rather than seeing depressing news all the time." Next to advice columnist Ann Landers, Bombeck is the most widely syndicated newspaper columnist in the country. "People say are you discriminated against [because of being a woman]? No," says Bombeck. "My business discriminates against no one who makes a lot of money."

It wasn't always so. Bombeck worked her way through high school and college, began her career as a copy girl at the *Dayton* (Ohio) *Journal-Herald,* and spent seven years writing obituaries, society and club notes and features for the women's pages. She loved writing features but didn't like straight reporting. "I can never get facts straight," she said. "It bored me." Her first column in the 1940s was "Operation Dustrag," which she has referred to as a sort of sick Heloise.

She took time off to have three children and returned to newspaper work at age thirty-seven, starting a column she called "At Wit's End," first for the *Kettering-Oakwood* (Ohio) *Times,* then for the *Journal-Herald.* Within a matter of weeks, the Newsday Syndicate picked her up and began distributing her columns. Familiar with syndicated columns that ran in the women's pages, which dealt with topics like sewing, gardening, gossip, or advice on relationships, Bombeck said she never thought in terms of writing a column herself. She was the only humor columnist in syndication when she started, she says. She didn't know how big it would get.

"Back in the 1960s, I was a woman in the suburbs and I didn't have a voice anywhere in this world . . . and I literally gave myself a voice through the column," she says. "It reflected me and I had to get rid of some of it. So I just started to write honestly of what I felt, whether it was good or bad or irreverent. It didn't make any difference. Those were the things I felt." In 1971, *Life* magazine dubbed her the "Socrates of the Ironing Board," a tribute to her homespun wisdom. That same year she moved from a thirty-acre farm in Ohio to Paradise Valley, Arizona.

Bombeck realized she wasn't alone in needing a voice, and over the years her column has reflected her changing perspective on the women's movement and society in general. Skeptical at first of militant feminists, she came to agree that women needed opportunities in addition to marriage and children. As her column has changed, so has her audience grown more diverse. About a hundred letters a week come from working women and homemakers, young and old, men and women. "It's done a 180-degree change," she says, "because you have to reflect the times."

The biggest difference she sees in readers is the increase in the number of people who tell her they're offended by what she writes. It makes it difficult to write humor, she says. "Never have I encountered such sensitivity among people. . . . It's to that point where you don't have room to move," she says. "I think people are on overload of the world . . . they can't take any more bad news, any more worries. . . . We are just assaulted with this to the point where we're angry, we're frustrated, and we don't know what to do any more—and it's very hard to lay humor on people like that."

Some topics, such as drugs, Bombeck finds too serious to tackle. Other subjects are voluntarily off limits, such as her children's dating habits or relationships, or anything that would embarrass her family. "No one sets the rules for you. You just have to set them for yourself," she says. "Oh, you still go for their bedrooms—the cockroach that hangs their coat up, stuff like that. That's safe territory for me and they know that. But I'm talking about things that might single them out and reflect them and make them different than anyone else. I wouldn't do that to them."

Bombeck is also protective of her mother, whom she says uses words like a James Thurber character. "It's all right for me to say she has a toilet seat that plays the theme from [Dr. Zhivago]. She thinks a lot of people have one," says Bombeck, laughing. "But there's a difference between making fun of her and laughing with her. You have to be sensitive about that."

How carefully she tends the fence separating the columnist's public persona and her private life was demonstrated the time she took her then-teenaged children to the Rose Bowl parade when she served as grand marshal. "They knew what I did for a living, but they didn't know so many people appreciated it," she says. "So when our car turned and went around the corner, all these people were screaming my name, and they said, 'What is this—that's our mother—what did you do?' They were truly shocked."

Not one to rest on her laurels, Bombeck says she is motivated by the insecurity of knowing that "some little Chicago housewife" might be writing a column that could replace hers. She has no intention of quitting, comparing the idea of ending her column to what she felt like when she stopped producing regular features for the television show "Good Morning America." "I said I'm never going to miss this job, except—except when I get out of bed some morning and think, 'Oh, that would make a great spot. That would be wonderful." The same thing would happen if she were to stop writing the column, she says: "I would get out of bed in the morning and see this story and say, 'Oh this begs to be put in perspective.' I would just kill myself if I didn't have an outlet for that."

With the exception of three to four weeks' vacation every year, when she says she "shuts down," Bombeck must be on. "Sometimes it's hard. Some weeks you don't have any ideas and you have to go with lesser ones than you want," she says. "But there are always those wonderful moments that you have that gem to go with. Everything goes together and it comes out right. That's a magic moment. I love it."

AT WIT'S END

Second Pregnancies Erase Any Modesty

Since Demi Moore's *Vanity Fair* appearance, which gives new meaning to "mother of all covers," I've read a host of male reactions. They range from "disgusting" to "shocking" to "breathtakingly beautiful."

As a mother, I feel bound to tell you: You're missing the point. This is Demi Moore's second child. I'll repeat that. This is Demi Moore's second child. Translated, that means modesty is no longer a word in her vocabulary.

I am willing to bet that before the birth of her first offspring, she wore weights in the hems of her maternity tops. She demurely crossed her legs at the ankles at all times and requested two sheets in the gynecologist's office. All that changed when she entered the hospital to deliver.

There is a stream of men we have never seen before who whip in and out of our hospital rooms like they are caught in a revolving door. They invade our bare chests with stethoscopes and throw back the sheets to "take a look at what we have here." They thump, probe, squeeze and push on every part of our bodies. They interrupt our baths to inquire about our irregularities and watch us struggle with hospital gowns that are too small to set a cocktail glass on.

There should be a sign over every delivery room in the country: *Here enters the last modest woman on the face of the Earth!*

When I delivered my second child, I shared a room with a young woman giving birth to her first. She was so modest she referred to her pregnancy as "something in the oven." When she was examined, she turned her head to the wall and bit her lips until they bled.

Two days after she delivered, she approached a man in the hall and said, "Doctor, I'm nursing. Does this look normal to you?" and proceeded to drop her robe. A nurse guided her to her room and told her she had just bared herself to a maintenance man.

The loss of modesty is a given. You have no control over it. From that day on, your body is never your own. Your children will not only watch you when you shower, they will bring along their little friends. When you are using the bathroom, they will unlock the door with a shish-kebab skewer. You sit at the breakfast table with your robe open. It doesn't matter anymore.

After I left the hospital following the birth of my first child, I somehow knew I'd never be the same again. At that time, what I was feeling didn't have a name. After this summer, I suspect it will be known as the Demi Moore syndrome.

[*August 4, 1991*]

Striking the Right Note

You have to know a little background to appreciate this column.

My husband and I both work out of our home. His office is next to mine. We share the same thermostat.

Every day after lunch, I take a 20-minute nap. When I return to my office, I pass the thermostat and adjust it to a warmer temperature. The other day, as I mechanically reached for the dial, I encountered the following note taped to it:

"Sleep-induced body temperature declines are not uncommon. Usually, the body temperature returns to normal within minutes of resumption of normal activity. Normal activity does not include hiking thermostats up and down."

It was signed "Mr. Science."

I want an unbiased opinion here. You don't have to give your right name or worry about reprisals. But don't you think there is something wrong with a man who keeps the summer temperature of a room the same as for fur storage? I mean, if this were a wax museum, I'd understand, but this is an office, where working in a coat is cumbersome.

I think the real problem here is that he secretly resents the fact that I can fall asleep in the middle of the day and at the end of 20 minutes awake refreshed. It's a gift. He cannot do this; he'd sleep right through prime time.

I marched into his office and told him I found his note patronizing. He said, "I find notes make a more lasting impression."

"What's the matter?" I said. "Couldn't get a stonecutter to record it properly?"

I returned to my office and put the note in a drawer with the rest of his epistles. There was one from the year we camped on a beach in Michigan. He attached it to a whisk broom and hung it on the flap of the tent. It read, "Do not track sand in the tent. A clean tent is a happy tent. Use brush on bottom of feet. Remember, the muck stops here." Signed, "Mr. Tidy Camp."

There were others. The little 3-by-5 card he covered with plastic and attached to the electricity meter next to the garage that read, "Give it a rest!" There was one he attached to his toolbox that read, "If you borrow these without permission, be prepared to go to jail."

I'll answer his latest note when I calm down a bit and when I can figure out how you spell the sound of sticking out your tongue and blowing a raspberry.

[*September 27, 1988*]

"I've Loved You Best"

It is normal for children to want assurance that they are loved. Having all the warmth of the Berlin Wall, I always have admired women who can reach out to pat their children and not have them flinch.

Feeling more comfortable on paper, I wrote the following for each of my children.

To the First Born

I've loved you best because you were our first miracle. You were the genesis of a marriage, the fulfillment of young love, the promise of our infinity.

You sustained us through the hamburger years. The first

apartment furnished in Early Poverty . . . our first mode of transportation (1955 feet) . . . the 7-inch TV set we paid on for 36 months.

You wore new, had unused grandparents and more clothes than a Barbie doll. You were the "original model" for unsure parents trying to work the bugs out. You got the strained lamb, open pins and three-hour naps.

You were the beginning.

To the Middle Child

I've always loved you the best because you drew a dumb spot in the family and it made you stronger for it.

You cried less, had more patience, wore faded, and never in your life did anything "first," but it only made you more special. You are the one we relaxed with and realized a dog could kiss you and you wouldn't get sick. You could cross a street by yourself long before you were old enough to get married, and the world wouldn't come to an end if you went to bed with dirty feet.

You were the continuance.

To the Baby

I've always loved you the best because endings generally are sad and you are such a joy. You readily accepted the milk-stained bibs. The lower bunk. The cracked baseball bat. The baby book, barren but for a recipe for graham pie crust that someone jammed between the pages.

You are the one we held onto so tightly. For you see, you are the link with the past that gives a reason to tomorrow. You darken our hair, quicken our steps, square our shoulders, restore our vision, and give us humor that security and maturity can't give us.

When your hairline takes on the shape of Lake Erie and your children tower over you, you will still be "the Baby."

You were the culmination.

[July 20, 1971]

JANE BRYANT QUINN

Personal finance columnist Jane Bryant Quinn says she's so bad at arithmetic that it's a joke. But that's the point. "Numbers are absolutely unnecessary" for managing money, she says. Her column, "Staying Ahead," preaches the importance of using common sense. "I want people to think about the nut of the problem and not just think it's numbers that have to be manipulated. The numbers are utterly incidental to the nut of the problem," she says, "and the nut of the problem is a common sense thing. Common sense is not hard and everything has it—almost everybody." It sounds simple, but her message has alienated many stockbrokers and financial planners.

She tells of a man who congratulated her after a speech, saying his son, a stockbroker, had refused to come with him. Quinn shakes her head. "I always think if somebody can come and hear me, maybe they'll get what I'm saying." She's saying that managing money is based on logic, not magic. "Financial people are always bringing out new products and they're almost always very complicated. You don't need any of that stuff. Only Wall Street needs them," she says. "People can do very well with their savings and their investments—with bank accounts, treasury securities, and no-load diversified mutual funds that buy stock. That's all you need. That's all I have. . . . They do well, they're low cost, you can understand them well enough to manage them yourself. You will not pay huge fees to brokers and lose that money off the top."

Quinn could pass for a stockbroker herself in her elegant suit and simple gold jewelry. But when she writes her column there's no question about whose side she's on. Many people think they're stupid about money, she says, and they believe in the myth of the financial genius who knows the magic secret to making money. "You don't feel this way in other professions, right? Nursing or teaching? A good nurse works hard," she says, "but there's this mystique of the financial genius where something drops from heaven." Over and over in different ways, Quinn tells her readers there isn't any magic secret, and she tries to cut through the maze of numbers.

Her no-nonsense approach is one of the strengths of her column, and she's as straightforward in person as she is in her writing, avoiding financial terms the way she does junk bonds. "My job is to write the column without the jargon," she says. "I use English and think sensibly about what I'm doing. Financial topics are logic, and I'm wonderful at logic. I think conceptually, I understand concepts, I can put them together and separate them. I can turn the prism and see something from a new direction. My mind works that way with great clarity."

A Hancock Award winner, Quinn is knowledgeable, authoritative, and "willing to tackle issues that relate to readers, not just economists," said Tim Kelly, editor of the *Lexington* (Ky.) *Herald-Leader,* which runs her column. "She's got a track record, and she obviously works hard at what she does. She's a reporter first and a columnist second." Quinn's column is often controversial, Kelly added, and the paper regularly gets letters about her column from people in the business world.

Aware of the influence her column has, Quinn says she forgets about it when she is involved in the actual writing. "When you are sitting in your office by yourself with your word processor, writing what you think about something, you tend to forget it has any influence whatsoever," she says. "I think in terms of 'This is important and I want people to know this.' I know the press has power, and I know my column has power, but I am not consciously aware of it." She believes "muscling around," using the power of the column, is the wrong approach for a journalist.

In gathering information, Quinn says she talks to everyone she can think of—"the hardest part is deciding who to believe." She then writes what seems to her the fairest and best of what she has learned. "I don't think it's my job to unseat this, demolish that, get back at this. That's not the way I think. My audience is you. I'm thinking about you." She spends a great deal of time on research because she knows that people trust her. "I work very hard at being right. That's the hardest thing about the kind of work I'm in," she says. "When you give a political opinion, everyone can instantly argue with you, and it hardly matters." But when Quinn gives her opinion, people act on it. "People out there will say, 'Let's do this, let's not do this.' They will give it to their financial planner or brokers," she says. "It's an incredible responsibility, and I do a tremendous amount of research, talking to people, worrying, biting my nails, checking back."

Her opinions are well grounded and usually fairly conservative. "I don't say, 'Here's this nifty partnership, go and buy this.' I don't believe in it," she says. "The fact is, I think you can make a hell of a lot more money doing it my way." Despite the time she spends on research, an occasional error creeps in. "I feel as sick at heart about a mistake today as the first time I ever got into journalism," she says. "I want to get in bed and pull the sheet over my head." She says it's especially distressing if she knows she could have avoided a mistake by making one more phone call. She knows putting out her opinion "invites people to shoot back at you," but she says she doesn't mind the attacks. "A mistake makes me sick, but an opinion I feel very confident about and am willing to defend."

Ideas are the backbone of a columnist's business, and Quinn has no difficulty thinking up topics. "Ideas fall on me from heaven. I have twenty ideas a day. I have wire baskets that just overflow with clips and ideas and things. I'm always digging out and throwing things away." Two questions guide her: Is the topic timely? and Would it be of concern to readers?

"This is a very difficult subject to write a national column about— you have to have some idea all the time about what's going on in so many different parts of the country," she says, noting for example that there are no second mortgages in Texas. "You must go all over the country all of the time." Some of her principal sources are the trade publications, specialists recommended by trade associations, and the chairs of various American Bar Association committees." I have a small number of steady sources," she says, "but the cast of characters is constantly changing."

Quinn does almost all of her reporting by telephone, which she finds frustrating because she prefers live interviews. "I was never so much aware of it as when I worked for tv," she says, referring to the eight years that she worked for CBS, "when you take your ten-ton pencil—the lights, camera, and crew—and you go see things. It was wonderful. You go all over the country to get your twenty-second sound bite." But telephone interviews are the most practical for her newspaper column. "My phone technique is what I would call your basic schmooze," she says. "I have a series of questions that I know I'm interested in, but I schmooze around a lot because things turn up in conversation that might lead you to another point you didn't know existed or another story. It's easier to schmooze in person, but I'm so busy I wind up doing most of it by phone."

She writes to the average person—"whoever that is"—and thinks in terms of a one-to-one dialogue with readers. She says the American public has gotten more sophisticated about money, and more people have money now than when her predecessor, Sylvia Porter, began writing her financial column forty years ago. Sometimes she angles columns to specific readers. A column on first-time homebuyers, for example, might appeal to younger readers, while another column on annuities might be read by older people. Quinn receives fifty to sixty letters a week from readers, and she reads all of them. Sometimes readers make suggestions that she pursues, but more people write to criticize her. "I hear from so many people who are sore at me," she says, "rarely from people who really like the column."

Her two newspaper columns a week, syndicated to about 200 newspapers by the Washington Post Writers Group, are written "right on top of my deadlines," she says. "There's no point in working ahead in my business. You write something two weeks ahead, and then right on top of it they pass a law, things change this and change that, interest rates go up or down, and you have to change." She loves gathering information, but writing is hard work. She rewrites again and again.

"Someone said a work of art is never finished, it's always abandoned," she says. "I will rewrite until they literally seize it from my hand and say stop." Quinn says the first draft is never easy, and that she doesn't know many professional writers who like writing. "Writing is hard. Writing is heavy lifting. Writing is labor. Writing hurts. It hurts your head and your shoulders and your body and you ache and you feel as if you've been moving stones all day. I always feel that." For Quinn, the fun is in talking to people, gathering information, reading the files, and pulling it all together. "Then you sit down and stare at the screen, and say, 'Oh, God.'"

Although she has an office at *Newsweek,* where she writes a regular magazine column, Quinn does most of her writing at home in Westchester County, about two hours by train from New York. When her children were young, the two-hour commute was a gift. "These were two hours out of my life that no one could get to me—there was no phone," she says. Quinn goes into the office to close the column, meet with her researcher and editors, and conduct some interviews, saying, "I can't write amidst a lot of noise and clamor." But writing her column is not as difficult as writing a book, and she says she can bang out a column on an airplane if she has to.

Quinn always wanted to be a journalist but says being a reporter again after writing a column would drive her nuts. "It's not the picture and it's not the name. It's the ability to say what I think about something . . . to say this is a good idea and I want to tell you about it. You can't do that as a reporter. I make my own judgments and I can go out and give my own opinions." Her philosophy has been always to take the job with the most responsibility. "That's the best and most interesting and most challenging and most exciting job," she says. "That's where I am."

Writing a column was the furthest thing from Quinn's mind when she went looking for a journalism job in New York City, armed with a liberal arts degree from Middlebury College in Vermont and several summers of experience writing for her hometown paper in Niagara Falls, New York. "I always knew I wanted to be a newspaper reporter. It's the only thing I ever wanted to be," she says. "I was always writing something." An American literature major in college, Quinn feels strongly that journalists should study liberal arts. "To be a journalist, what you should do most of all is furnish your mind with history, politics, economics, sociology, literature," she says. "Your skill, after all, is your writing."

But this was 1961, and she was hired by *Newsweek* to sort mail. "Those were the days when they took real smart girls out of college and put them on the mail [detail]," Quinn says. Her Phi Beta Kappa key in hand, Quinn figured she would work her way up. But the other women laughed. "Look around you, Jane, you idiot,' they said. I realized the men were all writers," Quinn recalls, "and the women were all older and older researchers." So she looked for another job, but soon discovered that writing jobs were reserved for men.

She recounts how she got an interview at *Time* magazine under false pretenses, by saying she was interested in working on a series of books on cooking. But when she revealed to the editor that she was really interested in writing news, he stood up and shouted at her that she had wasted his time by applying for a man's job. "I said, 'Why can't I have a job like this?' He said, 'It would upset our men,'" Quinn recalls, "and it was legal for him to say it. I was discovering for the first time, scales falling from my eyes, what I was up against."

Quinn finally got a job writing for the women's section of *Insiders Newsletter*, a *Look* magazine publication. Two weeks after she got the job, she discovered she was pregnant. She kept thinking she should stay home because so few women were in the workforce. But she was inspired by her editor, a smart, witty woman who was married and

had children. Eventually Quinn moved into her position. The consumer movement was just starting, and she found herself gravitating
toward consumer finance stories. "I found them fascinating and had a
knack for them. They totally involved me intellectually." When the
Newsletter folded, Quinn found work editing a financial newsletter
for McGraw-Hill. A few years later, when the *Washington Post* asked
her to write a personal finance column, Quinn was not interested. But
after McGraw-Hill promoted her but refused to give her the title of
publisher, reserved only for men, she decided to quit and try writing a
column. It was 1973. The gamble paid off.

"There aren't very many people who have the opportunity to
work for themselves and do work on their own. Common to women
of my generation, I had no future in an organization. So, like a lot of
other women who started their own businesses to get out from under
all this garbage, I went to work for myself," she says. "No one assigns
me anything. I'm self-employed. I'm on my own, I make my own
decisions."

One regret is that she and Sylvia Porter created "a new little golden
ghetto within the world of finance reporting. . . . Consumer reporting
has now become women's work. It just kills me. It doesn't matter how
good you are and how hard you work, they carve out your little world
as women's work." She and Porter would have been equally good at
covering economic policy, Quinn says. "I have often been sorry my life
didn't lead me to covering the Federal Reserve, because then I would
have made the world more broadly safe for women."

Being female has been an advantage at times. Quinn often ran
into what she calls the "little lady syndrome" and found it useful. "In
one way your femaleness is a handicap, but in another way it leaves
you an opening you can run through, if you know how to use it," she
says. "I don't mean sexually, but know how to use the fact they don't
expect anything out of you. Therefore they may be less guarded and
so you may learn something." Because her column has made her an
authority on personal finance, "I can't play that game anymore," she
says.

Her readers are men and women, and the question she is most
often asked is how to find good money managers and financial planners. "I don't have an answer. My feeling is people can do it themselves." That was the premise behind her 1978 book, *Everyone's
Money Book*. It's loaded with consumer information, from advice on
writing a will to buying a car or getting a mortgage. Her latest book,
published in 1991, is a financial planning guide, *Making the Most of*

Your Money, structured to help people order their finances. After finishing the book, she told her editor she wanted to write something irresponsible. Quinn laughs as she remembers the editor's response: "She said, 'Jane, you can't do it. Everyone does what they can, and you can't write irresponsible books.'"

STAYING AHEAD

Picking Mutual Funds

NEW YORK. Two new studies just came across my desk that help answer a question asked by millions of investors: "How do I pick a good mutual fund?"

You'll be pleased to hear that the answers are easy. (1) Pick a fund without up-front or back-end sales charges, and with the lowest possible annual fees. (2) Bond-fund buyers should pick one that's indexed to the market as a whole. (3) Stock-fund buyers should pick one with a persistently good record in the past. Superior stock funds tend to stay that way.

The word on bond funds comes from Lewis Altfest, a New York City financial planner and associate professor of finance at Pace University's graduate school of business. He studied bond-fund performance for the years 1974 to 1988, as well as for four shorter periods within those years.

In general, he found that bond-fund returns just about match the bond-market averages. Adjusted for the annual expenses you pay, however, they fall below average. In general, the higher the expenses the lower your return. (This study didn't even count front- and back-end sales charges, which penalize your yield even more.)

What's more, Altfest found no consistency. Just because a fund ranks above average this year doesn't mean it will repeat the trick. So looking at past performance records won't help you find a superior fund.

Moral: Your best buy in bond funds is an index fund with no load (no sales charge) and the lowest possible annual fees. (An index fund buys securities that mimic the action of the market as a whole; no attempt is made to beat the market in any way.) The lowest-cost bond-index fund for individuals: Vanguard's no-load Bond Market Fund, with annual expenses of 0.21 percent. (For information, call 800-662-7447 in Valley Forge, Pa.)

Looking only at high-yield bond funds (better known as junk funds), Altfest found that the game wasn't worth the candle. Junk funds returned only 1.5 percentage points more than corporate funds, and the study period ended before the big junk-bond defaults began. You are simply not earning enough extra money to make it worthwhile to take the risk. Since the junk-bond market crashed, you have probably lost money relative to the safer funds.

The word on stock funds comes from two finance professors, William Goetzmann of Columbia University and Roger Ibbotson of Yale. They studied stock-owning mutual funds, looking at successive one-year and two-year periods from 1976 to 1988.

For stock funds, they found, winners do repeat. A money manager who did well in the past has about 60 percent chance of doing well in the future, too. Similarly, there's a 60 percent chance that a poor fund will not improve. So in picking a stock-owning mutual fund, past performance counts.

Many academics believe that investment results are unpredictable; superior performance is purely a matter of luck, not skill. Goetzmann and Ibbotson beg to differ. Some stock funds are demonstrably better than others. In general, the higher they rank, the better they perform, long term.

With one exception: The managers at the very top of any fund performance list aren't necessarily the best, Goetzmann says. Maybe they run a biotech fund just when biotech stocks are hot. Maybe they run the Spain Fund just when Japanese investors discover Spain. When the Japanese bail out, the fund goes down.

Moral: Look for the funds that appear consistently somewhat below the very top—say, in the upper quarter of the mutual-fund rankings. Pick funds whose good records have lasted at least two to five years. And buy no-load (no

sales charge) funds. Sales charges lower your returns.

Two caveats to the stock study: (1) You can't count on superior performance every year, even from a top manager. Consistency wins, but only over longer periods. (2) Although good funds tend to stay good, there's no proof that very many can outperform the stock-market averages, over time.

So even stock investors should think about an index fund. Once again, the cheapest is offered by Vanguard: the Vanguard Index Trust.

[June 25, 1991]

Getting the Boot in Middle Age

If you lose your job in middle age, it means a lot more, financially, than six to 12 months of scrambling for another berth. Your standard of living is probably going to be permanently reduced.

This is the terrible, untold story behind 1 million forty- and fifty-ish professional people, middle managers and other workers now pounding the streets. Even if they find a new job at their old salary, they'll never be made whole.

First, they'll eat up savings that otherwise would have compounded until their retirement. So they'll enter old age without as large a cushion as they had planned.

Second, corporate employees won't get as big a pension as they expected. The value of a pension typically gains the most between the ages of 50 and 65, says Gerry Bell, a partner at the employee benefits firm, Kwasha Lipton in Fort Lee, N.J. If you switch jobs in your early 50s, your pension fund generally won't get the kick that continuous employment brings.

The most high-powered savings you possess are those in your company retirement account. That money is a mix of personal contributions (put into 401(k) plans) and pension contributions from the company. As long as it stays in a pension fund, it's tax deferred.

If you're laid off, there are three ways to keep that tax deferral: leave the money in your ex-company's plan until you retire; roll it into another employer's plan; or roll it into an Individual Retirement Account. If you take the money into current income, you'll owe income taxes on it plus a 10 percent penalty if you're under age 59 and a half.

Of workers eligible to receive lump-sum distributions from their pension plans over the past year, around 40 percent took part or all of the money into current income, according to a recent survey by the Profit Sharing Research Foundation (PSRF) and the Gallup Organization.

An earlier study, by the Employee Benefit Research Institute, put that figure even higher. Even if you build up your savings again, this precious, tax-sheltered stash is permanently gone.

Some 60 percent of workers kept their savings in some sort of retirement plan when they left their companies, says PSRF. But if they're unemployed, some portion of this money will most likely be spent at a later date. A smart way to handle lump-sum pension savings after a job loss is to roll them into an IRA and tap them as needed. This minimizes the taxes and penalties you pay and preserves your tax shelter for the longest time possible.

The haircut you take on your pension, however, is another story. Companies save on their pension payments by firing workers early and there's no smart way you can avoid that loss.

What makes those final years so important, in establishing retirement income, is that so many pensions are based on final pay and years of service.

Say, for example, that you started working for a company at age 30, got annual raises of 5 percent, and were earning $80,000 when you retired at 65. Your pension might come to $28,000 a year, Bell says.

But if you got the boot at age 50, you might get only $8,000 a year starting at age 65—and between now and then, the value of that $8,000 would be greatly eroded by inflation.

Early retirees often get an incentive payment that raises their retirement income, but not by enough to compensate for what they've lost. For example, the effect of lost raises isn't factored in.

Even if, by some miracle, you find a new job the day you're laid off—at the same salary and with the same pay raises and retirement plan—you'll still come out behind, Bell says.

Take someone who left Company A at age 50 with an $8,000 annual benefit and worked another 15 years for Company B, reaching a final salary of $80,000 at age 65. Company B would pay a retirement benefit of only $12,000 a year—giving you $20,000 total. That's $8,000 less than you'd have gotten if you'd stayed with Company A.

The longer it takes to find work, the smaller your pension is going to be. That's a special tragedy of early job loss. The moral for younger people: start socking money into a retirement plan the moment you can.

[*January 7, 1992*]

The Hidden Hazards of Divorce

NEW YORK. "I've accidentally ruined my former husband's credit and I'm sick about it," a reader writes. "I got into financial trouble and had to file for bankruptcy, and it went on his record as well as mine. Is there anything I can do about it?"

In this case, no. But the risk of catching cold when your ex-mate sneezes is something every couple needs to know about. Your credit record could be ruined if your ex-spouse gets behind on bills that you thought were his.

During a marriage, you often acquire debts jointly. You both sign for credit cards, car loans and mortgages. Therefore, the creditor looks to you both for payment.

If the marriage ends, you decide between you who is going to repay which debt. For example, the wife might agree to take over the loan on the car she drives. The husband

might agree to cover the personal loans. They arrange for the bills to go to their new addresses and then go their separate ways.

But what if the wife gets behind on her car payments? When the lender reports that delinquency to the credit bureau, it goes on both husband's and wife's report—because originally, you both signed for the loan.

So the husband could be getting black marks on his credit without even knowing it. If the car is repossessed, that will show on his credit record, too. The next time he applies for a car loan, he may be turned down.

The wife runs the same risk. If the husband doesn't pay his share of the loans, the lender will come after her. It does no good to argue that, under the divorce agreement, the husband is responsible for the debt. The lender wasn't a party to that agreement. The wife has to make up the missing payments (if she can), then go after the husband for the money.

Joint credit cards follow a similar rule. Separating spouses should immediately cancel their joint cards. But any debt on the cards remains their mutual responsibility, says Keith Coughey, group vice president of PNC National Bank in Wilmington, Del.

The biggest debt of divorcing couples is often the mortgage. It's not unusual for the wife and children to remain in the house while the husband makes the monthly payments.

As part of the divorce agreement, he might have gained title to the house—but perhaps didn't tell the bank about it. So the mortgage loan will remain in both names. If he doesn't pay, the bank can still come after the wife. In effect, she'd be forced to make payments on property she no longer owns.

In community property states, a creditor could come after you even for debts that you didn't sign for, if the purpose of the debt was related to the marriage, says divorce attorney Leonard Loeb of the Milwaukee law firm, Loeb, Herman & Drew.

Say, for example, that the husband buys a car, then defaults on the payments. If it's deemed part of the community, it will probably become the wife's obligation to pay, even if they've separated.

How can you escape these risky ties that continue to bind?

—Once you and your spouse have decided on which debt belongs to whom, talk to each of your creditors. Ask to have the debt transferred to the name of the person who will be responsible. However, the creditors don't have to agree. The switch will be made only if it appears that you can handle the payments alone.

—During your divorce negotiations, keep your joint bills up to date, even if it means paying for things that belong to your spouse. If your credit history deteriorates, your creditors may be more aggressive in requiring you both to remain responsible for the marital bills. That way, they'll have at least one of you to collect from.

—If the husband takes over the major joint debts, try to arrange for that to be recognized as part of wife's support agreement, Loeb says. If the husband goes bankrupt, the creditors can still pursue the wife, because she originally signed for debts. But she'll be able to sue her husband for the money back, because support agreements aren't dischargeable in bankruptcy.

—When one spouse assumes a major debt, try to get security, advises tax and family law attorney Marjorie O'Connell, Washington D.C. For example, if your spouse agrees to pay the mortgage, get that pledge collateralized by the money in his or her retirement plan.

There are many more angles to this debt story, so be sure that your divorce lawyer leaves you well protected.

                    [*April 7, 1992*]

GEORGIE ANNE GEYER

She was the first to interview Saddam Hussein nearly twenty years ago; she has talked into the early morning hours with Yasser Arafat and Fidel Castro, and interviewed the Ayatollah Khomeini. She has infiltrated and written about most of the major guerrilla movements in the world, and her life has been in jeopardy more than once. But Georgie Anne Geyer says that in some ways writing a column is harder than being a foreign correspondent.

"It's the pressure of having to give opinions three times a week. It's much tougher and it's much more independent," Geyer says. "I love it, I really do, [but] I feel like an entrepreneur because all the risk is mine." Geyer writes for Universal Press Syndicate, which distributes her column to more than 150 different newspapers. "I have this very good contract, but if the column doesn't sell, I won't make much money."

When she was a foreign correspondent for the *Chicago Daily News,* her work day overseas usually ended by 8 p.m., and she had as much as four months a year off. But a columnist's work never ends, she says. There's always research to be done, another piece to write. She remembers a friend warning her that writing a column is like being married to a nymphomaniac. It's nice, but. . . .

With her blonde hair, open face, and wide smile, Geyer made headlines in the early 1960s when she went with guerrilla fighters into the jungles of Guatemala on her first foreign assignment. She was twenty-seven, and there were no other women correspondents in Latin America. At home, most women journalists were still relegated to the women's section, writing society news and club notes. One gossip columnist reflected the era when he said Geyer "would be better

cast as a pretty school teacher than as a cool, nerveless foreign correspondent who thrives on hazardous assignments."

After three years of covering revolutions in Latin America, Geyer
began traveling the world, writing about change in the Soviet Union,
Middle East, and Far East. As her colleague and friend columnist Mike
Royko has noted, Geyer had an uncanny knack for sensing where a big
story was going to break next. Being able to forecast things is "almost
kind of weird, kind of strange. I'm always years ahead," Geyer says,
laughing at herself. "I'm so far ahead that people don't remember
what I said. That makes me mad."

When she was asked to compose the lead essay for the 1985
Encyclopedia Brittanica, Geyer wrote about "Disintegration in the
World." The subsequent breakup of the Soviet Union confirmed her
predictions. She also wrote a book titled *The Young Russians* in 1976,
but says she had difficulty getting it published because it was far ahead
of its time. The book accurately forecast what later happened under
the leadership of former Soviet Prime Minister Mikhail Gorbachev.
"The last few pages are absolutely prophetic," she says, "but everybody made fun of me."

By 1974, Geyer was feeling the toll of being away from home for
nine months of the year and decided to try writing a column. It was a
difficult transition for someone who still thought of herself as a
reporter; instead of filing straight news stories, she had to distill an
opinion three times a week. Reporting is still the backbone of her
column, and she considers it important for any columnist. "I find the
reporting columns easier. I'm more of a reporter than a theoretician,"
she says. "I find the ones who don't report soon get pretty weak."

Geyer "is a throwback to the old school of journalism. She's not a
hand-out artist," says Vince Davis, head of the Patterson School of
Diplomacy and International Commerce at the University of Kentucky, who has twice invited Geyer to speak at the school's annual
meetings. "She's out in the trenches getting the stories," Davis says.
"She's a role model for our students interested in journalism. She
shows you what a high-class journalist can be."

One of Geyer's strengths as a columnist is her ability to assess and
describe the political structure and power in a foreign country. She
trusts her instincts but also reads widely. From her study of history,
she knows what has happened before, which gives her confidence to
predict what will happen next. Self-assuredness developed during
years of reporting, and a willingness to risk speaking out ahead of her
time made it easier to voice opinions once she became a syndicated

columnist. "She's extremely knowledgeable about the Middle East and South and Central America," says Mary Lou Forbes, Commentary editor for the *Washington Times*. "She has achieved a knowledge that few columnists—male or female—have." Because Geyer is still a reporter as well as a columnist, "she actually breaks news in her columns," Forbes adds.

She's not afraid to take an extreme position if she thinks it's justified. She went to Yugoslavia in the late 1980s, for example, and wrote a column forecasting that it would collapse and illustrate what would happen next in the Soviet Union. "Again, I was prophetic. I go way out on a limb on things like that." She has made mistakes, usually when it's something she thinks she knows. "I don't make big mistakes," she says. "If I don't know, then I'm going to check it."

Geyer has always been concerned about getting the whole story, and she regards herself as a translator or interpreter of other cultures. Most Americans no longer read history nor do they understand simple cultural differences among other peoples, she says. "We're such limited creatures, trying to understand things, limited in our intelligence. People in other cultures are totally different, so that you have to take that into consideration. That's what's so interesting—to see their perceptions."

In order to understand other cultures, Geyer not only reads, she "looks around," she says, immersing herself in other cultures. Her keen observations lend force to her writing. The Ayatollah Khomeini she described as "a huge black moth of a man. His round white ayatollah's hat hovered precariously atop his head like an obstinate halo." Of Libyan dictator Muammar Qaddafi she wrote, "His eyes were the eyes of the Baptist preachers of my youth who did not believe in going to the movies or to dances or (presumably) to motels, even with Baptist boys. They were tight, fanatic eyes."

Her first impression of Fidel Castro went beyond the purely physical, beyond the legend of the big barrel-chested man in the khaki uniform. What surprised her was "the strange mixture of almost abnormal sweetness, like a favorite uncle's overly affectionate attitude toward his young kin, and a piercing and quite frightening coldness and ruthlessness—bordering on a total lack of feeling for others— behind the eyes."

Her fascination with the way Castro rose to power and held on led her to spend most of the last decade working on *Guerrilla Prince*, a thoughtful and not-so-flattering book about the Cuban leader. She says it "meant fitting everything together in a deeper form and making sense of the bigger picture."

Although some describe her as a conservative, she says she's not that predictable. "I'm not ideological and I'm not partisan. I don't identify with one party or with one type of leader," she says. "I'm a centrist, a moderate." She is angered that some papers label columnists conservative or liberal when the point of a column is to get people to think about the complexity of a situation or idea. Setting up two polar ideas "skews the national dialogue," she says. "I think this is just criminal."

The editor of *Washington Monthly* magazine, Charles Peters, told her once that she was the "least knee-jerk writer" he had ever known. Geyer considers that a great compliment. Her goal is to make complex issues clear for readers. "I'm reasonable, rational. That sounds dull, but it isn't. I don't want my column to be one where people say I know what Georgie Anne's going to say today." Peters also says Geyer shows courage in putting aside an ideological perspective in order to state the truth.

A friend told her that many readers probably knew her better than they know their wife or husband because she reveals herself, telling what she thinks and feels. "People like to pit themselves against you," Geyer says. "There's a person there."

Royko, who worked with Geyer at the *Chicago Daily News* when both were starting out, says she was a terrific reporter. "She works hard, not like some of these fruitcakes who sit in Washington and call up the State Department." The strength of her column comes from the fact that she's a great foreign correspondent, Royko says. "She knows what's going on in so many parts of the world."

Years of living out of a suitcase, ready to catch the next flight out to cover the next big story, meant giving up what might be considered a normal life. But it wasn't just the hectic schedule that kept her from settling down. She made a deliberate choice. Raised on Chicago's South Side, she knew she was expected to marry at a young age and have children. But she wanted more out of life. "It was the structure I didn't like. I loved those people, but I just didn't want to lead that normal life. I don't lead any kind of a normal life."

Travel has been essential for Geyer, who says she feels more alive in southern countries. Even after making the switch from foreign correspondent to columnist, she has kept up a wearing pace. When she's exhausted, she goes to the beach to swim and catch up on sleep for a couple of days. Then she's ready to go again. It's a question of temperament, she says. "I need a lot of intellectual, psychological, and emotional input."

Some of the things she did to get a story were foolish, Geyer says in hindsight, despite the fact that she was careful and calculating. Because she was intent on getting the real story of revolutions around the world, she often placed her life in the hands of fanatics and dictators. One close encounter happened in Angola, when she was whisked away by Marxist thugs and interrogated in a century-old prison. The memory of that incident stills haunts her; she has a sense that anything can happen at any time.

Geyer knew it was time to make a change when she accepted her mortality. "In those [early] years, in the mountains with the Guatemalans, I knew how dangerous it was, but I didn't think I could die. I was in my late twenties," she says. "It wouldn't make any sense for me to go with the guerrilla movement now—I mean, that's what you should do when you're twenty-nine or thirty. It makes sense for me to think through these deeper questions. I can put it together."

Although she moved to Washington, D.C., and settled into an apartment when she began her column, Geyer decided not to marry. She says she misses having a family, but that it wasn't meant for her. "I mean, I'd like to have three *grown* children. . . ." She breaks off with a laugh.

She dislikes being thought of as a role model for young journalists, saying it's too superficial an image of her. "When somebody says to me today, 'you're my role model,' I say, 'No I'm not. You are your own role model, you inside—don't try to be like me.' It's presumptuous to be like anybody else. I really have a lot of trouble with that."

Even while she was involved in the rush of daily reporting, Geyer constantly examined her way of doing things and tried to operate on an ethical plane. As a young woman she had to cope with gossip—most often the kind that implied she had slept with a source to obtain an exclusive story. For the most part Geyer has been able to laugh that off; she is rigorous about separating her professional from her personal life.

Priding herself on her integrity, she says one of her goals has been to get the whole story. It's something many foreign correspondents find difficult to do because of pressure from totalitarian regimes. "You either play their game or you don't play the game, and a lot of journalists play their game. I just won't do that, and I don't think any journalist should."

As a result, Geyer has not been allowed back into Cuba because she refused to write what Castro wanted. She tells of a well known wire service correspondent who says he gets into Cuba twice a year because he knows exactly how far he can go. "That's the way dictators and totalitarian regimes have controlled the crowds," she says. "None of us should do it. If none of us did it, the world would be a different place, because it's skewing the information."

Fascinated by psychology, Geyer has spent much of her journalistic life trying to figure out what motivates revolutionary leaders and how they maintain power, and trying to plumb the way in which cultures shape personalities. She is a realist, and she says she knows there's no perfect leader. "I'm not looking for Utopia, and I'm not looking for a great leader to round out my life or to give my life meaning," she says. "In fact, I don't trust great leaders. I don't trust charismatic leaders. They're doing something to you."

She still travels extensively—in one recent three-month period she visited Berlin, Warsaw, Belgrade, Athens, Israel, Gaza, Jordan, Kuwait, India, and Oman on one trip, Japan and Korea on another. Because of her travel, she has gotten used to cranking out her column in unusual places. At home, in the dining room she converted to an office, she uses an electronic typewriter hooked to a word processor. Sometimes she writes the column on a battery-operated electronic typewriter when she travels. But more often, when abroad, she writes out her 900-word column longhand on white paper and faxes it to the syndicate. Sometimes handwritten columns work better, she says, because it's a slower process that seems to allow more creativity. "When you're typing fast, I think sometimes the concepts don't get developed."

Her columns are a combination of commentary and feature pieces, which take longer to craft. She writes a page at a time, reads that, and writes the next page. Although she writes easily, churning out three a week means not every column will shine. The syndicate has told her she could do just two a week, but she thinks in a way that might be harder. "I have a funny feeling that if I were to do two a week, each one would have to be a jewel." Now, she says, "if I had to have the column in five minutes to call in, I would have the column. Really. I would sit down here and write something. I have a lot to say. I do a lot of research." Some of her research is done in libraries, but more is on the scene. "I'm a journalist for good reason," she says. "It's temperamental. I couldn't sit there all that time."

"She does out-of-the-way international stories in a way nobody else does—she's good, she's an excellent writer," says Mark Fisher, editor of the *Columbus* (Ohio) *Dispatch* Forum Page. Unlike some other Washington columnists, whom he called "Beltway pontificants," Geyer is "out writing from God knows where, traveling and digging for stories."

Most of her column ideas come from what she has seen in her travels, from attending conferences, and from her reading in current affairs. She says she's never at a loss for something to write about, but that the weekly triple deadline can be difficult to meet when there are unexpected problems. A couple of years ago, after a serious operation, Geyer took a week off from the column. But the next Monday she was back home, lying in bed, calling people, writing the 900-word column by hand on white paper, and faxing it to the syndicate.

Has she traveled enough? "I may have," she replies. "I was thinking about this, flying back over the ocean from Korea, and saying, 'I think I've seen enough of this.' Because I've been almost every place." She would like to delve more deeply into psychology, the way she did in her book about Castro, and is thinking about writing a book on the death of citizenship in America.

Now in her early fifties, Geyer says it's hard to get accustomed to being viewed as an authority on international affairs—she is no longer an ingenue. "I'm sort of looking for a new role. I don't know how to be a middle-aged columnist," she says. "I keep thinking I should go and get a serious suit—you know, that a woman of fifty would wear." She laughs. "I don't know how to do it."

As a young foreign correspondent, "my body was so strong I would just take it for granted, and I was developing my brain. But now it's the other way around, and my brain is supporting my body." She says a new role for her may be in mentoring young people. And there's one other thing she's never had time to do: "I'd like to write a real sexy foreign intrigue novel. That's not a compulsion, but it would be fun."

Feudal Farce in Bulgaria

MUKHOVA, Bulgaria. As one approaches the Bulgarian village, it looks quietly picturesque and beautiful. Red-tiled roofs huddle in the rolling central mountains near a large dam and reservoir whose waters gleam in the late spring sun.

Mukhova's major, Nicola Kiskinov, a burly, determined-looking man, had every appearance

of running a free election—
Bulgaria's first in 45 years—as he
stood in the town's primitive little
park, waving straggling voters in.

But as a matter of fact, like so
much in Bulgaria, the town wasn't
beautiful and Mr. Kiskinov's
elections were not straight. This
entire mountainous area is
ecologically poisoned almost
beyond its capacity to maintain
human life, and the elections were
rigged by the communists in the
feudal fiefdoms these villages really
are.

"There were 7,000 people here at
one point, and there are now 234
permanent residents here," the
mayor told me and several election
observers the day of the June 10
elections. "In 1962, the government
built the dam and migration
outward started. Now we have 90
percent old people.

"At first, the dam was very
helpful for energy and irrigation.
But then we had a problem when
a connected reservoir's wall broke.
Now the whole lake is poisoned,
and we can't use it for fish or for
irrigation. Before, we had 18,700
acres under cultivation here; now
we have 1,100."

The admission by feudal
communists such as this mayor that
their party has ruined this country
is, ironically, the one honest thing
in this tragically debauched land.

In pre-communist years, this
agriculturally rich country exported
half its harvests to Europe. Because
of the communists' forced
industrialization of the '50s and
'60s, young people left agriculture
for industrial factories that were
decrepit before they were even
finished. In 1913, Bulgarians

consumed more meat than they do
today; this is a country that looks
like Germany or France in 1910.

In addition to the political
economics that destroyed this rich
land, the communists simply
continued the feudal tradition. In
villages like these, for instance, the
mayor still tells the people where to
collect firewood.

"You have a single owner in
these towns and villages," noted
Genaro Arriagada, the brilliant
Chilean campaigner who directed
the electoral campaign against the
dictator Gen. Augusto Pinochet, as
he observed the elections here.
"You have the security forces and a
communist army, and a mayor that
is not a mayor but a projection of
the informers and the state police.

"It is always the same—under
Pinochet, under the Sandinistas,
here . . . the lower the cultural level
of the community, the lower the
vote for the opposition. The real
element is fear."

Did the simple, dependent
villagers think they would be
punished for voting for the
opposition United Democratic
Front? That was the outstanding
question. But even in towns such as
Mukhova, where the UDF was not
registered, bright, aggressive,
middle-class men such as architect
Damian Stoyanov still managed to
watch and speak out for the first
time.

"The mayor has directly
threatened a woman from putting
up UDF posters," Mr. Stoyanov
said, standing up like a bantam
rooster to the mayor in the little
square. "She was physically
intimidated . . ." So it went in
every town we and others visited

that pregnant Sunday in the last country in the Eastern Bloc to hold its first "free elections."

Finally, I thought to ask Mr. Kiskinov why, since he himself had so willingly delineated all the incredible failures of his party, he still remained a communist. "I don't consider the policy a total failure," he answered obliquely, "but errors and mistakes were made." The lord of the manor does not, after all, have to answer to irrelevant foreigners.

All day long, the people went to the polls with faces as grave and unexpressive as those stone lions that wait before so many museums of the world. They did not reveal for whom they had voted. When I asked one man, he smiled ambiguously and said, "Reason." Another added, "For tomorrow."

But I at least left the poisoned Bulagrian countryside that day with some answers. In place of the progressive "wave of the future" that the communists always claimed, all they really did was become the new feudal owners of these, their lands of poisoned waters and ubiquitous outhouses. They gave the world a kind of international feudalism, the final retrogressive farce of communism's own false theory.

[*June 18, 1990*]

[Taken from the Georgie Anne Geyer column by Georgie Anne Geyer. Copyright © 1990 by Universal Press Syndicate. Reprinted with permission.]

Kazakh Leaders Grapple with Change

ALMA ATA, Kazakhstan. This is Central Asia's "Wild East," where businessmen from Houston to Seoul are doing everything but riding Mongol ponies and sending the Khan's couriers running up ahead to get dibs on Kazakhstan's milk and honey—read, "oil and gold."

This city of elegant parks and old mansions is the prettiest for 1,000 miles in any direction, a city where roads formerly named for communism have been conspicuously renamed for the Silk Route that never went through here. It is where the activist and savvy "new government" is creating the biggest laboratory in the entire former Soviet Union for economic experimentation in a transition economy from communism to capitalism.

This is the one place in Central Asia where you can stay in a first-class hotel. There is reason for this. The Dostyk was the former hotel of the Communist Party Central Committee, and it has now fallen to the likes of us. One cannot expound upon the communists' behavior in the wood-paneled bedrooms here, but one can certainly appreciate the luxuries, after the stinking hotels everywhere else. And the fax girl is endearing when she says brightly: "There's no problem getting faxes through to Washington—Moscow's the problem!"

But above all stands out the incredible and unequaled cast of characters: businessmen of fortune, swaggering adventurers, frontier oilmen, and even a few serious scholars and politicians:

• In the elegant conference room of the presidency, the man unquestionably the star of the Kazakh show is President Nursultan Nazarbayev, who is holding court with the visiting French foreign minister's delegation. He is handsome and slick, with his blunt nose, carefully combed hair and wily eyes. But his face is nearly expressionless, and I find myself uneasily searching for some remote resemblance.

Then it hits me: the late Mayor Richard J. Daley of my hometown of Chicago! Just another oddity of beguiling Kazakhstan.

"Where do you want to see Kazakhstan five years from now?" I ask.

"I will answer the lady," Mr. Nazarbayev says gallantly, while the other men sniff. "Kazakhstan has many possibilities. I hope that in five years Kazakhstan will have entered the market economy. In those five years, we will lay the foundation from the old philosophy to new varieties of property . . . and then finally create a developed democratic state that is recognized by the world as a sovereign country. As for us, we will proceed according to the values of the civilized world."

An Asiatic empiricist, Mr. Nazarbayev has studied the economic "models" of South Korea, China and Singapore. Out of these, he came to the conclusion that, for rapid development, an area like Kazakhstan, which is at the moment poised between independence and remaining within the Russian Federation, must have a period of authoritarian-representative rule that develops the economy and leads to democracy sometime later.

• In a lovely old mansion of the former Communist Party, the unlikely economist who is Mr. Nazarbayev's leading adviser paces up and down, trying to figure out how to carry Kazakhstan, with all of its contradictory energies, ahead to a healthily privatized economy. An unlikely figure to find in the snows here, Dr. Chan Young Bang is a Korean-American professor from San Francisco—charming yet troubled.

"To be fair," he told me, "Kazakhstan is way ahead of the other republics—but changing people's attitudes is a tremendously difficult task." The shock liberalization of prices on Jan. 2 must go "hand in hand with privatization," he said, or it "doesn't induce a market."

While he admires Mr. Nazarbayev enormously, he remains deeply concerned that "there is no economic plan year. Nor can we have one so long as we are inside the ruble currency space, because our economy will be dictated not by us but by the policy—or lack of policy—of the Russian Federation. There is no market here—only one single seller. And the market means many sellers and many buyers."

• Finally, downtown in offices that cannot be charged with overspending on the niceties, in simple cold rooms with some burned-out light bulbs, another important player in the Kazakh drama comes forth.

Victor Cho, president of Kramds,

is a mysterious man to many Kazakhs. "Kramds—what does it do?" Kazakhs would ask me. "They are everywhere, they have banks, they are on television—but what do they *do?*" It is an interesting question.

Mr. Cho, a Kazakh of early Korean heritage who was one of the major communist state planners (and apparently a very able one), is obviously a tough hombre. "We would like to develop our corporation, using the economic situation in Kazakhstan to transform it into a transnational corporation with many branches," he told me.

In short, while it is very complicated, it seems that what busy Kramds has done is to get the best of the former communist enterprise chiefs together, to raise $200 million to form the company, banks and other new enterprises, and buy the stock from the old communist enterprises to be privatized, and then transform them into working businesses.

The whole setting is impressive. Kazakhstan is huge—six times larger than the Ukraine. It has a nearly 800-mile border with China, and it is about to begin a first-time train line to China. Planes, it is said, will soon connect Alma Ata to Europe, Istanbul and Tel Aviv on the West and Seoul, Beijing and Tokyo on the East.

Mr. Nazarbayev exults in coining new terms—a "social market economy," a "Central Asian Common Market," an economy built like that created by Ludwig Erhard in Germany after World War II (because he built a normal market out of a broken economy and a useless currency). Or as Vice President Eric Asanayev spiritedly told me, "We are ready to test all influences!"

Still, even in relatively hopeful—and enormously rich—Kazakhstan there exist the same psychological problems, which then become economic problems, of all of the formerly xenophobic and even mentally centralized Soviet Union. "They are buying and selling, but not producing," one American businessman told me. "It's still the old communist system, nothing more," a Turkish diplomat chimed in. "They want things from outside for nothing."

"There are things of value here, but no one owns them, so there is nothing you can do about it," said still another American would-be investor.

Meanwhile, most foreign businessmen carry their cash in—and out. Nobody trusts the erstwhile new banks, which often will not give people their money back. And everybody harks back to the now famous case of "the Chevron deal." Chevron actually completed a contract with the Kazakh government to explore for oil in their rich fields. But the government got cold feet, started to worry the old communist fears of "selling the national heritage to foreigners," and pulled back the deal for renegotiation.

Revolutions are so easy, compared with this. Adrenalin starts flowing; it will be a new world, a pure world. But this new process is so difficult, so painful, so gradual, so without absolute promise—and so without any other alternative.

[*March 4, 1992*]

Dangers Lurking in a Vanishing Sea

TASHKENT, Uzbekistan. The threat to this vast crossroads, this Central Asian republic, used to come from Moscow. It came palpably, in the form of autocratic orders, officious party bureaucrats and brutal security forces.

Today, probably the biggest threat to Uzbekistan's tentative new 6-month-old independence is a strangely amorphous one. It comes on the winds, carrying salt and poisoned dust as far south as the ancient city of Samarkand and even to Kyrgyzstan on the Chinese border.

The new threat emerges directly from the death of the once-great Aral Sea. Until recent years, the Aral was a vast, shallow, 25,659 square mile oval-shaped sea, the world's fourth-largest inland body of water. Today it is only a raw wound in the Earth. As underwater mounds of salt and pesticides now open and begin to poison all of Central Asia, the sea has become a Sahara with ships marooned in what was the center.

"The most dangerous thing, as the Aral disappears, is the dust and the wind," Professor Pirmat Shermuhamedov, president of the Aral Sea Committee, told me in his office in the lovely Writer's Union here. "Its dust rises to a height of 3 miles and it spreads to more than 3,000 miles around.

"They have found the dust of the Aral in the tea plantations in Georgia and on the territory of India. The weather now is very hot in Tashkent and in Kyrgyzstan. The scientists say that if we lose the Aral, there could be snow in summer."

But the devastation of the Uzbeks' very doorstep threatens far worse to come. The land mass of Uzbekistan, so traditionally rich agriculturally it has been for centuries the stuff of Central Asian legend, is chemically poisoned. And as for the Kara-Kalpaks, the historic Turkic people who have the lousy luck to live around the Aral Sea, they are now dying "unnaturally," their children born with mental retardation.

Mohammed Salih, the intelligent writer, parliamentarian and leader of the democratic ERK party, posed the reality in newly freed Uzbekistan. "The situation is not good," he told me, smoking Marlboros nonstop as he sat in his office on one of Tashkent's attractive old streets. "We have political problems, economic problems, problems in the standard of living. The levels of living have sunk very low."

Even after the first Uzbek elections of last year, in which the former communists won, barely, over Mr. Salih and his party, "Power didn't change," he said. "It is still in the same place."

But soon this impressive man, who, analysts say, would almost surely win a presidential election today, moved on to the real core of the problem: the catastrophic monoculture imposed colonially by Moscow for so many years. Uzbekistan remains a critical example of what the communist decisions of "the center" really did to these Turkic peoples.

"We've had monoculture in Uzbekistan for 70 years," he went on. "Eighty percent of the ground was given to cotton. But it won't be monoculture in the future. Today, we have cut it down to 60 percent, and we must begin to give land back to the people."

"When the head of the government was communist, the central government in Moscow looked at Uzbekistan as simply one of its districts," said Abdulalikov Irismat, the presidential press secretary. "In that era, we had to accept all the laws of the central government. It has been said that cotton makes only slaves, not free men. It is true that, in those years, everyone had to go to pick cotton—the students, the children, all the technicians, thousands from the factories and plants. Now, we are just beginning to mechanize cotton."

What happened in the Aral Sea area should stand as the primary example of ecological irresponsibility, madness and suicide of the entire 70 years of the Soviet Union. In its colonial quest for King Cotton, Moscow diverted not only the ancient waters of the Aral Sea, but also the waters of the two great rivers of Central Asia, the Syrdarya and the Amu Darya—all to irrigate cotton! As the waters began to recede, the rigid bureaucrats of Moscow refused even to acknowledge the changes.

Arrogantly, the masters of the Kremlin also simply imposed whatever cotton quota they dreamed up, thus mulcting rich soils. In his excellent book "The New Russians," Hedrick Smith tells the story of how, when a corrupt Uzbek communist leader suggested a cotton quota of 5.5 million tons of cotton, Leonid Brezhnev whispered, "Please, round it up. Add half a million more." And in that economic Disney World, half a million was duly added.

There is no question that on some levels things are better now in Uzbekistan. Individual Communist Party members are still in power in the presidency of Islam Karimov, but the ERK is very active, with an amazing 40,000 members; and the original "popular movement," Birlik, that sparked the changes toward independence, is actively watching over the entire situation. Uzbekistan plans to create its own army, and there is some movement toward bringing in foreign investment, but to date only some.

It is the overweening problem of the Aral Sea that hangs over this period of transition and waiting, like a wraith of what could happen elsewhere and everywhere. But the worst thing is that, when officials toy with "answers," they talk about diverting still more Siberian rivers to raise the Aral's nearly nonexistent water level, or they talk about diverting water from the Caspian Sea.

In short, they think about doing more of the same that killed the Aral Sea in the beginning. And this is the real problem in Russia and throughout these new "countries" of Central Asia. The mind-set has barely changed, and unless it changes—through education abroad, through seriously transforming programs and policies at home—the future will hold more Aral Seas, of the landscape and of the mind.

Meanwhile, the eerie thing is to travel across Central Asia and see the Aral Sea still etched on all the maps. It just isn't there anymore.

[*February 28, 1992*]

[Taken from the Georgie Anne Geyer column by Georgie Anne Geyer. Copyright © 1992 by Universal Press Syndicate. Reprinted with permission.]

ELLEN GOODMAN

At first, newspaper editors didn't know exactly what to do with Ellen Goodman's column. It didn't seem to belong on the op-ed page, but it didn't fit the feature section either. Seventeen years later, more than 400 newspapers run her syndicated twice-weekly essay, and Goodman's personal/political column has become the standard to which many newer columnists are compared. "Newspapers divided up life into these artificial segments because they had to section the paper. . . . It was a ludicrous segregation," Goodman says. "When I was first syndicated, it was a real issue in terms of sales because people didn't know where to put my column. It wasn't strictly [about] family, and it wasn't just politics."

Settled in a deep chair in a dark paneled room at Boston's Harvard Club, Goodman reflects on those early years as a columnist: "It was important to me to reflect the range of life experiences. It's as simple as that," she says. "As a person, you live with many concerns—you're concerned about your kids and you're concerned about nuclear warfare, and the fact that you can only write about one or the other is absurd. So that probably slowed [the column's] acceptance. A lot of people didn't know what to think. I didn't fit a niche." But Goodman wrote well and had a knack for identifying and distilling issues and trends, so she carved out a new niche for herself.

She plays as well in the Midwest and South as she does on both coasts. Dennis Ryerson, editorial page editor of the *Des Moines* (Iowa) *Register,* for example, says he uses Goodman's column because she "can take complex issues and distill them in terms we can understand; put them in a context we can relate to." Both Goodman and *New York Times* columnist Anna Quindlen's view of the world is "more personal and less technical; more heartfelt and more genuine" than that of some other columnists, he says.

An associate editor of the *Boston Globe,* Goodman considers herself a newspaper person, not a celebrity wordsmith. She lives in Brookline, the same quiet Boston suburb where she grew up, but she writes her column in the newspaper office. "A lot of people think, 'Oh, do you write at home in your garret while the children are napping?' I work for a newspaper," she says, "and the newspaper is very important to me. The limits and pushing against some of those limits has been important."

What has enabled her to sustain the column? What has nourished her over the years? "Roast chicken . . . and chocolate," she says in a characteristic blend of humor and seriousness. "Friends, family, and intellectual interests. If you stay interested, you probably have a good shot at staying interesting. I've always been interested in observing change." Her column has been successful because she never strays too far from the news, says former *Globe* editor Thomas Winship, who gave Goodman her first column in 1971. "She is the wisest of back fence counselors," he adds. Goodman's column was picked up by the Washington Post Writers Group in 1975.

Goodman's love of newspapers belies the fact that she never considered becoming a journalist and never wrote for her high school or college newspaper. A history major at Radcliffe College, she first thought of going into journalism when her older sister took a reporting job at the *Quincy* (Mass.) *Patriot-Ledger.* She graduated cum laude in 1963, got married, and moved to New York, where "people were interviewing overeducated young women for crummy jobs." *Newsweek* hired her as a researcher for its television department, and since she wasn't allowed to write for the magazine, she freelanced articles to other publications. She liked the people at *Newsweek* (coworkers included *Jaws* author Peter Benchley), but not the work. "It was really negative. I could only keep things out of the magazine," she says. "I couldn't get anything in. That was the nature of research."

The experience also brought her face to face with inequities in the job market. "This was 1963—the Civil Rights Act had not yet passed. It was legal to discriminate against women—something everyone forgets," she says. "They know it happened, [but] they forget it was legal." It was an experience that would fuel some of the anger expressed in her later columns.

After two years, her husband finished medical school and accepted a residency at the University of Michigan, so Goodman found a job as a reporter for the *Detroit Free Press.* "I did some of everything," she recalls, adding wryly, "I had no formal training, so I was unencumbered by knowledge." Two years later they moved back to Boston, where Goodman got a job at the *Globe* writing feature stories and occasional columns.

Goodman smiles as she tells about *Globe* editor Winship giving her a column on the op-ed page so that he could keep keep her opinions out of the news. "I was never shy. I was always opinionated," she concedes. "I was writing features that were sort of—not opinionated per se—but had a point of view." Several of her early columns were written about the fledgling women's movement, which she has continued to follow over the years. "When I started reporting on those issues, it made a direct hit—it was very much—Bingo!" Goodman first encountered the women's movement on an assignment for the *Globe* and immediately recognized that it would be an important issue. Her clearsightedness and ability to peg trends are often cited as strengths of her column.

"I pay attention," she explains. "I think it is reporting. If you start picking things up and have your ears open, and you hear something here and you read something there . . . and you talk to two people, and bunk, bunk, bunk, hmmmm," she says, mimicking the sound of a computer processing information. "Something's going on here." Most of her ideas come from the newspaper, which she defines broadly as encompassing news stories and advertisements. "The one thing you can count on as a text when you write a newspaper column is the news," she says. "Everybody by definition reads the newspaper or else they're not getting to the op-ed page." She says she never lacks for material and frequently reacts to news events as they are happening.

Nobody tells her what to write. "That's the good news and that's the bad news," she says, putting on a radio announcer's deep voice. She does try to balance serious columns with lighter ones, but it depends on what's in the news. When people tell her they want to write a column, Goodman's response is that they've got to have ideas. "I'm sure you have six great columns in you. That's the first . . . three . . . weeks," she says, drawing out the last few words. "Everybody has six good columns. You have to have led a really dull life not to have six good columns."

Goodman was a reporter for ten years before she ever wrote a column, and her reporting skills are invaluable in writing the column. "What people don't always realize is that the kind of column I write requires all the skills I ever developed as a young reporter," she says. A columnist also needs maturity, the ability to distill an opinion under pressure, and the confidence to make it public, she says. "You've got to figure out what you think—that's the name of the game. Writing a column is telling people what you think, and to do that you have to figure out what you think on deadline."

Most often Goodman picks a topic that interests her, not one that she's made up her mind about. "You often pick a subject because it's interesting, not because you know where you're going to come down," she says. "The idea that I'll only pick things [to write about] where I know how I'll come down is usually antithetical to the reason I'm writing the column." She invites readers to share her thought process, and says it's vital to acknowledge opposing arguments. "A column is very short. If you don't do that, then over time you don't gain the respect of people who are going to agree with where you come down sometimes and disagree other times," she says. "You want people to ride with you through the seventy-five lines, and you also want to provoke them to think about what they think." She is less interested in coming to a conclusion than she is in presenting the mixed feelings and values that she hears.

The downside of writing a column is, she says, that "you have to get up and do it over and over, but one of the good things is it focuses the mind." Readers frequently tell her she wrote what they were thinking. "It isn't really true, but I did write what they were thinking about. They had to go to work and do something meaningful—teach children, make sheets, whatever it was," she says. "My job was to go to work and write about it."

Goodman doesn't speak in terms of a mission for her column; her goals are more down-to-earth. "Like everybody else in the business, I'm conscious of stating a given idea clearly in the amount of time and the amount of space, in a coherent way that people will be attracted to, will understand, will read," she says. "It's a very small agenda. It's not to change the course of public policy. It's maybe to make people think about something, but on a given day it's to get it done, and to get it understood." If public policy is changed as the result of a column, so much the better, she says, but she doesn't approach column writing that way.

Columnists who judge their work by whether a particular bill passes, for example, are "in deep weeds," she says, "and you also start being owned by the issues." If a columnist's goal is to change governmental policy, to say what should be done, then she's actually a politician rather than a journalist, Goodman says. "You try to say for yourself and others, 'Here's something; let's look at it. Here's where I come down on it—and maybe make them turn the issue around and look at it a little differently."

Sometimes she would like to pull out all the stops to sway readers on political issues she feels strongly about, but she holds back. "There are a number of things that I care very strongly about, and I want to carry people along, but I hold back a little where politicians are concerned," she says. "So we're talking about a matter of degree." For example, although she was sympathetic with Democratic vice-presidential nominee Geraldine Ferraro, Goodman wrote a post-election column critical of Ferraro's commercial endorsements. "You can't be a card-carrying member of the Geraldine Ferraro right or wrong [faction], or you'd lose your brain," Goodman says. "You'd lose your integrity. You reserve the right to say when anybody screws up."

Some columns require more work than others. To be able to write about questions involving bioethics, for example, Goodman says she must read widely, talk to people whom she respects, and work through what they tell her. "If your name is on it, you do not want to pick up the paper the next day and say, 'What idiot wrote that?' You want to make sure what you think and that you've said what you think." Her commentary earned Goodman the Pulitzer Prize in 1980.

Goodman doesn't plan her columns far in advance, often writing her column as a story is unfolding. Sometimes things change unexpectedly and she has to perform emergency surgery on a column. She remembers, for example, writing about the Mapplethorpe obscenity trial on the assurance that the jury would not return a verdict before her column appeared. But the jury returned as she was sitting at the hairdresser with wet hair, and she had to dictate a rewrite over the phone. "It doesn't happen often, but there's a chill in the spine [knowing something might change]."

She prefers to compose in the quiet of her office, but Goodman says she is able to write anywhere if she has to. She takes a lap computer with her when she travels. Even after all these years, writing the column is never easy. "It's like the old joke," she says, " 'How much time does it take to write a column?' Answer: 'How much time do you have?' "

After she has gathered information and is composing at the computer, she listens to what she is writing. "It was a gag for many years in the [*Globe*] city room . . . that my lips would move because I'm listening to the sound of the words in my ear," she says. "I wasn't aware of that until people would kid me. I'm very aural." She pauses, realizing that her last word could be misconstrued. "That's 'a,'" she says pointedly.

As a columnist, her "voice" is literally the way her voice sounds—"like my talking to you sounds"—but it's also her perspective on the world. The tone of the column is conversational, often sparked with humor. She enjoys playing with language, and puns frequently sneak into her copy. A columnist's voice develops over the years, she says. "It takes time before you find a way. When you first write it's uneven, and when you write over time it becomes yours," she says, "even though on some days you're sarcastic, some days serious, some days melancholy, some days funny, some down and dirty, some days just playing around. Aren't you [that way] as a person?"

A characteristic or consistent voice should not be confused with predictability. "There's a voice that's mine, but there isn't a predictable outcome," she says. "There's a great difference between being predictable, which is that you know where that person is going to end up—and having a recognizable voice, which is you can hear the sound of that person thinking."

Although Goodman recognizes the potential influence of her column, she says she's not conscious of it when she's writing. Then it's just "me and the screen." The time she spends on each column varies. There's the rare, easy day when something happens and she reacts to it in print. But many more columns require a tremendous amount of reporting, much of which "ends up on the cutting room floor," she says.

Once she's taken a position, she's never changed radically, she says, though she has moved by degrees. She's not worried about taking a strong stance on an issue and later changing her mind about it because, she says, "you always have another shot at it." She admits that on occasion she has been dead wrong. Once, for example, she wrote a column urging Congressman Barney Frank to quit because he would not be able to function effectively in the wake of a controversy involving a homosexual relationship. "But he did, so I wrote about that." She shrugs. "You have other thoughts. . . . It's like dealing with children. People who can't change their minds and backtrack and say 'Oops, I screwed up on that one' with their kids, they've got real trouble."

Most of Goodman's writing relates to the column, but she is also writing a second book about social change. Her first book, *Turning Points,* published in 1979, grew out of a year she spent at Harvard in 1973-74 as a Nieman Fellow studying how people change. She also tried writing fiction at Harvard but says that didn't suit her. "All the fiction I wrote sounded like columns," she says. "I wasn't any good." When she came back she asked for a regular column. Her editor, Tom Winship, remembers her eyes "piercing with determination" and says he didn't dare tell her no.

As is true of many columnists, Goodman's favorite columns are not necessarily the most popular. "Very often people like a personal one, like [when] my dog died," she says. "I often like the ones in which I tackle something I find very perplexing, figure it out, and come out on the other side." Not all the columns shine. If a column doesn't work, Goodman says she doesn't want to read the paper that day. But on days when it does work, she finds it gratifying to "feel like you said what you meant, that you figured it out, and you did it in a persuasive, somewhat stylish way. I'm a very hard grader, though."

Goodman gets several hundred letters a week from readers of both sexes, some critical. She doesn't like that aspect of writing a column but says it's something she's learned to deal with. Practically by definition, columnists are faced with conflict. "When you tell people what you think, they tell you what they think of what you think," Goodman says, "in no uncertain terms." Her readers are always in the back of her mind, but her foremost obligation is to write for herself, she says. Second-guessing what's going to be popular is courting disaster. For example, a column in which she described General Norman Schwartz-kopf as a perfect man of the 90s, tough and tender, drew "a tremendous amount of shit," she says.

Once described by *Time* magazine as "a cool stream of sanity flowing through a minefield of public and private quandaries," Goodman's column has evolved and kept pace with the changing culture. "A column grows continually the way a person does," she wrote in her 1981 book *At Large*. "Old interests, like cells, slough off: new ones take their place. . . . The one constant is a desire to find a context and a meaning."

Goodman travels and lectures, and retreats when she can to her home in coastal Maine. Some of her columns are about too-busy people who are stretched in different directions, reflecting her own life. But she's doing what she wants. "There are lots of ways in the world to make a living per se, but when I write a column I'm doing it because I wanted to figure out what I thought, have some fun, be lively, and write," she says. "And if you start writing for other people and other reasons, you're dead meat."

When a Child Goes Off to College

It is a late-summer day when we migrate south. The two of us, mother and daughter, join that long caravan of families in borrowed station wagons and rented vans, moving the contents of a million bedrooms to a million dorm rooms.

The cars in our 60-mile-an-hour lane are packed to the hilt with student "basics." Stereos and stuffed animals pop up into my rear-view mirror in Connecticut. Guitars and quilts are strapped onto rooftop boxes in New York.

When we take a fast-food break on the New Jersey Turnpike, the wagon trains going south mix with those traveling north. One car carries Washington license plates and a University of Vermont sticker. Another has Maine origins and a Virginia destination.

As a driver on this journey, I have the sudden impression that we are part of a gigantic national swap-fest. Western parents delivering their children East to school, Eastern parents delivering their children West. Northerners and Southerners taking their young to teachers in other cities, the way their ancestors once apprenticed children to distant masters.

The symbolism of our trek doesn't escape either of us. Loading the car, driving it and finally unloading its contents into her new room, we are both companions and accomplices to her leave-taking from home. We are in this separation together.

Like the other parents in this ritual, I have offered more than my permission for this transition. I have proferred my approval, pride, pleasure, confidence. The young woman is taking off, and I am giving away her hand in independence.

What will I go home to? The room my daughter left behind is remarkably, unrecognizably neat. When we finished packing, it looked just like a guest room. Or— I will say it—an empty nest.

A long time ago, I thought that mothers who also had work that engaged their time and energy might avoid the cliche of an empty-nest syndrome. A child's departure once meant a mother's forced retirement from her only job. Many of us assumed that work would help protect us from that void. Now I doubt it.

Those of us who have worked two shifts, lived two roles, have no less investment in our identity as parents, no less connection to our children. No less love. And no less sense of loss.

Tomorrow, for the first time in 18 years, the part of my brain that is always calculating time—school time, work time, dinner time—can let go of its stop watch. The part of me that is as attuned to a child's schedule and needs as it is to a baby's cry in the night will be no longer operative. I don't know how easy it will be to unplug.

What do you do with all the antennae of motherhood when they become obsolete? What do you do with the loose wires that dangle after 18 years of intimate connection to your own child? What use is there for the expertise of motherhood that took so long to acquire?

I will go home to a new demographic column: households without children. Are these families? I will enter the longest and least-heralded phase, that of parent and adult child.

I am not altogether unprepared. This summer, my husband and I laughed about our impending freedom. We imagined the luxuries of life without the deadlines imposed by children: working late when we need to; falling asleep without waiting to hear a car pull into the driveway; making last-minute plans.

When the absolute priority of children sloughs off, emotional space will open our lives. But will that space also have the empty look of a guest room?

My friends who have taken this trip many times before tell me wryly that Thanksgiving comes soon. One friend has calculated his own ironic formula: The higher the school tuition, the shorter the school year. Another tallies up her long-distance phone bill.

But today it is only my traveling companion who makes me feel at ease with this journey. "This is exactly what I want to be doing now," she says excitedly as we graze through the local salad bar for our last lunch. Hours later, on a street corner in a strange city, I hug this tall young woman and tell her, "Go fly." It is time.

[*September 16, 1986*]

A New Parental Battle: Countering the Culture

Sooner or later, most Americans become card-carrying members of the counterculture. This is not an underground holdout of hippies. No beads are required. All you need to join is a child.

At some point between Lamaze and PTA, it becomes clear that one of your main jobs as a parent is to counter the culture. What the media deliver to children by the masses, you are expected to rebut one at a time.

The latest evidence of this frustrating piece of the parenting job description came from pediatricians. This summer, the American Academy of Pediatrics called for a ban on television food ads. Their plea was hard on the heels of a study showing that one Saturday morning of TV cartoons contained 202 junk-food ads.

The kids see, want and nag. That is, after all, the theory behind advertising to children, since few 6-year-olds have their own trust funds. The result, said the pediatricians, is obesity and high cholesterol.

Their call for a ban was predictably attacked by the grocers' association. But it was also attacked by people assembled under the umbrella marked "parental responsibility." We don't need bans, said these "PR" people, we need parents who know how to say no.

Well, I bow to no one in my capacity for naysaying. I agree that it's a well-honed skill of child-raising. By the time my daughter was 7, she qualified as a media critic.

But it occurs to me now that the call for "parental responsibility" is increasing in direct proportion to the irresponsibility of the marketplace. Parents are expected to protect their children from an increasingly hostile environment.

Are the kids being sold junk food? Just say no. Is TV bad? Turn it off. Are there messages about sex, drugs, violence all around? Counter the culture.

Mothers and fathers are expected to screen virtually every aspect of their children's lives. To check the ratings on the movies, to read the labels on the CDs, to find out if there's MTV in the house next door. All the while keeping in touch with school and, in their free time, earning a living.

In real life, most parents do a great deal of this monitoring and just-say-no-ing. Any trip to the supermarket produces at least one scene of a child grabbing for something only to have it returned to the shelf by a frazzled parent. An extraordinary number of the family arguments are over the goodies— sneakers, clothes, games—that the young know about only because of ads.

But at times it seems that the media have become the mainstream culture in children's lives. Parents have become the alternative.

Barbara Dafoe Whitehead, a research associate at the Institute for American Values, found this out in interviews with middle-class parents. "A common complaint I heard from parents was their sense of being overwhelmed by the culture. They felt their voice was a lot weaker. And they felt relatively more helpless than their parents."

"Parents," she notes, "see themselves in a struggle for the hearts and minds of their own children." It isn't that they can't say no. It's that there's so much more to say no to.

Without wallowing in false nostalgia, there has been a fundamental shift. Americans once expected parents to raise their children in accordance with the dominant cultural messages. Today they are expected to raise their children in opposition.

Once the chorus of cultural values was full of ministers, teachers, neighbors, leaders. They demanded more conformity, but offered more support. Now the messengers are Ninja Turtles, Madonna, rap groups, and celebrities pushing sneakers. Parents are considered "responsible' only if they are successful in their resistance.

It's what makes child-raising harder. It's why parents feel more isolated. It's not just that American families have less time with their kids;, it's that we have to spend more of this time doing battle with our own culture.

It's rather like trying to get your kids to eat their green beans after they've been told all day about the wonders of Milky Way. Come to think of it, it's exactly like that.

[August 15, 1991]

Few Doubting Thomases in the Senate

It was her word versus his. Just a he-said, she-said sort of thing, as Sen. John Danforth had put it, dismissing the "October surprise," the "smear campaign," the "eleventh hour" accusation of sexual harassment that had thrown Clarence Thomas' sure thing into full disarray.

Who was this "she" anyway? The senators who found her "credible" called her Professor Anita Hill. The others called her "the woman," or "this lady," or even, in the strange case of Sen. Alan Simpson, "the lady who was lured."

Before Hill stepped into her televised Oklahoma classroom, measured and earnest, dignified and strained, the Senate's Judiciary Committee had dismissed her. Before Hill said, "It is an unpleasant issue. It is an ugly issue," they had decided to deal with her charges the old-fashioned way. Among themselves.

Anyway you cut it, some of these men had known since mid-September that the former head of the civil rights enforcement agency was accused of violating a woman's civil rights. Anyway you run the sequence of events, they had known before the committee vote that a Supreme Court nominee had been accused of sexual harassment as defined by that court.

But like businessmen running a private corporation, they handled this "delicate matter" discreetly, among their own kind. Why, Arlen Specter, the very model of judiciousness, had gone to Thomas and gotten a forceful denial. Dennis DeConcini had "made the judgment, right or wrong, that he was credible to me." It was her word versus his. They took his without hearing hers. They didn't tell the rest of us.

Would it have been better if Hill had gone public earlier? Sure, although anyone who wonders why she was reluctant can listen to the messages on her telephone tape. Did the senators have any legitimate reason for protecting Thomas' privacy? Sure, FBI files are full of scurrilous attacks.

But anyone with half an investigative eye open could have discovered that Hill was "no kook," as Sen. Paul Simon put it. And anyone doing his job should have understood that this is a subject that deserved as much attention as Douglas Ginsburg's tokes of marijuana.

This portrait of men in power is not pretty. Capitol Hill is not just a place where you can bounce checks with impunity and discriminate without fear of the law. It's a place where men can listen to Thomas' straight-faced claim that he had no opinion on abortion and then question Hill's credibility.

If these men kept the lid on the charges of sexual harassment, however, it was not just to protect Thomas. To many, Hill is their worst nightmare. The woman who rides out of the past waving a charge. False, of course, or maybe true.

Women have always lived with a sense of vulnerability. They have been vulnerable to rape, harassment, abuse; on the street, at work, even at home. Slowly, they have won some tools of self-defense. In the shouting match of his word against hers, it is not always or only his that is heard.

Date rape, battered-women's defense, sexual assault. With each modest change in attitude and law, there has been a stunning overreaction on the part of many men. Where women feel vulnerable to male assault, men feel vulnerable to a woman's accusation.

Rape is still vastly underreported. Twice as many men kill their wives as wives kill husbands. Sexual harassment remains as widespread as it is hard to prove.

Yet when a Willie Smith is arrested, how many men think: Any woman could accuse me. When a battered wife who killed her husband is granted clemency, how many think: It's open season on husbands. And when Thomas is hit with a charge, how many think:

You can't even ask a girl out anymore.

In real life, false accusations are few, maybe even fewer than false acquittals. But in fantasy life, they are the "reverse discrimination" story lines of the time, the female pit bull attack on the ankle of innocent man.

Her word is not always the right one. The chore of proving in public what happened in private remains as difficult as ever. There is no assurance that airing Hill's charges and Thomas' countercharges would lead to a crisp cleancut winner.

But it was not for the all-male Senate committee to silence "her word" before it was spoken in public. At the 11th hour and the 59th minute these senators finally heard, loud and clear, the voices of women. The women they represent.

His word, her word. This is our word to Congress: Listen up.
            [*October 10, 1991*]

JANE BRODY

When she was four, Jane Brody told her father she wanted to be a veterinarian. Fine, he said, Cornell has a college of veterinary medicine. That was 1945, and Brody grew up believing she could do anything she put her mind to. "If you wanted to do something, you did it," says the author of the nationally distributed *New York Times* column, "Personal Health." "I never had the feeling that things were not appropriate for me to do. There were never those kinds of barriers, either emotionally or intellectually."

Brody describes her father as a "women's libber" who helped shop, cook, and wash the dishes; her stepmother always worked. Brody says she didn't understand the women's movement at first because she had never experienced discrimination. When there were barriers, she broke through them. In 1965, for example, with just two years of reporting experience at the *Minneapolis Tribune,* she applied for a job as a science writer at the *New York Times.* Asked if she would be willing to write women's news, she said no.

The executive editor told her she had "a lot of nerve" applying, since other applicants had twenty years' experience and stacks of clippings. "I said, 'Mr. Rosenthal, if I didn't think I could do this job, I wouldn't be here'—and as I said it I thought what am I saying?—but that was exactly what he wanted to hear. He liked my writing and he also liked what can only be called chutzpah." At twenty-four, she became a science writer for the *Times.*

A.M. Rosenthal doesn't recall that first meeting with the young Jane Brody, but he was impressed with her from the beginning: "I do remember thinking she was first rate. She was very good, had a great deal of knowledge and wrote succinctly." Her writing reflects the way she is, "very direct, very feisty, determined, and brave," Rosenthal says.

Brody had majored in biochemistry at the New York State College for Agriculture at Cornell, but after working part time as a biochemist, she realized "you could spend years researching something before you would find out what question to ask." It was isolating and "took too long to get to the point where it was interesting to everyone else," she says. Still intrigued by the way living things work, Brody looked for an avenue that would enable other people to share her fascination. In her junior year, "just to keep myself from going crazy with school work," she edited a student publication. "I woke up one day and said 'I love this. Why don't I do this?'" So she earned a master's degree in science writing at the University of Wisconsin and worked for the university news service covering the medical school. When a science writing position she had been promised at the *Minneapolis Tribune* failed to materialize, she left the *Tribune* and joined the *Times*.

After reporting on science and health for the *Times* for eleven years, Brody was asked to write a personal health column. Although she had dreamed of having a column some years earlier, the offer came at the wrong time. Her two sons were old enough that she could begin to travel and do "adventure stories," and she was afraid a column would tie her down. "I didn't want to be burdened with something that had to appear every week, regardless, come hell or high water," she says. But she decided to try it, and at the end of three months "It was obvious that I was enjoying it and it was very well received. The *Times* loved it, readers loved it, and I was having a great time."

Former *Times* managing editor Arthur Gelb remembers asking Brody to write the column. "She exploded," he recalls with amusement. "She said it would take her away from the mainstream of science reporting." Gelb told Brody he wanted the column to be in the mainstream, and that she could choose her subjects and set the tone of the column. "It was immediately a success. In fact, it was such a success that doctors became furious every time she wrote the column," Gelb said, "because phones would ring all over the country with patients asking questions. Doctors for the first time were being questioned thoroughly by their patients."

Initially, Brody had thought of writing the column jointly with a physician but is glad she didn't because it would have constrained her. Physicians must be cautious. Columnists are paid for expressing their opinions and must meet deadlines. "You can't give advice if 'it depends,'" Brody says. "We can sit on the fence forever, waiting until every *i* is dotted and every *t* is crossed, trying to get the absolute, definitive truth—but we'll all be dead waiting. One has to come to grips with the best available evidence and say this is what you should do. And that's why I write the column and [the physician] doesn't." When the material doesn't allow her to come to a decision, she lays all sides out as clearly as she can and lets her readers decide.

As she sits and talks in the red-papered living room of her brownstone in Brooklyn, Brody's energy makes her small frame seem spring-loaded. Without stopping the conversation, she jumps up to get a magazine, answer the phone or bring a visitor a glass of water. She practices what she preaches about the benefits of regular exercise, sandwiching the interview in between swimming and writing her column.

Brody is known around the world for her science and health reporting, but she says her reputation for being on the cutting edge of science has been both a benefit and a curse. One of the hazards of being ahead of everyone else is that others have attacked her views. But in almost thirty years of science writing, Brody says she's made only one mistake. It happened because she broke her own rules—what she calls "Brody's Postulates"—when she wrote that there was a link between hair dyes and cancer. Carcinogens have been found in hair dye in laboratory experiments, but clinical studies have not shown the cancer risk. That was the problem.

Her rules stipulate that a relationship such as the one between hair dye and cancer must make biological sense, and that laboratory evidence, population evidence, and clinical evidence all must support the observation. In affirming the link between cancer and hair dye, she broke her own rules. But her insistence on those standards has served her well in other cases, enabling her to point out flaws in studies by researchers at institutions such as Harvard University and the Sloane-Kettering cancer institute.

One such study linked the use of oral contraceptives to cervical cancer, finding a three times greater incidence of cancer in pill users than in women who used diaphragms. "Ipso facto, the pill causes cancer. Like hell it does," Brody says. "The diaphragm protects against cervical cancer; the pill doesn't cause it." To detect the flaw in the study, Brody had to know about patterns of cervical cancer, which acts something like a venereal disease.

And when Harvard researchers published findings in the New England Journal of Medicine relating coffee consumption to pancreatic cancer, Brody said, "Hogwash." There was no lab evidence, no societal evidence, she says, and the epidemiology contradicted the observation because coffee drinking had been declining while pancreatic cancer was increasing.

Where does she get this certainty about science? "I have no idea," she says. "A lot of it is gut feeling." But she also has a tremendous reserve of facts and the ability to make connections across disciplines. During her first ten years as a science writer, she studied medicine, attended medical conferences, and read medical journals and related publications.

She no longer has time for conferences, but still reads widely. Now, however, the sheer volume of information makes it almost impossible to keep up. "One of my concerns is that I'm losing touch with all the details you need to have stacked up there," she says, pointing to her head, "to make sense out of every new piece of information." In order to stay on top of the subjects she deals with in her column, she leaves certain big and demanding subjects to her *Times* colleagues to cover, such as cancer research or the science of AIDS.

Her thoroughness often surprised her sources when she was a young woman trying to get information from scientists who were mainly older men. "I knew my stuff. I didn't pick up the telephone to talk to anyone until I had read the whole background stuff, and so I spoke their language," Brody says. "I used their words, I knew their science and they knew it from the first question I asked. They quickly got the feeling they were talking to a colleague, not a journalist. They expected me to be this little flighty know-nothing, and when it was readily apparent that I wasn't one of those, that intrigued them and so they stuck with me." Physicians also began to trust her because she checked the accuracy of what she had written with sources. The refusal by many journalists to let a source read a story prior to publication is a "cockamamie principle," she says. "I think it's stupid. I have them read it for accuracy. I let them know in advance they're not to change style unless style makes something wrong."

When she began reporting in the mid-1960s, Brody says, she was paid less than her male counterparts and given less risky assignments. For example, even though her science beat at the *Times* included sexual topics, a male was assigned to write about the groundbreaking Masters and Johnson study on sexual behavior "because they did not think it was proper material for a woman."

She later broke long-established unwritten rules at the *Times*, pressuring the paper to use direct, accurate language for sexual acts and body parts. Savoring the memory, she says she was the first to get the term "sexual intercourse" on page 1 of the *Times*, and to get the words "ejaculation" and "penis" in the paper. It took four years for her to persuade the paper to run a column on masturbation. "She helped us ride over taboos," recalls former executive editor Rosenthal. "We began to print what had made [past] editors spin like tops."

"There was so much squeamishness," Brody says. "Most of those battles involved sex . . . because the *Times* was the newspaper of record, the family newspaper, the good, gray *Times*." She tells of writing about a new birth-control method that involved putting cervical mucus on a kind of litmus paper. The editors cut out the description of the test because the term "cervical mucus" bothered them, she says. "I blew my stack."

Another time she wrote a story based on sex researcher Shere Hite's anecdotal material showing that the overwhelming majority of women do not have orgasm without direct stimulation of the clitoris. "Get this in the *Times*, right?" she says, snorting derisively. "They held it the first night." Brody tells of going to see Arthur Gelb, who showed it to his wife. "She said, 'Do you know how important this is? Do you realize how many divorces are caused by men's failure to know this?'" The story ran.

Although Brody has often challenged the medical establishment, she enjoys the respect of physicians and other health care professionals. Practicing physicians frequently distribute her columns to patients. Others say patients often clip and bring in a Brody column and ask for their reaction.

She decides what to write each week "by default," using a principle she calls critical mass. "I get an idea for something, start pulling material together, keep an eagle eye open for new information, some peg or something, and when the material reaches a critical mass and is ready to write, I sit down and reread the file and maybe make a couple of phone calls." Sometimes a chance remark prompts her to tackle a topic. A column on sudden death in athletes, for example, was sparked by a comment she overheard in a ladies' room: A woman asked a friend whether such deaths could be prevented. Some ideas are pegged to the season, and others are related to the development of new medication. "I get ideas all over," she says.

"She is extremely well informed, always bubbling with ideas," said *Times* science editor Nicholas Wade. And after more than twenty years of doing her column, her writing is still fresh. "I'm sure in some way it must come from her vivacious personality," Wade added.

"She's a delight to be with. . . . She has a knack for getting people to tell her their stories . . . and a lively interest in people."

Readers often say she has a sympathetic approach. Brody says that's probably what Gelb recognized when he asked her to write the column in the first place. "I am an empathetic person, the kind of person who sees somebody struggling with something on the street, a total stranger, and offers to help," she says. "I see somebody standing with a map on the corner, I say, "Where do you want to go?" My husband often tells me to mind my own business. But that's my personality, my nature. I'm not comfortable minding my own business when people seem like they're in need of assistance."

"She was empathetic," Gelb agreed. "She knew how to take complicated health subjects and make the information simple to absorb without lowering her journalistic standards. She was a genius at that. She was able to communicate some of the gobbledegook that doctors were saying. She broke it down into understandable language."

Early on Brody came to the conclusion that a lot of the things that made people sick were in their own hands—how they lived, what they did or didn't do, what they ate, whether they moved, how they managed stress, what substances they abused, whether alcohol or cigarettes, and even whether they used seatbelts. "Combined with the economic situation, the practicality of it all said to me that we should be preventing some of this instead of just patching people up afterward." She wants people to understand what goes wrong with them and give them the opportunity to avoid it.

Over the years, Brody has become "sort of disgusted with traditional medicine" and increasingly interested in what people have done for millennia to keep themselves healthy—things that have been tossed aside as unscientific. She has written about alternative healing methods and tried to focus on what has been substantiated. "Most old wives' tales are based on some real physiology—who would have dreamed that sticking needles in people would do what it does?" she asks. "Scientific medicine has its limits. It's time to bring back some of the traditional medical techniques that have time-honored value." Brody's interest in alternative medicine is reflected in two books she co-authored, *You Can Fight Cancer and Win* and *Secrets of Good Health.*

And her interest in good health extends to the kitchen, where she uses natural ingredients and experiments with new combinations. Her kitchen is paneled in warm brown wood; she designed the cupboards herself. Spices and herbs line the shelves in glass bottles. Cooking is a passion, "the only way I can express myself in artistic fashion," she says. Her concern about healthy eating coupled with her love of cooking prompted her to write *Jane Brody's Good Food Book,* a collection of essays on nutrition accompanied by recipes. On this day, a huge stockpot of vegetable and bean soup is simmering on the stove; later she will deliver it to a local shelter for the homeless.

Time started getting especially tight when Brody began writing books in addition to her weekly column and regular science articles. The one thing she doesn't have time for is answering the mail from readers. She says it overwhelms her. "I no longer have time to read it, much less answer it," she says. "It's just gotten out of hand. I used to spend weekends answering mail. When I started writing books, I simply couldn't do that." But no additional books are in the works— she finds the editing and publication process "horrendous."

Writing her first book on nutrition in 1980 was perhaps the hardest project she's tackled, but she calls it her greatest achievement. *Jane Brody's Nutrition Book* started out to be a debate on a number of questions about nutrition. But in typical Brody fashion, she got little more than a chapter written when she realized there was no debate— she saw a better answer for each of the questions.

Knowing that nutrition was a little understood area, Brody expected to be attacked as a quack by physicians, dieticians, nurses, and chiropractors. Instead, dieticians recommended the book, physicians told their patients to buy it, and it is still used by schools and colleges in courses for non-nutrition majors.

"It was the most courageous thing I ever tackled, while I had a full-time job and kids and a house," she says. "That book was the first popular nutrition book to reach the best seller list that was not a diet book. It was not a big gimmick. It was straight, honest, and down the line. I was very proud of that. It still is my crowning achievement."

It is that same honestly that has earned Brody a loyal following. Readers "trust me more than doctors because I stand apart from doctors," she says. Over the years many have written to ask for help. She understands their desperation but doesn't always have time to respond. "Sometimes I'm asked things totally beyond what any journalist should be asked . . . even if I were a physician. They assume a God-like knowledge that nobody would have. This person's been to seventeen doctors at ten institutions and has been unable to solve the problem. How am I going to know?" she says, empathizing with readers. "I understand exactly what happens when you're faced with an unremitting condition for which there's no treatment and no diagnosis. You hope that somebody apart from this who sees it all might have seen something and have an answer."

Once, when a friend said she was suffering crippling pain, Brody thought that the condition sounded like something she had researched and written about and suggested acupuncture. "It helped, but I can't do that for everyone," she says. Mail from readers overwhelms her. Someone at the office sorts it for her, and she takes the "fan mail" home and stuffs it in a shopping bag. "I feel bad. I think there are treasures in my reader mail, but when I read it I feel obliged to answer it," she says. "It's become prohibitive."

Brody writes at home, on a quiet street near Brooklyn's Prospect Park. Once a week she goes to the *Times* office in Manhattan for a meeting with other science writers. The only negative aspect of working at home is lack of interaction with colleagues, she says, but she prefers that to being interrupted. She describes her working style as being focused for short periods: "I constantly interrupt myself, but when I work at home I interrupt myself as opposed to having other things interrupt me when I'm not ready to be interrupted." She balances the hours spent on the telephone doing research and in writing with physical activity—biking, swimming, ice skating, or walking the dog, Max.

Brody is her own best authority, but she also quotes medical experts if she is writing about something new to her or about a controversial subject. If she's writing a column on nutrition, for example, "I know it cold," she says. "I don't see a need to hang it on somebody." But where a column contains highly detailed information or potentially risky advice, she seeks out sources who speak from positions of knowledge and authority.

"Column writing is a lot like writing books; it's tricky business," she says. "It's an awesome responsibility and I don't take it lightly. I'm a real middle of the roader. I'm not a far-out person," she says. "I've never been a fringe person, so that the chances of my giving off-the-wall advice are very slim."

She describes her writing style as stream of consciousness and says the wonderful thing about the computer is that the mechanics of writing no longer get in her way. Sometimes, if she has put in many hours researching a topic and interviewing people, she takes a break before she writes. Once she has completed the research, she can write a column straight through in an hour and a half.

She has enjoyed using her column as a tool to find relationships

between unrelated fields that could advance research or the understanding of a problem, such as the connection between osteoporosis
and exercise. She says, for example, that some physicians routinely
prescribe calcium tablets for women without understanding that the
only way to build bone mass is through exercise. "Why I'm different
from physicians who specialize, who know so much more about their
field than I'll ever know," she says, "is that I can relate column a to
column z." She has no regrets at not pursuing a career in science or
medicine, saying, "As a physician I couldn't begin to reach the number
of people I reach."

When she retires Brody plans to write about natural history—
insects, plants, and flowers. She had considered retiring at fifty, but
that birthday is past, and her editor says the subject hasn't been
discussed since. "I like the variety involved in journalism," Brody says.
"The most wonderful thing is you can never be bored. You may be
bored for twenty-four hours or a week, but you can never be bored
long-term because the subjects keep changing."

PERSONAL HEALTH

"You will live long and enjoy life."

I know full well that this paper
prophecy, which I found in a
fortune cookie the other day, comes
with no money-back guarantee of a
good or long life. But while many
people are content to accept
whatever fate life may have in
store, in the 15 years I have been a
medical and science writer, I have
come to believe that I can and
should adopt reasonable measures
to help preserve my health and
prolong my life.

I know that the measures are no
guarantee that I will still be spry at
90. I also know that many of the
recommendations are based on a
still-incomplete understanding of
the major killing and crippling
diseases. Some, in fact, may turn
out to be wrong.

But I am convinced that my
future health largely depends on
how I care for myself in the present,
and I try to live in accordance with
what I consider the best available
medical knowledge. It isn't always
simple, but I have discovered that,
contrary to what some people
might think, it's not a life of misery
and deprivation.

First, I want to respond to some
of the more frequent comments of
those who meet me or write me: I
am not too young to worry about
my health. I'll be 38 this spring,
and, anyway, I think it is never
too early to start taking care of
yourself. I am not thin by nature
but by design and constant
vigilance. I like to eat and, guided
by reason and self-control, I eat

everything I like. I exercise daily, even though my workday is regularly 10 to 12 hours long—I make time for the things I consider important. And, most important of all, I enjoy my life.

My guiding principle is moderation. Except for an absolute ban on smoking, I am not a fanatic about anything, unless you think it fanatic that I am determined to try to realize the prophecy in my fortune cookie. Now for the details:

Diet

I eat pretty much in accordance with the dietary goals spelled out by the Senate Committee on Nutrition and Human Needs.

Carbohydrates account for about 60 percent of my calories, protein for 10 to 15 percent, and fats, 25 to 30 percent. This is considerably less fat and considerably more carbohydrates than the average American consumes. Contrary to popular belief, starchy foods (complex carbohydrates) are not fattening; ounce for ounce, they contain less than half the calories that fat does and no more calories than pure protein. My daily cholesterol intake is about 250 to 300 milligrams (the amount in one egg yolk), less than half that of the typical adult American.

About a third of my day's protein comes from vegetable sources, particularly grains. Among the animal protein foods I most frequently consume are skim milk, low-fat cottage cheese and yogurt, chicken, turkey breast, small quantities of well-trimmed beef and pork, boiled ham and fish.

My family of four regularly dines on a total of a half-pound of slivered meat or chicken, stir-fried with lots of fresh vegetables and served with hefty portions of rice, bulgur (cracked wheat) or pasta. We rarely (maybe once in three months) have a slab of meat such as a roast, steak or chops for dinner. The average portion of such cuts of meat would triple the amount of meat each person consumes.

Spaghetti with meat sauce and a big salad is another supper favorite. So is homemade soup—lots of vegetables (including potatoes), small pieces of meat and/or chicken, rice or bulgur and/or noodles in chicken broth. The soup is a great way to use up leftovers, relieving the table-clearer of the "obligation" to eat those few hundred extra calories that often remain at the end of a meal.

Another use for leftovers is a favorite breakfast of mine— fried rice or bulgur mixed with whatever's left from last night's supper, perhaps supplemented by a scrambled egg white or slivers of boiled ham or turkey breast. The latter ingredients, incidentally, are usually consumed in sandwiches (on whole-grain or pita bread) for lunch a couple of times a week.

I eat eggs as eggs once a week, discarding one of the two yolks. (If you have a dog, the yolks you don't eat will give your pet a glossy coat.) My children love pancakes and French toast for breakfast. In both I discard one of every two yolks; pancakes are made with fat-free buttermilk, polyunsaturated oil and whole wheat flour. I top my serving with sliced banana and a dash of cinnamon sugar instead of syrup.

Rather than buying cakes, I make my own cakelike breads, laden with nutritious things like fruit, nuts, wholegrain flour or oatmeal, buttermilk or orange juice and polyunsaturated oil instead of the highly saturated fats used by commercial bakeries.

Because my diet is well balanced and includes lots of fresh and stir-fried vegetables, salad and whole grains, I see no need for vitamin supplements. Even without vitamin C, I have had only one two-day cold in the last four years, despite the fact that my young sons undoubtedly bring home all sorts of viruses from school.

I don't keep potato chips, pretzels or other high-calorie, salty, low-nutrient snack foods in the house. When I'm overcome by the urge to nibble, I make unbuttered popcorn (high in fiber, low in calories) with just a little salt.

I don't worry much about food additives because, other than bread and cereal, I eat relatively few processed foods. If once a year I want to dress up a fruit salad with maraschino cherries, I do it— despite the suspicions about red dye.

Despite the care I take with my daily diet—or, more accurately, because of it—I don't hesitate to splurge now and again.

Once a year, for example, I make blinis (buttery Russian pancakes) served with caviar, sour cream, chopped egg and melted butter. Another annual favorite is pumpkin soup made with half-and-half and topped with a dollop of salted whipped cream. Italian sausages are an occasional treat.

Weight Control

I once weighed a third more than I do now. I was always on a diet, and after a week of eating library paste and toothpicks, my willpower would run out and I'd gorge on everything I loved and had missed all week. Or else I would put nothing in my mouth all day, then eat nonstop all night. Eventually, I became obsessed with food and weight, and the more obsessed I was, the fatter I got.

Then one day I realized that I had to learn to live more sensibly with food. I stopped dieting and started eating like a normal person, three reasonable meals a day. No more binges, no more whole bags of potato chips or pints of ice cream and no more going hungry. And, lo and behold, I lost weight. It took two years to reach what I consider a normal weight for my size and bone structure, but I never gained it back. Here's how I do it:

I never skip a meal. That only makes me hungrier for the next meal and increases the likelihood that I'll overeat. Besides, when I'm hungry I'm irritable and impatient and I can't write. I consider breakfast and lunch my most important meals; they provide me with the energy I need to work productively and run around all day. I usually consume two-thirds or more of my day's calories by 2 P.M., just the reverse of what most others I know do.

If I've had a big lunch, I eat only a salad and a piece of bread for supper (then I often eat the leftover supper for breakfast the next day). If I've had only a sandwich for lunch, I eat a small portion of the family dinner plus the salad. If we're planning to have a big dinner out, I have a large breakfast and small lunch.

I don't consume much alcohol—

at a dinner party, one drink plus wine with dinner; at home, a small glass of wine with supper. I find that in addition to the calories in alcohol, it diminishes my will power, and I tend to overeat if I overdrink.

•

I must admit, though, that I have a sweet tooth (diminishing in intensity as I age). I keep it pretty well under control by allowing myself one or two sweets a day, usually two cookies and a slice of homemade sweet bread (for example, pumpkin, cranberry, zucchini or banana bread).

In a restaurant, I usually have fruit for dessert; in someone else's house, I'll eat a sliver of the pie or cake that's served. Ice cream, a lifelong passion, is consumed by the tablespoon instead of the scoop and only flavors I find irresistible; that way I don't feel deprived.

I weigh myself every day, sometimes twice. My weight usually fluctuates within a three- to four-pound range. As soon as I hit the top of that range, I increase my vigilance. But I don't cut out, just down.

Exercise

When an injury kept me bedridden for six weeks last year, I discovered that I could, through determination, keep my weight down even without any exercise. But I have a lot more leeway in my diet when I'm active. Currently I swim a quarter-mile three times a week, jog two miles three times a week, play tennis one to five times a week (depending on the season), ride my bike often and walk lots. Whenever possible, I use footpower

instead of cars, taxis, subways, buses, elevators and escalators.

This activity adds far more to my life than the few hundred extra calories I can eat each day. It is a great tension reliever and relaxant. I find that I get angry and frustrated less often and get over my destructive feelings more quickly than I used to when I exercised less regularly. And I sleep like a baby— about six hours a night—even though I always have a lot on my mind.

In sum, then, unless you have a chronic illness like diabetes or are genetically prone to an early death from heart disease, you need not become an extremist or an ascetic, nor do you have to give up everything you love forever, to live healthfully and enjoyably. Through the principles of moderation, you can have your cake and eat it too. All you have to do is decide it's something you want to do.

[April 4, 1979]

Masturbation: Coming out of the Closet

Changes in American society are drawing new attention to the form of sexual expression most widely practiced, yet least talked about: masturbation. Compared with the 1940's and 50's, when Alfred Kinsey did his studies, many more people today say they approve of sexual self-stimulation and perform it fairly often.

Various surveys have revealed that younger adults are more likely to approve of masturbation and say they practice it than those in older groups, but also that more older people now say they masturbate than did in Kinsey's day. Such findings are believed to reflect a greater willingness to talk about masturbation, as well as an actual increase in its practice.

Greater reliance on masturbation may result from such factors as the increased number of Americans who are divorced or widowed, the number of young adults who live alone, the increase in two-career marriages that often involve frequent separations, fear of sexually transmitted diseases, including acquired immune deficiency syndrome, and newer approaches to treating sexual problems.

Though long shrouded in secrecy and guilt, masturbation in recent years has been considered quite useful in sex therapy. Many therapists regard it as a means of sexual self-discovery as well as a safe and easy way to release sexual tension.

Dr. Mary S. Calderone, president of Siecus (the Sex Information and Education Council of the United States), said an increasing number of sex therapists now agree that "masturbation has a specific role to play in the sexual evolution and total life cycle of the human being."

But however normal or useful masturbation may be for many people, Dr. Helen Singer Kaplan, a psychiatrist and sex therapist at the New York Hospital-Cornell Medical Center, said that the practice is not essential to normal development and that no one who thinks it is wrong or sinful should feel he or she must try it.

"Those who have not masturbated, for cultural or religious reasons, can have perfectly normal sex lives as adults," Dr. Kaplan said.

From infancy onward, many if not most human beings purposely stimulate the genital area, Dr. Calderone said. The late Dr. René A. Spitz, a Denver psychoanalyst who studied young children, observed in 1962 that emotionally healthy infants whose mothers were close and caring were more likely to masturbate than those who had rejecting mothers or were orphaned. Dr. Spitz reasoned that the latter groups had failed to learn from their care-givers about the pleasures of touch.

Rarely do small children reach orgasm. Rather, they seem to use genital self-stimulation to gain pleasure, reassurance, comfort and relief from anxiety, according to Dr. Calderone and Eric W. Johnson, authors of "The Family Book About Sexuality" (Harper & Row, 1981). Children may turn to pleasurable self-touching to relieve anxieties totally unrelated to sex, such as those stemming from the arrival of a new sibling or problems at school, they said.

Dr. Calderone and other experts urge parents not to chastise children found masturbating, but merely to suggest, if necessary, that such activities be done in private.

The sexual pressures that emerge during adolescence cast masturbation into another role: that of relieving sexual tension and learning how the body works.

"By the time they enter college, about five out of six males are masturbating," according to Lorna J. Sarrel and Dr. Philip M. Sarrel, co-directors of the Yale Sex Counseling Service, who have periodically surveyed students.

In 1969, the Sarrels reported, a third of the women in college said they masturbated, but starting in 1973, "there was a sudden and steep rise in the number of women students who said they masturbated."

"From 1976 on, the statistic has been fairly consistent, and now about 70 to 80 percent of college women say they are masturbating," the Sarrels reported. Ms. Sarrel, who has a master's degree in social work, and her husband, a physician, are authors of "Sexual Turning Points: The Seven Stages of Adult Sexuality" (Macmillan, 1984).

As Dr. Calderone and Mr. Johnson view it, masturbation is "a rehearsal for mature sex." They state in their book that adolescents "need to find out how their bodies perform sexually."

"Masturbation is a safe way to do this," they write, "because it does not involve another person."

Dr. Calderone sees masturbation as a means of preparing for later sexual interaction with a partner, since it can help individuals understand their own particular sexual needs and better appreciate those of others.

Dr. Lonnie Garfield Barbach— a clinical social psychologist and sex therapist at the University of California at San Francisco and author of "For Yourself: The Fulfillment of Female Sexuality" (Doubleday, 1975)—said that masturbation is "one of the best ways to learn about your sexual responses." She is one of many therapists who now encourage

women to use masturbation to achieve orgasm. Men, too, have been aided by this technique, both to achieve orgasm and to overcome psychological impotence or premature ejaculation.

The studies conducted in the 1960's by Dr. William H. Masters and Virginia Johnson on human sexual response found that although masturbation was not preferred to sex with a partner, orgasms achieved by masturbating were usually more intense.

Dr. Kaplan, who practices at the Payne Whitney Psychiatric Clinic at the New York Hospital-Cornell Medical Center, said that based on her clinical experience, those who masturbate during adolescence seem less likely to develop sexual problems as adults.

A prominent sex educator in New York, Dr. Michael Carrera, author of "Sex: The Facts, the Acts and Your Feelings" (Crown, 1981), said that in a great many relationships, "mutual masturbation plays a significant role as part of the lovemaking repertoire."

"It may be an end in itself or a part of the buildup to other sexual acts," he said. "Either way, if both partners are at ease about masturbation it can be mutually satisfying."

Like any form of sexual expression, masturbation is sometimes abused or misused. As Dr. Kaplan noted, "Some people who haven't faced the anxiety involved in sex with a partner may take refuge in masturbation, using it as a compulsive substitute for love and intimacy."

Dr. Irwin Marcus, a co-editor of the psychoanalytic text

"Masturbation: From Infancy to Senescence" (International University Press, 1975), said that masturbation becomes a problem "if it interferes with social development, if it's a sign of withdrawal from relationships or if a person becomes overladen with guilt because of it."

Despite the sexual liberation of the last two decades, the belief that masturbation is immoral or harmful remains widespread. In the late 1970's, a study of 1,100 families in Cleveland by Elizabeth Roberts, David Klein and John Gagnon found that 40 percent of parents viewed masturbation as immoral, sinful and harmful.

Many people who are now middle-aged or elderly were told when they were growing up that masturbation would destroy their minds and health and cause insanity. Later it was said to cause warts and pimples and make it impossible to respond normally during sex with a partner.

Given the tenacity of attitudes about sexuality, Dr. Bernard Starr and Dr. Marcella B. Weiner, gerontologists in New York who wrote "The Starr-Weiner Report on Sex and Sexuality in the Mature Years" (McGraw-Hill, paperback), were astonished to discover in the late 1970's that many of the 800 men and women over age 60 who volunteered to participate in their study said they masturbated or at lease condoned the practice.

When asked in formal interviews what they thought of the fact that "many older people masturbate to relieve sexual tensions," 85 percent of the women and 76 percent of the men surveyed said they approved. Slightly less than half the respondents said they masturbated; this was a dramatic increase, at least in reported incidence of masturbation, from the 1950's, when almost none of the older respondents in the Kinsey studies said they masturbated.

Dr. Starr and Dr. Weiner also noted that masturbation was not limited to older people who had no partners. Rather, 40 percent of those who said they masturbated were married and living with their spouses. This finding points to another common role for masturbation at all ages: that of relieving sexual tension when your regular partner is unavailable, ill or not in the mood for sex.

As Dr. Robert N. Butler, a former director of the National Institute on Aging, and Myrna I. Lewis, a psychotherapist, wrote in their popular book, "Sex After Sixty" (Harper & Row, 1976), "Solo sex resolves sexual tensions, keeps sexual desire alive, is good physical exercise and helps to preserve sexual functioning in both men and women who have no other outlets."

Masturbation may also be gaining favor among younger people as a form of "safe sex" in this age of acquired immune deficiency syndrome and other serious diseases that are transmitted sexually. An unmarried woman in her 30's, who asked to remain anonymous, said she now prefers masturbation to a succession of male partners.

"At least I know that I'm healthy," she said, "and I want to stay that way."

[November 4, 1987]

The Surprising Benefits of Helping Others

Last Christmas I gave my husband a special gift that, unlike the many sweaters, shirts, pajamas and gloves of the past, he could not say he neither needed nor wanted. I gave him my pledge to cook each week for a homeless shelter run by his favorite local charity. He said it was the most thoughtful gift I'd given him in 22 years, but to my surprise, it turned out to be even more of a present to myself.

Every Sunday from December through April, I dug into the depths of my freezer and cupboard for forgotten ingredients and combed the markets for seasonal bargains and store specials that could be combined into a tasty dish that would be easy to heat and serve and that would provide 12 homeless men with at least one nutritious meal a week.

I had fun expanding my culinary imagination and skills by trying to make delicious, economical dishes without overloading them with fat, salt or sugar. After a few weeks, pleased with the results, I increased the quantity prepared so my husband and I and the shelter staff could also partake of the weekly creations.

Having tasted the rewards of volunteerism, I moved on to another project in the spring: working with my husband and other neighbors to spruce up our local park. In addition to joining monthly weekend cleanup crews, I adopted my husband's routine of picking up garbage while walking our dog in the park. After a while I noticed that others equipped with plastic shopping bags and rubber gloves were also collecting trash.

In this season of gifts, there are probably millions of people ready to curtail the commercialism and consumerism and think instead about giving a gift of themselves. Volunteering is hardly a selfless act, if for no other reason than doing something nice for other people can make you feel very good about yourself.

Unexpected Benefits

As some 89 million Americans have already discovered and researchers have documented, volunteering can enhance self-esteem, foster a sense of accomplishment and competence and act as an antidote to stress and depression. In fact, some studies have shown that people who volunteer their services tend to be healthier and happier and live longer than those who do not volunteer.

A decadelong study of 2,700 people in Tecumseh, Mich., showed that men who did no volunteer work were two and a half times more likely to die in the study period than men who donated their services to others.

While skeptics may believe that people who volunteer are healthier and happier to begin with, many volunteers insist it is the other way around. My husband started working in the park to fight off emotional depression. His justifiable pride in the many erosion control projects he completed was a more effective antidepressant than any medication.

Some physicians have recognized

the health benefits of volunteering. Dr. Dean Ornish, a heart specialist at the University of California Medical School in San Francisco, urges his patients to help others as a way of countering the self-involvement and hostility that seems to raise their cholesterol levels and induce angina.

An unmarried New York woman discovered that helping to care for hospitalized children with AIDS remarkably reduced the stress she was feeling over her tiresome job and frustrating social life.

Voluntary participation can often be used to develop skills that could lead to a rewarding new job or hobby. Through volunteer work, you could test your talents and interests in a career you may be considering.

By volunteering in a shelter for battered women, one woman realized that she was unsuited to the career she was pursuing in clinical social work. But another volunteer, a business executive in his 60's who spent a summer vacation building outhouses in a national park, discovered a latent talent for carpentry that became a lucrative retirement activity.

Volunteers over 60

A growing legion of retired and elderly people devote spare time to helping others. Among the most popular activities is the Foster Grandparents program, in which volunteers over 60 are teamed with children who are emotionally or physically handicapped, abused or neglected, in trouble with the law or have other special needs. Volunteers regularly visit the children and try to involve them in creative projects or learning experiences, or they are just a friend.

A foster grandparent might help tutor a learning-disabled child, uncover artistic talent in an emotionally disturbed child or even teach a delinquent child mechanical skills that could be translated into a money-making opportunity.

In another program of Senior Companions, physically able volunteers over 60 do the shopping, banking, cooking or cleaning for those who are housebound. Senior Companions also transport the elderly to medical appointments and community events.

In New Orleans, volunteers in Repairs on Wheels play Mr. Fix-It for the elderly who live in their own homes. Throughout the country, volunteers can help Meals on Wheels deliver nourishing foods to the frail or housebound elderly.

Retired executives can advise budding entrepreneurs through a 12,000-member national organization called Score, for the Service Corps of Retired Executives. Volunteers 50 and older are also welcomed by the Peace Corps for service abroad, and by Vista, its domestic counterpart.

Many other volunteer opportunities open to people of all ages can provide direct or indirect health benefits to recipients. They include visiting children in hospitals or foster care homes, providing entertainment and aid in nursing homes, operating bookmobiles and humor wagons in hospitals, mobilizing community assistance for a family devastated by an accident or death, or providing food or a helping hand for a shelter for battered women or the homeless.

Your community's well-being might also be fostered by such volunteer efforts as organizing or participating in a neighborhood recycling project and planting flowers or trees in public parks.

Former President Jimmy Carter and his wife, Rosalynn, used their participation in Habitat for Humanity not only to help rehabilitate neighborhoods and provide homes for the needy, but also to counter their own feelings of displacement after leaving the White House.

Even if you are plagued with an emotional disorder, drug problem, disability or chronic disease, your participation in a volunteer program or support group concerned with the problem can help others as well as yourself. Note the well-established success of Alcoholics Anonymous and its many offshoots, such as Narcotics Anonymous, Neurotics Anonymous, Gamblers Anonymous and Overeaters Anonymous.

Continued participation in support groups, even after you feel your troubles are behind you, can help reinforce your own gains and enable you to encourage others who are still struggling with a similar problem.

[December 1, 1988]

DOROTHY GILLIAM

When she graduated from the Columbia Journalism School and got a job as a reporter at the *Washington Post* in 1961, Dorothy Gilliam was determined to avoid being stereotyped as a black reporter. But the hot stories of the 1960s involved civil rights, freedom marches, and welfare issues—and Gilliam soon plunged in. Now she purposefully tries to give her readers the perspective of an African-American woman. "That voice is enormously important because there are so many pressures for persons to be more conservative, to be anti–affirmative action," she says, "to be more white."

Her weekly column appears on the front page of the *Post*'s Metro section. The *Post* doesn't run pictures with columns, but Gilliam says most readers know she is black. She has been writing the column since 1979 and is well known in Washington. And she's also known in journalism circles as a pioneer, one of the first black women to crack the predominantly white male-controlled media.

In spite of the authority and credibility she has established over the last decade, Gilliam says there's still a risk that her column will be dismissed as fringe opinion because the mood of the country has turned conservative. "The real key is for columnists to be taken seriously, not to be marginalized," she says. "Women and minorities always have to worry about that." The shift to a more conservative climate has caused her to modify and adapt her approach while holding fast to her beliefs. "It's more challenging to write in ways so that you are taken seriously, but still espouse the view in which you believe."

Finding a way to touch all her readers is especially challenging. "I want to connect to readers. I care about the respect of black readers, of oppressed people, as much as I care about the respect of congresspeople," she says. "I have to be honest and tell what I see and how I feel—and when you have conservatives and neo-cons all around, it's much more difficult."

Gilliam resumed her column in early 1992 after a year's leave from the *Post,* which she spent as a fellow at the Freedom Forum in New York, studying racial diversity in the media. Her research will feed directly into her columns, and she expects it to result in a booklet on strategies to encourage diversity in newspapers. Freedom Forum director Everette E. Dennis says Gilliam has added the argument of economic viability to the moral authority argument generally put forward as the reason for newspapers to hire more minorities. He says her argument reflects a change in strategy and style, and would be more effective. "Being right doesn't cut it in a recession," he observes. "I'm impressed that she's now taken the tack that it's not only right but good business, that it ties to circulation issues. It's far more than do-gooder stuff."

Gilliam's year-long leave from the *Post* gave her time to regroup and refocus her energy. After writing a twice-weekly column since 1979, "I was feeling burnout," she says. "I was conscious of the responsibility of the column, of saying something. It's a hard market in Washington—you have to try to say something significant in an interesting way all the time. [Editors would say] 'What did you do for me today?'—not yesterday. I felt like I just needed to take in for a while instead of give out."

The time off from column writing gave her the chance to think in a different way. "Doing a column, you take in for two days and then pour out," she says. At the Freedom Forum "it was a slower absorption process. You could listen, read . . . and I was in New York, in an entirely new setting." The year also got her started on another book—the story of her life and work, wrapping in issues of racial diversity.

A tall woman who carries herself with regal self-assurance, Gilliam is dressed in black this day, with a vibrant African scarf draped across her shoulder. She is in New York attending a national conference on multiculturalism in journalism. She speaks slowly in a resonant deep voice, as she searches for words to describe her role as a columnist. "It's important to hold onto the sense of who I am," she says. "I think to be different is OK. I fought for that right. I didn't want to be a stereotyped. I'm coming to understand who I am as a black woman and as a human being. I think that my caring and concern and willingness to stand up for what I believe is characteristic of that kind of voice. It's worth having at a newspaper."

The daughter of a preacher, Gilliam was born in Memphis and moved to Louisville when she was five. "I liked from a very early age to talk," she says. To impress her father, "I said poems in church. Before I was four, I could recite 'The Night Before Christmas'. . . . I was a star performer." Her father died when she was fourteen, and her mother took a job as a domestic to help support the family. Gilliam doesn't remember ever wanting to be a newspaper reporter or columnist, but she read a lot, mostly fiction. At home she was encouraged to speak out.

Her entry into journalism was accidental. She had been working as a secretary at the old *Louisville Defender* while attending Ursuline College, and was asked to fill in for the society editor. "I realized what a key it was to opening doors," she said, "to seeing people like lawyers, doctors, the upper stratum of black society." She later transferred to Lincoln University in Jefferson City, Mo., and also attended Tuskegee Institute in Alabama, both predominantly black schools. She says her education helped build her confidence and gave her courage to speak out.

After college she found work in Chicago with the magazines *Jet* and *Ebony* before returning to school to get her master's degree at Columbia. She interviewed with the *Post* after graduation but spent the summer in Kenya with Operation Crossroads, a forerunner of the Peace Corps. From Africa she sent several stories to the *Post,* and when she came home the paper offered her a job as a general assignment reporter. It was three years before passage of the Civil Rights Act, and things were rough on a black reporter in Washington. Gilliam remembers the setbacks she encountered in trying to cover stories other than those about blacks and women. Once, for example, sent to an elegant apartment building to interview a centenarian, Gilliam was stopped by the black doorman who could not believe she was supposed to come in the front door.

Finally she realized that she was missing some of the great stories of the day by continuing to be a general assignment reporter and trying to avoid being a black reporter assigned to black issues and events. She began writing stories about the black community, about poverty, and about the welfare system. One of the memorable stories she covered was James Meredith's entry into the University of Mississippi.

Gilliam worked until her first child was born in 1963 and returned soon afterward, but said she was unprepared for the maternal feeling that would overwhelm her. So when her second child was born she took a leave, returning to the *Post* in 1972 as an assistant editor in the

newly-created Style section. Working with good writers was satisfying, Gilliam says, and it encouraged her to write a book on Paul
Robeson, which was published in 1976. But after seven years on the
desk she felt restless.

"One of the tasks I had set myself was to bring coherence to black
culture," she says. "I had done some hiring. But things were changing.
The newspaper was changing. Things were more conservative."
Gilliam proposed two options to *Post* editor Ben Bradlee: That she be
named editor of the paper's Sunday magazine, or that she be given a
column. She remembers Bradlee saying, "Take your time. Write some
longer stories with a point of view and we'll see how it evolves."

Bradlee, now *Post* vice-president at large, says he told Gilliam to
try a column because she was a decent writer and moved around town
in circles where no one else moved. "We had nobody talking for that
segment of our audience," he said. "We were becoming aware of
shortcomings in local coverage, but none of us were as prescient as we
should have been. The credit belongs to Dorothy. When she got going,
she did a good job."

Gilliam began writing her column in 1979 and says her early
efforts were pretty rough. It was hard to make the shift from traditional news reporting, which attempts to be objective, to expressing a
point of view. Column writing is a tricky balancing act, she says, and
she's still working on refining it. "It's a combination of elements—the
shaping of my own thoughts and feelings, my own opinions. [Figuring
out] what's too little, or too much; what's persuasive, what's naive,"
she says. "I grew up in public."

Readers have to feel the columnist is a human being to whom they
can relate, Gilliam says, adding with a smile, "I'm definitely very
human." She appreciates the *Post* giving her time to find her own
voice, especially since editors didn't always agree with what she said.
"It takes a certain kind of very tolerant, broad-minded visionary
editor to understand that it's important to truly have diversity," she
says. An editor must be willing to run opinions that he or she doesn't
accept or understand, if they're well stated and convincingly argued,
Gilliam says.

Although there were probably many columns that people disagreed with, especially those on racial subjects, she says Bradlee only
questioned one column in ten years. He told Gilliam he would have
liked her to rethink it. That column, written in the aftermath of a Ku
Klux Klan rally in Washington, condoned violence, comparing the
situation to times of war. In hindsight, she says condoning violence

was something she should not have done. "As I have learned more about white culture, I've learned you don't ever condone any damage to personal property," she says. "It's not that I don't respect private property, but something so onerous as the Klan. . . ." Her voice trails off, but her body is rigid with the anger she still carries. Feelings like that are what make her columns resonate, she says, "personal emotion, anger, love—any deep feeling."

Her ideas come from everywhere. "In a sense, when you write a column, you're always on—as you move about the city and community and attend events," she says. "That's what's most exhausting." Writing a column two times a week may not seem like a lot, she says, but "in ten years I wrote over a thousand columns." Gilliam's column was syndicated briefly in the mid-1980s, but the syndicate went out of business.

Now that she is back at the *Post,* her challenge will be to establish a different rhythm. In addition to the once-a-week column, she will do longer pieces for the paper's Outlook section. "It will be an opportunity to stretch out a bit and do things in depth," she says. "I'm pleased with the prospect. I think one column a week will be enough to give me continuity of voice."

Many of her ideas come from the news, and she also has an agenda that involves politics, education, and social change. "In addition to 'topic A' columns, I have highlighted four or five areas that interest me and have tried to build up contacts in those areas," she says, listing politics, including black and local politics; education; racial diversity in the media; young people; new technology in media and in employment; and multiculturalism in society. She sees her column as reflecting a different experience. "As this country gets more diverse, we've got to arrive at the point where we can understand, appreciate, and value difference," she says. "The presentation of a different voice, a different perspective—all of that is terribly vital to our growth and development as a nation." Too often black journalists feel the pressure of homogenization, she says, and are absorbed into the mainstream.

"Her significance as a columnist is in terms of a very humanistic approach to local issues and problems," says Freedom Forum director Dennis. "She doesn't beat you over the head with the racial angle, although it's always there. . . . She's very steady, very consistent." Dennis adds that Gilliam has a following not only in Washington but among young minority journalists. Gilliam doesn't look at herself as a role model but says it's a reality. "I certainly feel a responsibility—

more than I should. It's probably female guilt—the responsibility of [being] another voice there is very real to me."

The editor of the *Post*'s Metro section says Gilliam "often speaks to and connects with a number of clusters of readers that we often don't connect with—but that can't be defined by race and gender." She writes as a black person, a woman, a member of the middle class, a longtime Washington resident, and a parent. "And she writes a little bit against the grain," says Milton Coleman, assistant managing editor for metropolitan news. "She can connect with all of those people."

Aware of the power of her medium, Gilliam says one of the worst things for her is to make a mistake. Her main concern is to report as thoroughly and fully as she can before she gives an opinion. "So if I'm critical or attacking or applauding, I've got to know every aspect—I seek to know every aspect." Gilliam says she's made mistakes and admitted them, and that her opinion on a subject has often evolved or changed. Writing about former Washington Mayor Marion Barry in the 1980s, for example, Gilliam says she tried to be fair and praise him when he did well. She wrote columns critical of the *Post* when she thought the paper based stories about Barry's drug use and womanizing on hearsay and rumor. But later Gilliam changed her mind and called for the mayor's resignation. She says she was the first to demand that he resign, even before the *Post*'s editorial board did so.

Ideas are abundant, but writing does not come easily. "It is an area that I struggle with a lot," she says. "I would love to be facile and beautiful, but it's not my strength. It's a constant struggle." Although she still doesn't think of herself as a writer, she acknowledges that time in itself has made her a better wordsmith. "Writing is an old person's game," she says. "By that time you have the wisdom and understanding to bring something to it."

Freed of the deadlines imposed by getting out two columns a week, Gilliam says she hopes writing will become less onerous. "I want to stop the struggle and let the writing come," she says. "What I like to do is to try to absorb everything I can. Then it all pours out." She always feels anxiety until she starts the actual writing process. To get herself started, she does a rough outline of what she wants to say, then writes the column through. After showing the piece to one or two other people, she rewrites. It usually takes her about two hours to write a column, although she says she can do it in twenty minutes if she's clear enough on the piece beforehand.

Gilliam's columns usually provoke a response, and she says her readers represent every level of society. Sometimes readers are irate. "I get quite a bit of hate mail," she says. That bothers her, but she figures it goes with the territory. "If I'm going to have the temerity to be critical, I've got to take the lumps." A columnist is always vulnerable, she says. "Writing a column is like growing up in public. It's a pretty vulnerable position, especially with the visibility of the *Post*. You do something wrong, you get a hundred letters; you do something right, you don't hear."

She says she weighs that vulnerability against other things that are important to her. Born in the South at a time when society was rigidly segregated, Gilliam knew she would face obstacles. But she has also seen and experienced many changes first hand. "I'm a new old woman—or an old new woman," she says, "because I've been affected by the gains of the black movement and the women's movement. I lived through them." Much of her time since the mid-1970s has been devoted to increasing opportunities for minorities in journalism, and she has found that fulfilling.

"It's important to me to be excellent in my craft, to try to excel in being a writer, and it's just as important to me to be a change agent in the industry, that's the other part," she says. "When I think of what I want to do in active journalism, this kind of writing is it. So you have to take the risks along with the rewards."

You Define Yourself

While some people have been endowed with as much ambition as Patricia Roberta Harris had, few people have possessed the drive and intelligence to convert that ambition into monuments of success. In the best of those few, ambition combines with humanism to create a sense of mission. Pat Harris, the rail car waiter's daughter who became the first woman to hold two Cabinet posts, was among the best.

A problem with being an ambitious and successful black woman is that one often walks down corridors of power where few blacks or women get to enter and roles and purpose can easily be misunderstood. And so it was Pat Harris' lot to have to defend herself against charges that she was aloof from the problems of the poor.

Yet many blacks, like many whites, misunderstood this remarkable woman and questioned the importance of her accomplishments for the black community.

"I fought her being named to the Cabinet," recalled D.C. school board member R. Calvin Lockridge, "because I thought that she wasn't black enough. I felt she did not relate to the black community."

Later, Lockridge recognized his mistake. He got to know Pat Harris and realized that he had been judging her "on her outer appearances" and, in his words, "my own feelings of inferiority" in the face of her knowledge and skill. Eventually, he became an ardent supporter of Pat Harris and supported her unsuccessful bid to become mayor of Washington.

This irony, which Lockridge alluded to, is that Pat Harris was often distrusted because she was too intelligent and sensitive. This greatly angered one of Harris' closest friends, Dr. Pearl Watson, who, at Harris' funeral yesterday at the Washington Cathedral, said in her eulogy: "It has always been very distressing to me that anyone, especially the Johnny-come-latelies" would question her commitment.

One of the sad byproducts of the wonderful things that emerged in the '60s for black people is that anyone pursuing excellence is often accused of "acting white." The notion that excellence is associated only with whites was a thought that was repugnant to Pat Harris. She believed that blacks could achieve anything they wanted if they didn't buy society's low opinion of them, and, in turn, attempt to hold each other back based on that opinion. This may be her true legacy, one that black children today could benefit from: "You define yourself."

Until more black people begin to define themselves, black children will be faced with two subtly conflicting messages from the world: one will say, "Strive for excellence," and the other says, "But only whites are excellent." Pat Harris probably laughed at this line of reasoning from the time she was a child.

But as I listened to several speakers at Pat's funeral, I couldn't help but feel that the real legacy that she left to black people and to the country as a whole may be the reminder that we should always respect each other's differences. No matter how we talk, carry ourselves, or even dream. As racial oppression subsides, we must be careful not to oppress one another.

We need to let Pat Harris' life be a new yardstick. We shouldn't think that what she attained is impossible to emulate. She wouldn't want that.

What she would probably want to see for all of us, black and white, is that we try to judge each other not on our outward trappings, mannerisms or even associations, but on our individual commitment to justice and equality. By that yardstick, Pat Harris belonged to the black community even as she walked with presidents, popes and kings.

[March 28, 1985]

Robinson and a Pioneer's Heart

"Thoughts of death
Crowd over my happiness. . . ."
—Sterling Brown

Ever since the news of his death, I have been remembering the sound of his laugh: full-bodied, in turn mirthful or disdainful, but always infectious. Max Robinson was larger than most of us in life, and if his weaknesses—the things that "got him through the night"—were glaring, it was only because his accomplishments were stunning. He was not a man of moderation, but then again, a moderate man could not have achieved as he did.

The first black to anchor a local television news program in Washington, the first black journalist to anchor a network TV news program, Robinson was a pioneer—and therein lay his very large measure of joy and his pain. "Max felt strongly that he was the first black to succeed in this little corner of the world," said Peter Jennings, his former coanchor at ABC News and now sole anchor of "World News Tonight." "He felt he had to live up to it all the time. God knows, that would be a burden for any man."

Pioneers have no rules to follow, no codes of behavior. They define the rules as they go along. The judgments of them are made after the fact. And so, after his death Tuesday at age 49, some of his colleagues said his faults did him a disservice. But by judging him today as if the rules already had been in place, they may have misunderstood the parameters in which a pioneer operates.

Robinson often was out there alone, on the cutting edge of change when he went to work for Channel 9 in 1969 and for ABC News in 1978. Few people can understand the loneliness of a pioneer. He was seen as a role model, and the hopes and dreams of many people were tied to his meteoric star. He was blazing a path, and, if he fell, he fell for all those holding on to his coattails.

In his last public appearance, a speech at the Howard University communications conference in November, Max told his audience of young would-be journalists: "I'm not recommending that you be an old hardhead like I was, and stubborn. I'm not recommending my way. . . ." But in 1969, it may have taken a hardhead to rack up his achievements. And perhaps he was not merely possessed of demons, but also exhibiting ordinary reactions for a person in an extraordinary situation.

As he fought his losing battle with AIDS and came to peace in the last couple of years, less concerned with money and more in touch with how blessed he was to have good friends, the recognition brought him to tears. Quoting his late father in that Howard speech, he said, "Maybe I should have cried sooner." But he could not have cried sooner, because the bright, shining faces that understood him so well in 1988 were not there 20 years earlier.

Just as he had to bear the mantle of being a novelty in his work in media, so too did his substance abuse problems occur at a time when there was little understanding or support for sufferers of that disease. Today, those addictions are better understood, and sports stars, television personalities and film stars openly admit their addictions and receive treatment with job security and little loss of public face.

There wasn't any such sympathy for Max. He missed the funeral of his coanchor Frank Reynolds, where he had been scheduled to sit next to First Lady Nancy Reagan, because, it was said, he passed out after having several drinks and taking prescription pills. He didn't answer the door of his Chicago apartment when a network car arrived to take him to the airport. Furious executives chastised him for messing up—again. I don't imagine anybody suggested sending him to the Betty Ford Clinic.

Where do pioneers go for help when they are living in a fishbowl? In those days and perhaps for some even now, they cannot go anywhere; they push through somehow. When Max finally checked himself into a hospital for alcohol abuse and depression in 1985, it was too late to save his career.

So he fought others and he fought himself. Max told The Washington Post that "one of my basic flaws has been a lack of esteem . . . always feeling like I had to do more. I never could do enough or be good enough. And that was the real problem." But doesn't that statement aptly define the role of pioneer? Television, with its reliance on ratings, is precarious for everyone, but even more so for the trailblazers. How could he ever do enough or be good enough when

he was being pressured from above and below?

He longed not to feel the pain, not to be alone, to be an insider. But he couldn't do it because that is not in the nature of a pioneer. If the trailblazer can't bend, he occasionally cracks—as I did when I heard the news of Max's death. But Max never broke. Despite the pressure on him to be everybody but Max Robinson, at the end, he was simply Max, and that was enough.

[*December 22, 1988*]

A Sweet Remembrance of Fathers and Daughters

Growing up, I was a daddy's girl. I can still recall the way he called me to come into the house from play some evenings, extending the final syllable of my middle name in his deep Tennessee drawl. He died when I was 14. But I began losing him several years before, when the illness that would later take his life began to strike with full force.

Only in recent years have I begun to understand fully how powerful that relationship was in shaping every area of my life.

It was not surprising, therefore, that an acclaimed new book, "Sweet Summer: Growing Up With and Without My Dad," by Bebe Moore Campbell, had a special resonance for me.

The book is the story of Campbell's life after her parents divorced when she was still a quite young girl. It was then the pattern developed that shaped her life. She lived in winter, spring and fall with her doting mother and grandmother in a north Philadelphia row house.

But it was in the summers when she came alive in a special way—months she spent with her father in North Carolina. Though he long used a wheelchair as a result of a car crash, he drove with great speed from the South to the North every June to pick her up.

"There are gifts that only a father can give a daughter: his daily presence, his solemn declaration that she is beautiful and worthy," writes Campbell. "That her skin is radiant, the flair of her nostrils pretty. *'Yeah, and Daddy's baby sure does have some big, flat feet, but that's all right. That's all right now. Come here, girl, and let Daddy see those tight, pretty curls, them kitchen curls.'*"

The powerful bond between her and her father that carried from her from childhood to young womanhood is Campbell's focus. Indeed, the death of her father, George Moore, in 1977, left her with a void that is yet unfilled. "When my father died," she writes, "old men went out of my life." Even today she chafes because she is surrounded by women, "overexposed to femininity."

From the eagerness with which she awaited summer respites from the loving, but perfection-demanding women who raised her, to the "surrogate fathers" with whom she sought to fill her northern seasons, Campbell reveals a sensitive and seldom seen side of the black male. "No horror story

here about demented black men," writes poet Haki Madhubuti, with a sigh of relief.

Yet it is the problems of some black men—drug violence, fewer going to college, estrangement from their families—that prompted Campbell to tell her father's story. "I thought he might be a good source of inspiration," she said in an interview. "He couldn't walk, didn't make a lot of money but still wanted to be a good father."

The other crucial theme in her book is that little girls need fathers, or father substitutes, a message that society doesn't pay sufficient attention to. Although the disasters that can ensue when little boys do not have male role models have been copiously recorded, no societal chorus has echoed that need for girls.

Studies have shown that girls who grow up without fathers or substitute fathers often exhibit low self-esteem in the later relationships with boys and men, evidencing a fear of abandonment that makes them more accepting of relationships that are brutal or otherwise unhealthy for them.

How many of this generation's teenage mothers are the result of the prevalence of female-headed households and absent fathers is something we probably can only surmise. Most of today's teenage mothers do not even expect the fathers of their children to be responsible, and the fathers lack even a perception of what it means to be a father.

Even among more responsible adults, when separation or divorce occurs, a father may be too angry at the mother to write a check for his children.

But it is important for him to communicate with the children, give to them, take care of them.

"Some of these fathers are redeemable; they can do better," says Campbell.

[June 22, 1989]

JUDITH MARTIN
(Miss Manners)

The picture with her column shows the formidable Miss Manners in a high-collared blouse with a brooch at her throat, her hair piled up like Queen Victoria. But the real Miss Manners, Judith Martin, has no desire to return to the past. "The assumption is that if I like good manners I must want to go back in time. Well, I have no desire whatsoever to go back in time," Martin says. "I'm trying to order the future."

She is annoyed by people who think she's a dinosaur, but she doesn't convey her displeasure with raised voice or bad words. Instead, sitting ramrod straight, she uses precisely chosen words to demolish the uninformed. "It is a minor annoyance," she says, "to have people think that this is some sort of ultrareactionary desire to go back to a past that educated people know never existed."

Sipping tea in an elegant women's club, her silvery hair perfectly coiffed, her shoulders back and her ankles crossed, Martin calls it ridiculous to think there was ever a time when everyone was well behaved. She wears high collars because she likes them, she says, not to pretend to be living in another century. Although she jokes about having been in school with Queen Victoria, she does not like being thought of as a comic actress. "I'm really not an act," she says. "I'm a writer."

Martin's satiric column answers questions from readers ranging from the predictable, such as how to ask for a date or refuse an invitation or whom to invite to the wedding, to the offbeat, such as a delicate way to tell your husband he snores. Once a week she writes an essay that examines some aspect of American society. Her column is syndicated by United Media to more than 250 newspapers.

Often described as the modern-day Emily Post, Miss Manners

deals with questions that might have mystified her predecessor, and some that certainly would have made her blush. Only one has had Martin stumped—and it's not something Emily Post had to deal with. "We need a public, presentable name for a couple who are together socially but who are not married," Martin says. "One didn't used to recognize such a thing." She's tried several terms, but nothing has worked. One reader suggested "paraspouse," but when she tried that one out on a radio call-in show, people thought she was saying "parasite," so she discarded it. Her interest in etiquette parallels her interest in language. "I don't like sloppiness in language," she says, "I don't like misuse of it."

Some questions are so far out that Martin suspects readers make them up, but sometimes she answers them anyway. "I don't have an investigative branch that says did you really spill your tea or are you just trying to fool me?" she says. Occasionally she wonders in print whether some of the situations her readers tell her about are fiction, such as the woman who asked what she should do about her daughter's wish that the bridal party at her wedding be nude. But always Martin gets letters from readers saying such situations are real.

Martin writes with authority, yet her writing is liberally laced with wry humor. Sometimes her answers are flip, the humor teetering on the edge of insult. She says she doesn't intend to embarrass readers. "I write funny because I see the world as a comedy of manners and I can't help myself," she says, "but I would be extremely upset if I thought I had humiliated anyone."

"I think that people read her as much for the humor content as for the advice," said Mary Hadar, editor of the *Washington Post* Style selection. "She's a very entertaining read, and I think she does give darned good advice." Her writing has a formal tone, and yet the reader is constantly reminded that much of her message is tongue-in-cheek. A paragraph of elegant phrasing is likely to be a prelude to one of Martin's zingers.

Martin was a fulltime film and drama critic for the weekend sections of the *Washington Post* when she began writing "Miss Manners" for fun for the *Post*'s Style section. "The mail came in like that," Martin says, snapping her fingers, "and I started answering letters. I thought this would be funny, really just a lark in my spare time. I had no idea that it would snowball." Martin left the *Post* in 1983 to work full time at home on the column.

She also has published two novels and several volumes of advice.

Her etiquette books sometimes run 800 pages or more, and their titles suggest the sweep of the endeavor. They include *Miss Manner's Guide for the Turn-of-the-Millennium*, published in 1989, and the earlier *Miss Manners' Guide to Excruciatingly Correct Behavior*. "I suggested they publish them with wheels so that people could drag them along," she says, smiling at the thought.

After World War II, etiquette writers began telling people to say and do whatever felt comfortable. Martin takes a different approach. In person and in her writing she doesn't equivocate, saying, "It's no use being wishy-washy." Drawing on her own experience growing up in the 1950s and on common sense, she says she has no difficulty rendering judgment. "If you ask me a question, I presume you want an answer," she says, "and if I throw it back at you and say, 'Oh, do whatever you feel like,' then I've wasted your time."

She compares her role to that of a judge. The law may be clear, but each situation is complicated by motivating circumstances or conflicting laws. "I'm not just reciting rules or I would have come to the end of it a long time ago," Martin says. "I'm looking at the individual cases and saying, 'What are the rules and how do they apply here?' There are many conflicts. Motivation is very much taken into account." For example, she says, if you don't come to a dinner and don't let the hostess know, it looks like a clear breach of etiquette. But if it turned out that your mother died, or you got stuck on an airplane and couldn't call, it wouldn't be a crime. On the other hand, it would be terrible manners if you just decided you didn't feel like coming. "You have to weigh all these factors the way a judge and jury would," Martin said. "Here's the law, the law is clear, but how does it apply in this case?"

Her comparison of etiquette with the law is no accident. Martin has been researching the philosophy of etiquette and has spoken to law school classes and to philosophical societies. She draws a comparison between natural and positive law, with natural law being universally applicable. Positive law, on the other hand, involves rules that apply in a particular time and place. "In etiquette, which is a sort of sub-legal system, the universal [or natural] law would be respect for others," she says, "but whom you respect and how you show that respect could differ wildly."

Martin dismisses the criticism of those who say etiquette books are not necessary because one can be guided by great moral principles, such as respect for others. Those who say etiquette is just common sense are wrong, too. "It's not common sense, because if it were, I could put down in Kyoto and you would know how to behave," she says, "but unless you had studied it, you wouldn't."

People are naive in thinking that because they mean well, they don't need rules. "Etiquette has us behaving very often much better than we genuinely feel," Martin says. Honesty, for example, is a noble concept but sometimes hard for other people to take. An honest comment can be cruel, even if meant well. "People learn these [rules] the way they learn language, without thinking about it," Martin says. "They're not aware of it, they think 'Aha, we can just be natural.' You can't in civilized society." The idea that natural is better than artificial is "such a charming idea, one hates to point out what a disaster it was," Martin says. "Meaning well is not enough." Just as people can't communicate without a common spoken language, they can't get along without a language of behavior in common.

As a reporter for the *Washington Post* in the 1960s, covering the White House and diplomatic missions, Martin wrote that she would be happiest reporting on the small things, "silly or perverse, that inevitably creep into every master plan." She's doing exactly that in writing about etiquette. "A great deal of etiquette is conveying things through nuance, symbolism, phrasing, all those little things," she says. It's focusing on "the little telling detail."

Martin's understanding of American culture and society is most evident in her Sunday column, written in essay form, in which she tackles a range of subjects that include the changing face of business and family life. Political columnist George Will once said of Martin that she wrote political commentary. She responds: "In a larger sense of restructuring society, there could hardly be a more political idea than changing our concept of the workplace." In her book *Common Courtesy* Martin advocates a restructuring of the business world to recognize that both men and women have personal lives.

"The modern professional world is still designed for an employee who is constantly available because he does not have a family. He only has a wife who has a family," she wrote. "The pattern of the man always free for duty because he has a sham family and social life, which is actually entirely run by a woman, is disappearing; both men and women are less willing to settle for half a life." Martin says personal and business worlds have been divided by gender, with the woman's world centered around home and family, and the man involved in business: "Obviously this means that both of them have a sadly deprived life," she says. Although women have moved into the workplace in increasing numbers, the pattern has been retained of a worker who is totally available and mobile—in short, a worker who has a wife to take care of the family.

"Obviously, if you have a woman in a job or a man married to a woman who has her own professional responsibilities, this doesn't work," she says. "What has happened in our time is that the woman has taken over the male pattern, and nobody makes up the slack." She says her own story might have been different if she had not had a housekeeper when her two children were young. Writing a column that tells thousands of people how to behave is easy compared with the confidence it took in the early 1960s for her, as a married woman with two young children, to buck societal norms and go to work. "It takes knowing that you are right about what's good for you, no matter if the whole world tells you not."

There's a pervasive misunderstanding of what constitutes good manners, Martin says. "There are people who mistakenly think the only system of manners is the ladies first system. In fact, in the workplace it's highly inappropriate. In the workplace, gender is not a factor in etiquette, rank is." Bad manners are personified by a man who treats a woman socially on the job, whether he flirts or expects the woman to perform a social function, such as getting coffee. "That person has to be stopped. He's doing real harm," she says. "I cannot imagine a system of true good manners based on the idea that you put down some people based on gender or anything else.

Reciting gender-based behavior in the workplace does not mean throwing out traditional courtesies. "I do not discard the charming things when they are not harmful," she says. "Nothing could be ruder than taking an intended kindness and treating it rudely—I mean the man who offers a seat on the bus and the woman spits in his eye." Other little frills and courtesies of life should also be retained, such as honorifics before a name, she adds. Some people are so afraid of offending others they simply do away with the Mr. or Miss and address the person by his or her whole name, as in "Dear Sam Smith," which Martin considers silly.

An English major at Wellesley College, Martin likes to say she majored in "gracious living," her byword for what well-educated young women were being prepared for in the late 1950s. After graduation, she "accidentally" got a job as a copy girl at the *Post,* and she jokes that by the time she thought about what she wanted to do, "I had so much overtime there was no turning back."

She worked first as a general assignment reporter, then joined the *Post*'s newly created Style section in 1969. She later became film and dramatic critic, fulfilling a longtime dream. The "Miss Manners" column, at first a sideline, kept getting bigger. "People always say, 'Did you see a need?' Sure, I went out and polled everybody and they said what we're really missing is etiquette," Martin says wryly. "On the contrary, all you had to do was say the word and they'd burst out laughing. But apparently I'm not as eccentric on that score as I thought."

Why is the column so successful? "The simplest thing of all—I have always used the very simple method of 'It amuses me, it might amuse someone else.'" Since she has so much feedback, receiving 200 letters a week, Martin feels she has an ongoing dialogue with her readers. She only answers letters through the column, choosing those that interest her the most. She also reads widely. "I love reading," she says, "and besides, it's a tremendous etiquette aid for situations where you have to sit and wait for someone."

Rarely at a loss for words or a strong opinion, Martin is apt to begin sentences with words such as "obviously," "clearly," "doubtless." Telling other people how to behave suits her well. She says with relish, "Everything I do is an act of audacity."

MISS MANNERS

Etiquette Frowns on Bigotry

The word should be out by now, Miss Manners would have thought, that adult society will no longer tolerate the open expression of bigotry. Every week there seems to be another painful story about a career that is ruined because some prominent person has made an obviously prejudiced remark.

Yet those caught never fail to be surprised that a negative generalization about people based on their race, religion, gender or national origin could offend the targeted group, much less the society at large.

Stunned, they make one of the following replies:

"You see? They're oversensitive."

"Can't anybody take a joke any more?"

"You shouldn't listen to what I say when I'm angry, because I get out of control."

"Everybody knows I'm not a bigot, so I can say what I want."

"I was only saying what everybody else thinks."

"Well, their objections interfere with my freedom of speech."

These people have reckoned without the power of etiquette. They think they can do anything they want as long as it's not illegal.

Woe unto them, Miss Manners murmurs darkly.

Unfortunately, this stance is particularly prevalent on college campuses. Administrators who believe in freedom of speech with all their hearts (as does Miss Manners) seem stymied when that is cited on the side of incivility and intolerance. Dedicated to the airing of all points of view, they nevertheless realize that nobody can teach or learn in an atmosphere of hate and harassment.

Well, of course not. Civilization cannot function without a system of etiquette that prevents us from living in a state of mutual antagonism, even though it is true that law cannot condemn this without endangering freedom.

In situations where members of the society do not have the maturity to enforce restraints upon themselves, those charged with looking after their welfare must make explicit etiquette rules binding on anyone who freely elects to participate in their community. Universities have always had some sorts of restrictive rules. One of the pleasures of attending college reunions is recounting how one got around these rules, and bemoaning the fact that the rules have been softened for current students.

Etiquette has always been the primary force in charge of banning offensive speech that does not actually constitute an immediate danger, although Miss Manners admits that it has not always done as vigorous a job of enforcing this as it should have.

Law has a difficult time stopping people from wounding one another with words. It can, in its weighty way, prosecute people for slander and libel, and, with more difficulty, mental cruelty and harassment. But anything short of this is not apt to be covered.

Etiquette should also make sure it is not condemning anyone unfairly. The weapon of social disapproval, while less threatening than fines or jail, is a powerful one and should not be abused.

But etiquette acts swiftly, having little trouble telling the difference between a genuine joke or legitimate observation, and an insult. As its concern is maintaining civil surface behavior, it is deaf to excuses about anger or the honesty of expressing offensive thoughts. The past record of a presumed offender in fighting bigotry certainly counts in establishing that the remark may have been misinterpreted, but it does not give license to transgress current standards.

The argument that criminal intent is mitigated by one's psychological state has not made much of a dent on etiquette, which doesn't really believe that other people can shove words in your mouth.

DEAR MISS MANNERS—We received an engraved invitation to an open house in honor of a young couple. There was no mention of an engagement or marriage.

In the lower right-hand corner of the invitation were the words "silver, china, crystal."

Is this the ultimate in tackiness and a major breach of etiquette? Also, shouldn't open houses be held after a couple marries and not before?

GENTLE READER—Who says

these people are getting married? As Miss Manners understands it, they are merely shopping for silver, china and crystal. You may cooperate with them in this enterprise or not, as you choose.

There is such a thing as the legitimate open-house party, not to be confused with a wedding reception. At an open house, often held to welcome friends to a new house, guests do not require their hosts to produce a marriage certificate.

On the other hand, there is no such thing as a legitimate social event at which hosts demand outright that guests furnish their houses.

[July 15, 1990]

Etiquette's Role in a Free Society

Does everyone except Miss Manners believe that we must choose between having a free society and having a livable one?

That the only way to preserve human rights is to give up on humane behavior?

Miss Manners believes that would be a sad commentary on America. It would amount to an admission that in order to achieve fairness, we have to renounce civilization.

Yet Miss Manners always hears people on both sides of current issues of behavior arguing from these shared assumptions. Whenever the flaunting of obscenity, bigotry, and personal or

symbolic disrespect (such as flag-burning) are discussed, it is with the underlying presumption that there can be nothing whatsoever to restrain any individual's impulse, no matter how damaging or outrageous it may be, other than the full force of the law.

Nobody seems to question this premise, but only whether we ought to try to outlaw all behavior we don't like, or to tolerate being daily affronted and disgusted.

"Lock 'em up," says one side.

"Let 'em sue," says the other.

This is not a proper choice.

We seem to have a national crisis that calls for—Miss Manners!

Miss Manners starts from the assumption that everyone wants to have a harmonious, nonabrasive, perhaps even pleasant society. She includes everyone, even those whose chief goal in life is to offend others, because it is impossible to be outrageous unless there is a minimal expectation of civility to violate. You can't shock anybody who doesn't have any standards.

Yet she also assumes that every American recoils from the idea of compromising free speech and other liberties. Even those driven to distraction by other people exercising their rights don't really want to give up their own. They just want their own standards, which they chose in freedom, to be universally compulsory.

The difference between Miss Manners and all these other people who want it both ways is that she knows of a system to restrain offensive behavior, which does not interfere with our constitutional rights, because it is not a part of our legal system.

This is called etiquette. What

ought to restrain people from shouting epithets, flaunting obscenity, desecrating national symbols and otherwise upsetting their fellow citizens is etiquette.

True, it doesn't always work. Even Miss Manners has noticed that—especially Miss Manners, in fact. Being a voluntary system, etiquette cannot, by definition, be forced upon others, which is why Miss Manners is devoting herself to persuading them instead.

But she would appreciate her fellow citizens' help. And no, she doesn't want them to run around telling other people how rude they are, or to punish offenders by escalating the rudeness into violence. Miss Manners sometimes despairs of achieving a better world, because such nastiness is so often the first thought of those who profess to be on the side of manners.

The approved methods for enforcing etiquette are:

Self-restraint. You do not have to do everything unpleasant that you have a right to do. Nor do you have to bring everything you do to public attention. Controlling yourself to avoid causing unnecessary affronts to others is the price you pay to live in a community.

Child-rearing. Contrary to the great experiment of the last few decades, allowing children to rely totally on their own judgments or those of their peers did not result in the children's becoming happy or artistic. Kindly discipline seems to be as important for happiness as it is for creativity.

House rules. Athletics seems to be the only remaining area in which no one questions the idea that if you want to play the game, you must abide by the rules. But the fact is that you cannot run anything— a class, a dinner party, a town meeting, a club, a household, a ceremony, a courtship—unless everyone involved agrees to abide by certain standards of behavior, and those who do not accept the terms are banned.

Social consequences. Much as Miss Manners admires tolerance, the effort to show those who outrage society that society is unshockable and uninsultable has gone too far. In the public area, miscreants should not be protected from reasonable social disapproval.

Miss Manners remembers when those arguing for a constitutional amendment protecting the American flag from desecration argued that without such a law, "everyone" would be burning flags. Are they?

Well, no. Even among those who might be tempted, an awareness of the fury such an etiquette violation arouses is inhibiting.

[*June 30, 1991*]

Respect for Privacy Is Rare

Privacy? Does anyone remember the concept of privacy?

As difficult as it may now be to imagine, Miss Manners recalls a time when etiquette rules successfully prevented people from telling everything they knew and asking about everything they wanted to know.

Those who failed to guard their

own privacy were condemned as blabbermouths and bores, rather than admired as examples of health and openness. Those who failed to respect the privacy of others were considered busybodies, rather than volunteer therapists or students of moral character.

Miss Manners, who has lived in the world for some time, not altogether a stranger to juicy conversation, is not in the least surprised that people are interested in talking about the private lives of themselves and everyone else. There will always be occasions when confidences and even non-vicious gossip are acceptable.

But she is shocked at the lengths people will go to, in order to put a virtuous cast on blatantly inappropriate instances of the ancient and ever annoying sin of failing to mind one's own business.

The modern argument for revealing everything about oneself to friend and stranger alike is that it is therapeutic to confess, virtuous to keeping nothing concealed, and philanthropic to set an example of imperfection for others, who might otherwise brood about being the only people in the world ever to have had troubles.

For probing into everything about everyone else, there are two justifications, depending on whether you actually know the people.

If you deal face to face with the objects of your curiosity, even if you are hardly acquainted with them, you congratulate yourself for doing them a service, no matter how much you may have made them squirm. You tell yourself that such investigations

have the object of forcing them to enjoy the therapeutic, virtuous and philanthropic benefits just described, even if they are led to do so kicking and screaming.

When your curiosity concerns public figures whom you don't know, the argument is that these people have an obligation to be role models and must be held to account when they fail. Never mind that they were not modeling private behavior until you helped force it out into the open. First you snoop, the self-righteous formula goes, and then you get indignant that what you have uncovered does not bear public scrutiny.

An increasing number of people seem to have come to believe that the more hidden part of one's life is, the more likely it is to reveal character that will manifest itself in public action, thus making it the public's business. Miss Manners has noticed that in the case of elected officials, this relieves their constituents of the boring task of following and evaluating public action at all. You skip that and get right to the more titillating private actions that you then claim might taint the public ones.

Well, Miss Manners regrets spoiling everyone's fun, but etiquette is never going to turn around and condone old-fashioned snooping, no matter how colvoluted a psychological case is made for it. One can gossip about others, either behind their backs or from the safety of simply reading about them, but one cannot pretend that this is commendable.

For one thing, the virtue of honesty does not cancel out the need for exercising the other virtues. Is Miss Manners the only person to recognize this? Honesty does not cancel out either a transgression or the obligation of consideration for the feelings of others. Sometimes it even takes second place to the virtue of kindness to others.

Owning up to one's sins is not the same thing as atoning for them. Miss Manners admires the spirit of forgiveness, but is puzzled when people behave as if no crime should be held against anyone, provided only that the criminal doesn't try to hide it. "It wasn't that he went around chopping people up," is the sort of thing one hears, "but that he lied about it."

There are cases of private offenses, such as adultery, in which the sinner who makes a confession "to get this off my conscience" has committed a second transgression if this relief makes another person suffer. Discretion is a virtue, too, when it means continuing to bear one's own burden of guilt rather than foisting it off on an innocent person.

Discretion? Does anyone remember discretion?

DEAR MISS MANNERS—I have a friend who does something in restaurants that I find quite off-putting—he tries to get chummy with the waiter, even in the nicest establishments.

"Where were you born?" he might ask. Or "How long have you been working here?"

It seems to be a response to the copious quizzical looks that all attentive waiters give. But I drop my silverware (figuratively, of course).

He says that he's just trying to be friendly or disarming. Am I wound too tight? Or is he wound too loose?

GENTLE READER— Somebody's wound wrong. Why would a responsible person want to disarm a waiter who is probably balancing a plate of hot food somewhere above the region of that person's head?

It is one of the trials of modern service jobs that the clients feel free to be chummy with people who may well not wish to socialize with them if given the choice. Miss Manners recommends that they fend off any unwelcome attention by answering relentlessly, "Very good, sir," or "Whatever you say, madam," no matter what the nosy question.

However, she does not want you to take her sympathy as license to correct the manners of a friend. That, too, is an example of cheeky intrusiveness.

[*March 29, 1992*]

MONA CHAREN

A case of teenage insomnia and a late night radio talk show influenced Mona Charen's decision to become a conservative political columnist. Growing up in a family of Democrats in a liberal New Jersey community, she listened to a show hosted by a conservative Jew that reinforced her conservative leanings. "It was significant to me because it made it okay to have those views and be Jewish," Charen says. "The Jewish community does tend to be quite liberal. . . . In those days it came with mother's milk that you would be a member of the Democratic Party."

Instead, Charen has forged a conservative philosophy that underpins a column dealing with American politics and society, reportedly one of the fastest growing in the country. Her twice-weekly column is syndicated by Creators Syndicate, Inc. Charen has been called a "conservative Ellen Goodman" by *National Review* editor William F. Buckley and has been compared with George Will. She relishes challenging Will for a share of the op-ed space some newspapers allocate to a conservative viewpoint. "I am a conservative who grew up among liberals and therefore I know how to speak to liberals," she says. "I think I have a sense of what people get exercised about . . . and frankly, with all immodesty, I would say that I write well . . . I try to be lively and interesting."

Although her parents were mainstream Democrats, they were willing to listen to their youngest child and only girl. "You had to be able to talk fast and loud and get yourself noticed because nobody would turn to you and say, "What do you think?" she recalls. "There was some sexism in my family as in all families, but one reason I've been able to do what I've done is that they took my opinions seriously, and I was listened to and acknowledged. There was no sense that 'You're just a girl and what you say doesn't matter.'"

Charen's conservative epiphany came at age thirteen, when she discovered the weekly *National Review* and developed something of a crush on Buckley. "To my thirteen-year-old eyes, he had everything— he was glamorous . . . hilariously funny," she says. "I didn't see his affectation as a problem. He was brilliant. That's what appealed to me." In her senior year at Barnard, she interviewed Buckley for a yearbook story, which led to an internship at *National Review* after graduation. Her job involved answering mail and operating the type-setter, but she also wrote occasional editorials. At twenty-two, filling out her first income tax return, she listed her occupation as "pundit."

It was not merely wishful thinking; the stint at *National Review* had confirmed her desire to be a columnist, but she figured she needed some credentials first. So she earned a law degree from George Washington University in Washington and then went to work as a speechwriter for First Lady Nancy Reagan. "I'm still trying to live that down," she says. Later she joined Pat Buchanan's staff in the White House communications office, leaving the administration in 1986 to work as a writer for U.S. Senator Jack Kemp's re-election campaign.

She had taken a job writing a semi-monthly opinion column for the *Republican Study Committee Bulletin,* read by Republican members of Congress, when she decided to try getting a column syndicated. Although the *Bulletin* commentary was 2,000 words—about three times the length of her newspaper column—it gave her confidence that she could put her thoughts together on deadline.

"I approached a syndicate or two and said would you consider taking me on? I knew I was doing it the hard way," she says. But Creators Syndicate took a chance on her. Since the column debut in 1987, her client list has grown to about 100 newspapers, including such major metro papers as *Newsday,* the *Washington Times,* the *Boston Globe* and the *San Francisco Chronicle.* "It's enormously gratifying," she says. "I feel a sense of such accomplishment. I've done it all myself. No one handed me anything. It's a very competitive field. Beyond all those hundreds who are syndicated are thousands who want to be."

Sitting in the dining room of her house in Falls Church, a suburb of Washington, Charen says she made only $8,000 in her first year of syndication but was willing to be patient, "even if it didn't immediately ignite. I knew it would take time." Although she acknowledges that column writing is a tenuous business, she retains her optimism. "I don't look down, I look up," she says. "I don't think about the people who are dropping away because I don't think that will happen to me." Even in a Democratic administration, a conservative voice is needed, she says.

Conservatism may underpin her columns, but Charen is not stuck on an ideology. She cites letters from readers who say they like her column because it's clear she has thought through where she stands. "I do have a fairly consistent conservative point of view," she says, "but I hope and I believe, and I've been told, I'm not predictable." For example, she blistered the Los Angeles Police Department for the Rodney King beating, while her former boss, Pat Buchanan, took the more predictably conservative tack in his column, writing that the police gave King an unforgettable lesson in driver education.

"I try to be honest, approach everything fresh and look at both sides. It's very important to be fair and to think things through. I'm not a partisan Republican for the sake of being Republican," Charen says, citing Buckley's influence. "He always provides an intellectual context for why he believes what he believes. I too try to come at things from a philosophically consistent point of view."

Mary Lou Forbes, Commentary editor of the *Washington Times*, said she added Charen's column because she is "very representative of the new young visionaries who came along during the Reagan years." Forbes describes Charen as "an extremely lucid writer, always on top of issues, never afraid to take a strong stand. I consider her among the best columnists writing today."

Charen says she assumes her readers are intelligent but not necessarily well informed. She thinks in terms of "a cadre of people like me," but doesn't picture an individual reader when writing. "They're interested in public affairs," she says. "If you provide them with facts and you show them how you came to your decision, they may agree or disagree, but at least they'll be more informed." Gentle and soft-spoken in person, Charen enjoys peppering her columns with wicked barbs, and she takes her gloves off when she writes. A column about the federal luxury tax, for example, called it "a perfect illustration of the Democratic Party's inability to understand the workings of a capitalist economy."

She writes to change people's minds. "I am not writing to the converted, which is what some conservative columnists do. . . . I'm interested in persuading people. I think I'm well situated to do it because I grew up in an environment where I was used to people disagreeing with me and I'm used to having to justify why I thought differently," she says. "I like to set out an argument that will make people think, and that will make them look at the same tired arguments we've all heard in a new way."

She receives about thirty letters a week from readers, both men and women, and says she feels guilty about not answering but doesn't have time. She notes a difference in the general tone of letters since she first started the column. Initially, some letters were outraged, asking her how she dared say such things. "As I became better known and got a name, I stopped getting those letters," she says. "I still get 'I disagree,' but with more respect." Her columns on political/cultural issues such as federal government spending for AIDS research stir readers most. That's what she's after—not only to persuade but also to generate debate. She tries to keep from being influenced by reaction to her columns, saying, "I don't want it to dull my sword."

As a columnist, "You have to be somewhat sharp in the things that you say. You have to put a fine point on things, and sometimes that's going to affect people," she says. "You go further, put a sharper edge on something than you would at a dinner party because it makes for more lively writing and reading, and it's for the purpose of engendering debate." It's evidently working. Charen's column draws more mail and comment than any other columnist on the *Columbus* (Ohio) *Dispatch* op-ed page, says Forum Page editor Mark Fisher. "It's pretty evenly balanced between those who love her and those who loathe her," he added. The paper uses Charen because she's provocative and an excellent exponent of the conservative point of view, Fisher said, adding, "She's well connected and she writes well. She can fling those barbs with the best of them."

Charen sees her voice as important not only as a conservative but also as a woman. "Women need to see their perspective on the world presented," she says. "Obviously, no one can speak for all women and I don't claim to, but I do have a feminine perspective . . . and I've written things that have gotten an enormous response from women, saying, 'This is exactly how I feel.'" Charen is critical of feminist spokeswomen who support the sexual revolution and denigrate family life. They "claim to speak for women, but don't."

Acknowledging that she appears to be living out a feminist ideal, Charen says she supports a different kind of feminism, one that respects a woman's role as wife and mother and advocates employment opportunities for women. "I'd be the first to demand to be taken seriously," she says. "I've certainly struggled with that. It *is* harder being a woman. There is still a view that women aren't as serious as men, are somehow a lesser sex. That is a struggle, and I've been on the ramparts as far as that goes, but I think the feminist movement has been a disaster."

Her stance has garnered her a following among conservative women's groups and pro-life groups, although she has little in common with them. "We are not the same kinds of people, we didn't grow up in the same environments. . . . They probably don't laugh at the same things I do," Charen says. "Yet I say the kinds of things they're dying to see in print and that they see all too rarely."

A theme to which Charen repeatedly returns in her columns is the disintegration of family life and the general decline in American morals and standards. "I do really believe that the cultural decay that's been going on in this country for the last twenty-five years has been a tragedy," she says. "And I think it's probably the greatest threat this country is facing."

The hardest part of writing a column is settling on a subject, which produces "that slightly panicky flutter in your stomach when you think, 'I wonder if I've got a topic.'" She gets column ideas from reading and keeping aware of current events, trends, and ideas. She reads a number of national newspapers and several conservative magazines, as well as the generally left-leaning *New Republic* magazine. She also watches C-Span, which lets her be at home with her young son instead of attending a press conference. "I have the luxury as a columnist of writing about whatever moves me," she says. "The whole world is a theater from which you can draw topics."

Charen also tries to avoid writing too many columns on a single issue, and she keeps up with other columnists in order to keep from writing about the same thing every one else is. "I model myself a lot on George Will," she says, "in the sense that he's somebody whose eye roves across the landscape and settles on whatever he thinks needs writing about." Occasionally she writes more playful or intimate columns that provide a glimpse of her personal life. After she married, for example, she wrote a column on whether to take her husband's name. (She has kept her own name professionally.) The most personal column she ever wrote was also the most difficult—it talked about her decision to adopt a child. "I said here's what I've been through with infertility, here's the resolution. It was so personal, so close to my heart," she says. "I made myself vulnerable to the whole world." One reason for writing the column was to explain to readers that she would be taking a month-long maternity leave, highly unusual for a syndicated columnist. She also wanted readers on her side in case any editor was going to use it as an excuse to drop the column. "Nobody dropped it," she says. "I got hundreds of letters—an incredible outpouring of love and support about the adoption from people who were adopted, who had adopted, and who had never adopted but had kids and said everything is taking care of them. Giving birth is not what makes you a parent."

Two of the letters were hurtful, particularly the one from a reader who told her "God knows what he's doing and chose to make you infertile for a reason." "When you make yourself vulnerable and you tell the truth about yourself and talk about something that personal," she says, "you open yourself up for that."

Charen is not the sort of columnist who writes about what's happening around her kitchen table, but she does reveal the kind of person she is in her columns. Readers write to say they wish they knew her personally. "My response is 'I think you do, if you're a faithful reader of this column over time.' I pour a lot of myself into it, and so I think people do know me in a way." She smiles. "They don't know all my bad habits."

In writing a column, she typically begins with an idea culled from a newspaper or magazine and then researches it. "I never want to be a chin scratcher," she says. "I feel a responsibility to present the facts to readers. I don't think that what I think is as interesting as what I know." She considers herself as much a reporter as a columnist. "That's one reason I feel I can't leave Washington," she says. "My phone bill would be too unaffordable. I have a great network of people here that I can call upon."

Charen's extensive connections in the GOP and her ability to criticize conservative politicians when necessary were factors that led Patrick McGuigan, chief editorial writer for the *Daily Oklahoman,* to add Charen's column to the op-ed page. McGuigan said Charen writes elegantly and appeals to younger readers. "We needed her in order to reach an important component of readership—women who are conservatives but not past the age of fifty."

After Charen finishes gathering information, it takes her about two and a half hours to do the actual writing of the column. She does only one draft, revising as she goes along. About 10 percent of the columns are done straight out of her head. "It's a screed," she says. "You know, it just flies onto the computer." An editor at the syndicate looks over each column for typos, but there's no other editing.

Charen loves the English language, and it shows in her writing. "I make an effort to keep my language as precise as I can, and try to choose the right word," she says, "but I will sometimes steer away from a word if I think it's not widely understood by newspaper readers." On the other hand, when it's down to a choice between the right word, which may not be so well known, and a word that's less clear, "I will choose the right word and hope that people will either look it up or glean the meaning from the context," she says.

She works at home, where she has a word processor and a fax machine, and seems unperturbed by a constantly ringing telephone, a visit from the plumber, interruptions by the cleaning woman, and the demands of her infant son. She says it's not always this busy. Her own mother worked outside the home, and it has given her mixed feelings about whether that's a good idea. "I felt the price that is paid by children who have mothers working and they're not around," she says. "I work at home and I made sure I could do that so that I could be here for my children."

"This is the greatest job in the world. I have total freedom," she says. "I get to write about what interests me. The ups and downs of who's in and out don't affect me. [Former chief of staff] John Sunnunu's up; John Sunnunu's down. Mona Charen keeps writing."

Worshipping the Condom God

Are we becoming a nation of condom worshippers? Is the humble latex that was scorned for its failure rate when I was in high school now the answer to our woes? If you listen to Phil Donahue, Rep. Patricia Schroeder (D., Ca.) and the House Select Committee on Children, Youth, and Families, you might think so. The committee has issued a respectfully-received report called "A Decade of Denial: Teens and AIDS in America."

The title so suits the current liberal agenda—begin the condom propaganda with a satisfying slam at the 1980s. The "decade of greed" now gets a new sobriquet. The "chair" (her usage) of the committee is Rep. Pat Schroeder, condom-hawker-in-chief. Schroeder agrees that abstinence is the best protection against AIDS, but she wants to be "realistic." Kids are going to have sex no matter what we say. After all, Schroeder insists, "We've been talking abstinence and 'just say no' for more than a decade, and the teen pregnancy rate is going up and so is the sexually-transmitted disease rate."

Now be serious. Anyone who thinks that the dominant social message to teenager during the past decade has been the virtue of virginity is living in a time warp. The last time the culture transmitted that message, John F. Kennedy was in the White House and the Dick Van Dyke Show was in the top ten. Today we live in the world of "Married with Children" and "Two Live Crew." Virgins are considered rare enough creatures to get their own hour on the "Geraldo" show, just after transvestite accountants and men who sleep with their mothers-in-law.

Nevertheless, the Democratic majority of the House committee sees a scandal in our collective approach to the issue of teenagers and AIDS, and recommends—surprise!—more federal dollars for AIDS education and school-based health clinics (read: condom dispensaries).

Liberals are not honest about sex. They claim to believe that abstinence is best for teens, but they don't mean it. In their hearts, they think people who promote abstinence are fundamentalist freaks. If they truly believed that sex was bad for teenagers, they wouldn't be pushing condoms at them. The comparison with drug use is apt. Imagine school-based clinics to distribute clean needles. "Well, we think abstinence from drugs is best, of course. But let's be realistic, they're going to do it anyway, so they might as well protect themselves." It would never happen. Why? Because not even liberals believe that drug use is acceptable. And the answer to unacceptable behavior is prohibition, not facilitation.

In their eagerness to believe that condoms provide the magic solution to the problems of sexual promiscuity in the age of AIDS, liberals ignore some basic facts of teenagerhood. One is this: Disbelief in one's own mortality is endemic to teenagers. That's why so many die in accidents. Another is this: Teenagers are, more than other people, acutely sensitive to shame. If the culture makes virginity shameful, as ours now does, not even the fear of AIDS will make teens chaste. Promiscuity is motivated far, far more by conformity .than by hormones.

But the entire House committee report, with its emphasis on governmental action, is misconceived. The minority report, issued by the Republicans, gets to the heart of the matter. "Cultural problems demand cultural solutions," says the minority, quoting William Bennett.

"It appears," the report goes on "that teens are seeking love and we are giving them biology classes. Teens are seeking guidance about whether to engage in sexual experimentation and we are merely listing options for them. Teens are seeking to belong, to be given a sense of community with shared values, and we are giving them a hall pass to see the school nurse."

Positive cultural change is possible. The recent turnaround in attitudes toward drunk driving is illustrative. Groups like Mothers Against Drunk Driving helped to make it shameful to get behind a wheel tipsy. Handing out condoms with a wink and a nod in every junior high in America is guaranteed to make the problem worse.

[*April 16, 1992*]

Wake Up Call to Whom?

The claptrap quotient following the wilding in Los Angeles reached record proportions. Half a dozen leading Washington figures called the riot a "wake-up call" to America about the wages of ignoring poverty and injustice. TV newsman Jim Lehrer asked a panel of guests whether they could feel "compassion" for the looters, murderers, and arsonists!

George Bush was surprisingly sober and hard-headed. He struck exactly the right tone, and projected true leadership (which raises a subsidiary question about why he has heretofore been so loath to resort to prime-time TV speeches). But in the hours following the verdict, the president's was a lonely voice. The media machine had cranked up and was spewing out a torrent of garbage. The Los Angeles Times ran a story on May 2 headlined "Looting Assumes Trappings of Justice If System is Seen as Failing, Experts Say." The article offered helpful analysis about why parents would want to loot with their children in tow. With schools and day care centers closed, explained the Los Angeles Times, there was nowhere else to put them. Lord Acton said, "There is no error so monstrous that it fails to find defenders among the ablest men."

While the jury verdict in the Rodney King case certainly appears to be a terrible miscarriage of justice, it is the mayhem that followed—and the response to it—that deserves center stage and must be treated as the main story.

It was misreported from the first. Throughout the riot, television and newspapers depicted the violence as an expression of rage at the jury verdict. Nonsense. The pictures of those looters and murderers conveyed something very different. There was a carnival atmosphere. The looters were grinning and strutting. "Hey, man, it's bargain basement," crowed one thief. One of the murderers who smashed a large object on the head of a truck driver gave the high five sign. Moreover, many of the thugs were not black but Hispanic, and it can hardly be argued that they were motivated by rage.

The King case was only the spark that fell on an ammunition pile. What happened in Los Angeles last week was not, frankly, all that different from what happens every day in cities across America. Random, senseless violence committed by people who grow up without love, without families, without churches, and without hope. We know how to create monsters: bring children into the world and then abuse and neglect them. We know all about it. In fact, we've raised it to the level of government policy.

The other great fatuity of the week was the refrain: "This is just like Watts in 1965. Nothing has changed." Good God, we've spent two and a half trillion dollars in a well-intentioned, but fatally-flawed attempt to eliminate poverty. All of the institutions of this nation have been fighting racism and discrimination—even to the point of reverse discrimination against whites.

What those who cry "Nothing has changed" have difficulty facing is that the solutions we've tried—massive federal outlays of income support, housing, and food stamps—have had unintended, but disastrous consequences for the poor. We've created an underclass devastated by pathology.

The worst tragedy that could come of last week's horror would be a return to the failed policies of the past. If we're serious about improving the lot of the poor, we will heed the recommendations of Housing and Urban Development Secretary Jack Kemp and permit public housing tenants to purchase their homes. (Owning property is the beginning of conservatism.) We'll reform the welfare laws so as not to reward fathers for abandoning their children. We'll repeal the law that prohibits welfare recipients from saving money. We'll establish enterprise zones to attract businesses to depressed areas. And we'll permit parents to choose the schools their children attend.

The Los Angeles wilding was the harvest of liberalism. For twenty-five years, liberals have congratulated themselves on their "compassion" and refused to confront the true consequences of their policies. If the riot was any kind of a wake up call, it was saying that the Great Society backfired.

[*May 4, 1992*]

What Makes People Good?

The two thirtysomething women are lively, articulate, and full of laughter. There is about them no air of self-conscious piety, no showy religiosity. And yet to meet them is to experience the very best that human beings can be.

Cathy and Ann, both white, middle-class midwesterners from large families, have teamed up to offer themselves as foster mothers for some of the neediest children from the District of Columbia. Until last week, when seven-month-old Dion was adopted, Ann and Cathy were caring for three children.

Dion was healthy, but the other two were tormented children. Alonzo is now two-and-a-half years old. Before he was born, while still in his cocaine-smoking mother's womb, he suffered a stroke. Cocaine, Ann explains, causes "cerebral accidents." Today, Alonzo needs round-the-clock care. Severe cerebral palsy has left him unable to perform the most basic functions of life, like coordinating sucking and swallowing, which sends him into spasms of gagging. Ann and Cathy feed him four times a day through a stomach tube. They suction the mucous from his mouth and throat six times a day. Pneumonia is a constant fear. This child cannot walk, nor talk, nor crawl. But in the year he has been with Ann and Cathy, he has started, on very rare occasions, to smile.

His younger half-brother, Tony, 18 months old, is also cocaine affected, though not nearly as severely. He has respiratory problems requiring medication, and delayed development. Like his brother, Tony too was premature, weighing only two-and-a-half pounds at birth. Today he is walking and beginning to babble. He still wakes up in the middle of the night arching his head back and gasping in a desperate attempt to open an air passage. And Ann is there, to administer the medication that will ease his suffering.

Yet this house, this haven, is not a mournful place at all—quite the contrary. Ann and Cathy are as proud and delighted with their charges as any parents could be. "It's like watering a plant," says Cathy. Cameras click to capture childish grins, and hugs and cuddles abound.

Ann had been working as a pediatric nurse in a major Washington, D.C. hospital. She made it her voluntary task to monitor the troubled newborns who had been discharged from the preemie ward. It meant venturing into neighborhoods that were unsafe, and shelters that were ghastly. "I would bring formula," she said, "because often that was the only way I could get in the door." Once inside, Ann would check on the baby's progress . . . and the mother's.

A wealthy benefactor read of Ann's extraordinary service and offered her the use of his farm in the Virginia countryside. The offer came just after Ann and Cathy had met at a lecture on C. S. Lewis and found kindred spirits in one another. They had talked of renting an apartment in the District—but the farm was a godsend.

In the year that Ann and Cathy have been foster mothers, they have cared for five children including one AIDS baby. Neither has had a full night's sleep in 12 months. Cathy commutes an hour and a half each way to her job at a Washington, D.C. law firm.

What makes people do such things? We spend so much ink and effort studying evil—why not pause to ask what makes people so inspiringly good?

Neither of these women would claim saintliness. They say modestly that they are merely "putting feet" to their faith—living their Christian commitment. One is Catholic, the other Episcopalian. Each has lived through a phase of doubt about God, and as Cathy says, "cynicism is, in many ways, the spirit of the age." But both have come back not just to faith but to a walking, living, breathing expression of that confidence in God's existence.

The children, they insist, are the special ones. The women feel blessed to be able to touch those lives with a love and support they would not otherwise have had. "If you write about us," they urge "let people know what a huge difference they can make in the life of just one child."

[*May 18, 1992*]

JOYCE MAYNARD

Joyce Maynard wears vibrant colors—an apricot top, matching espadrilles, and pants splashed with bright flowers. Her hair is short. The New Hampshire house where she now lives is quiet. Gone are the blue jeans, the home-cut shoulder-length hair, the children clinging to her legs. "Some people don't recognize me," says the author of "Domestic Affairs," a syndicated column on family life. She wears her hair short as a symbol of newfound independence.

As a homemaker questing for pefect motherhood, Maynard wrote a weekly column about the small details of life in a nuclear family. But after writing the column for five years, she left husband and children to be with her dying mother. She never went home. Instead of writing reflections on days spent sponging crumbs off the counter or changing diapers, Maynard began writing intimately of her mother's death, her decision to leave home and to divorce, and about falling in love again.

Those columns drew sharp criticism from several editors, and many readers wrote to say they felt betrayed. This was the woman who led a life just like theirs. Some papers dropped the column. Maynard no longer filled a niche on the feature pages, and the column was not what editors had been led to believe when they bought it. Syndication fell from a peak of forty-five to about thirty, Maynard says. She continued to write the column for two more years but didn't pick up new newspaper clients and finally wrote her last piece in the summer of 1991.

She thinks editors of the papers that dropped her column overreacted, and that most readers would have come around eventually. "Anybody who's lived, it takes a lot to shock them," she says. "I think these editors have this very archaic vision of women and family, who suppose that the American public can't take divorce." Maynard acknowledges that some readers were upset and disapproved of what she did, but even those people didn't necessarily want the column stopped.

Standing in the remodeled kitchen of her house, Maynard remembers the intensity of the reaction when she left her three children and their father in Hillsboro and moved twenty miles away to Keene. "Not only did I leave, I didn't take the children with me. . . . People just launched into me—newspapers, editors—for being a bad mother," Maynard says, mimicking an imagined editor: " 'How can we publish the column of a mother who's deserted her family?' "

Editors ignored the fact that the children still had two loving parents and were going to be one parent short whoever they were with. "In their vision I was this wild woman who had left her family," she says. Newspaper editors' rigid vision of sex roles "was a real barometer of thinking on how far we have and have not come."

Her dramatic departure was unusual for a woman, and many female readers could no longer say their lives were just like hers. "It was a very frightening and somewhat incendiary piece of news that I was leaving my marriage," she says, "because people had been writing me for years to say they so identified with me, their life was so much like mine—and then I say I'm leaving my marriage. I think they overidentified; because I'm leaving my marriage does not mean their marriage is doomed."

Men also wrote to blame her for the breakup of their marriages. Maynard looks exasperated. "I left my husband and then their wife left them and they blamed me. I don't heap loads of guilt on myself and say I'm a homewrecker across America," she says. "The person's marriage was over, anyway. All I did was tell my story."

Since their divorce, Maynard and her husband have worked out custody arrangements. The children spend summers with their father and live with Maynard during the school year. It's summer, so her children are away, but their pictures are tacked up on the refrigerator; Maynard had a steel panel bolted to the side when she discovered magnets wouldn't stick to the door. In the basement are games, building sets, and an air hockey table. A huge dollhouse occupies one end of the living room. Maynard bought it for herself.

Outside, purple, blue, and orange flowers bloom in a garden Maynard finally has had time to plant and cultivate. She pours another cup of coffee and curls up in a wicker chair on the porch, remembering how readers would tell her that they drank their coffee with her. Her intensely personal style evoked deep loyalty among regular readers.

Editors at the *Sacramento* (Calif.) *Bee* discovered that when they dropped "Domestic Affairs." *Bee* ombudsman Art Nauman said "scores of readers, mostly women . . . voiced vigorous disapproval." The column was reinstated the next week. Nauman said the decision to kill the Maynard column "was based on the belief that it had strayed from its original intent—a sort of home and hearth theme— and that perhaps she had lost her constituency."

Readers let them know otherwise. "Clearly, the column has an impressive audience which relates to Maynard in ways the Bee's editors simply didn't discern," Nauman wrote in a column explaining the paper's decision. Susan G. Sawyer, promotion manager for the *New York Times* Syndication Sales Corp., which introduced Maynard's column in 1984, said Maynard's readership was like a cult following. Loyal readers "would come out of the woodwork and surprise client-editors with their enthusiasm," Sawyer says.

The *Minneapolis Star Tribune* dropped Maynard's column twice, bringing her back once because readers complained. But the "continuing soap opera" became too much, said deputy managing editor Linda Picone. "It was as if she was writing a journal. There was no introspection," says Picone. "It was all very shallow. She was spewing her life out on the page."

Picone says she was able to live with the decision to reinstate the column because it filled a niche in the paper's Variety section for a young woman's articulate portrayal of family life. But Maynard slipped out of that niche when she left her family. Picone says readers became voyeurs of Maynard's life.

Managing editor Tim McGuire disagreed with her decision, arguing that it wasn't right for the paper to hold out its own standards as right if readers wanted the column, Picone says. That thought is echoed by Paula Anderson, editor of the *Lexington* (Ky.) *Herald-Leader,* which dropped the column about three years ago. Maynard's detailing of the problems in her marriage posed a moral dilemma for editors who had bought what they thought was a family life column, Anderson says. "Do we reflect society . . . or do we set a higher moral tone? I don't think the newspaper should hold anyone to moral standards."

Anderson says the *Herald-Leader* had dropped Maynard's column because, somewhat ironically, it was too predictable. "There was this office joke that she was always in the damn station wagon," Anderson says. But Maynard contends readers and editors could have seen the changes coming. She doesn't think her earlier columns painted a portrait of anything close to domestic bliss. "It was always the story of struggle. I was to a discomfiting degree telling tales on us, not because it was such a cheerful thing for me to do," she says, "but because I felt a really strong sense of mission that if I were writing a story of family life at all I better do it in an honest way. . . . I never wanted to leave some woman out there under the delusion that I had it all figured out, [so] what's the matter with her."

Although she was accustomed to receiving around a hundred letters a week, she was surprised at the response to her final column. In the two weeks following her last column, Maynard says she received a thousand letters. Many readers told her they would miss her deeply. "So many women are isolated when raising children," Maynard observes. "Many of them write to me about the importance of friendship, that they feel as if they've lost a friend, that the friend has moved away and left no forwarding address."

Her last column, like many before, was about parents and children. But instead of being a eulogy for nurturing mothers, this one was a defense of a mother's right to be a person, not simply the embodiment of society's expectations. "It's not just children who grow. Parents do too. And as much as we watch to see what our children do with their lives, they watch us to see what we do with ours," Maynard wrote in her farewell column. "I can't tell my children to reach for the sun. All I can do is reach for it, myself."

After her mother's death, Maynard had begun reflecting on her obsession with being the perfect wife and mother. As the year wore on, she dealt in her column with the disintegration of her marriage. The need to be honest propelled her. Raised in an alcoholic family where the word alcohol was never mentioned, Maynard says she had learned the value of naming things. "I couldn't say 'I guess my life isn't as figured out as I thought, so I better stop writing the column.' That was the very moment to keep on doing it. You don't stop going to the doctor when you get really sick, and the column was always an examination of life." Some readers and editors evidently felt they got more than they bargained for when the column changed, but she says she thought it got much more interesting.

She didn't set out to create the controversy. Her goal in writing "Domestic Affairs" was to make meaning of her life, to validate the experience of "women who didn't hear in a lot of other places that what they were doing mattered." Maynard says she tried to find meaning in repetitive childcare and household tasks like changing diapers, telling herself, "I was doing nothing less than launching human beings and helping to determine their sense of what kind of a world they were going to grow into and what their place in it was.

"This sounds pompous," she says, searching for words to describe her philosophy, "but all of us are about the business of figuring out what's the point of life. There has to be meaning. And the minute that you see it that way, every experience is transformed, even including death."

She remembers her mother's response to being told she was dying of an inoperable brain tumor. "Her first words were, 'How amazing. Isn't that interesting.' That's how she lived. Once you view your life as interesting, it's not the worst thing to be said about something that it hurts, that it's painful, because you're really learning something."

Maynard knew in the spring that it was time to end the column and began preparing her farewell message. But in typical fashion she wrote the last column in an hour, two days after deadline. Although she says she wasn't written out, she realized that the children were becoming more vulnerable to her writing about them. "I've lived a very public life my whole adult life, that's my own particular way of dealing with existence on the face of the earth. . . . If the only choice were 'Do I feel comfortable telling my own story in the newspaper?' I'd say yes— but my story involves the stories of many other people too . . . my husband and my children, and I can't make that decision for them."

Maynard always wrote less about her husband than she would have liked and more than he wanted. "It was always a fine walking of the line. He would have preferred that I not write a column about our life at all." It is a decision every columnist must make every time she writes—how much to reveal to readers, how much to hold back. Because her children were young, privacy was never an issue, but she told them early on she would prefer they never read her column. "I tried to anticipate what they wouldn't be comfortable with and not write it in the first place," she says. "I don't think there were too many times when I violated that . . . I made a couple of mistakes."

Once, for example, after she wrote that her six-year-old son had encouraged a visiting child to drink water from the toilet, he was teased at a birthday party. Maynard realized too late that she had set him up for humiliation. Another column she feels uneasy about involved revealing her dislike of a friend's children. Readers told her they were surprised she would write about a close friendship that way. "Sometimes I broke my own rules for no better reason than it was Monday morning and I was desperate," she says. "I was never desperate for material but desperate for something I felt strongly about."

Raised in Durham, New Hampshire, Maynard began writing for her neighborhood newspaper in grade school. In her freshman year at Yale she vaulted to the national stage when the *New York Times Magazine* published her essay "An 18-Year-Old Looks Back on Life." The cover piece made her a spokeswoman for her generation, something she considers ironic, since her life had hardly been typical. Her father was an artist and professor of literature and her mother was a writer and television talk show host with a Ph.D. from Harvard.

Although she prefers not to talk about it, Maynard's article on her generation's alienation resulted in a year-long alliance with the reclusive author of *Catcher in the Rye*, J.D. Salinger. The piece also led to publication of a book in 1973, *Looking Back: A Chronicle of Growing Up Old in the Sixties*. She used the royalties to buy the house in Hillsboro.

In 1978, after a brief stint of reporting for the *New York Times*, Maynard married, moved back to rural New Hampshire, had three children, and began writing about children for women's magazines. At first she told herself it was temporary and that soon she would write about more important subjects. "It sort of crept up on me that it was interesting and that I had a beat—the 'home front beat'—as interesting as any that I could find in the pages of the *New York Times*."

Her first stab at column writing came when she was asked to write a piece for "Hers," the weekly *Times* column written by women. After she wrote a second set of "Hers" columns, the *New York Times* Syndicate Sales Corp. approached her about writing a regular column. She had just given birth to her third child and options were limited. "We were at a point of utter financial disaster and I had to do something," she says.

Along with her weekly syndicated column, Maynard continued to write fiction. Her most recent novel, *To Die For,* a fictionalized account of the New Hampshire high school teacher who persuaded two students to kill her husband, was published in early 1992. After researching it, Maynard did the actual writing in two weeks, she says, working around the clock when her children were with their father. After closing out her column, Maynard went to California to write screenplays for a situation comedy based on the life of a syndicated columnist.

Although she has other book projects in mind, what she misses most about the column is the relationship with readers. "If some cataclysmic event occurred in my life, I'd want to tell the readers. It would be very frustrating not to tell them, because they would give me so much support."

DOMESTIC AFFAIRS

Our Mess Is Growing on Me

Don't ask me why, with all three of my children due to celebrate their birthdays in the next four weeks, I'd feel compelled to suggest to my son Charlie that we hold a Valentine-making party. But that's what I did last week. And then, of course, Willy wanted to ask one or two of his friends to join the crowd, and Charlie wanted to invite a couple of his guests to sleep over after the party. Then one or two of the others got wind of the sleepover plan. And before you could say "Tension Headache" there were ten children trouping into our house after school on a Friday afternoon, carrying paper doilies, scissors, glitter, sleeping bags, toothbrushes and stuffed animals. "You must be crazy," said one of the mothers, as she dropped off her son. "You're going to have one terrible mess to clean up tomorrow."

In preparation for this event I'd covered our dining room table with newspaper and set out a vast array of craft supplies: ribbon, lace, construction paper, glue, sequins, buttons, stickers, and a box full of old post cards and catalogues to cut up. Somewhere along the line (but not in a cemetery) I'd acquired a huge boxful of plastic flowers, which seemed ideal for gluing onto valentines, along with wallpaper samples and gold paper and pieces of old costume jewelry. Our local video store had been clearing out used video cassette boxes at a quarter apiece, so I'd laid in a supply of those, figuring they'd make great three dimensional

valentines, to put treasures in. And they did.

By four o'clock our house was a mess. Popcorn popping, paper scraps covering the floor, glitter everywhere. But the funny thing was that though our house was a wreck, the valentines were beautiful, and the children—far from having lost control—were as focussed and concentrated and harmonious a group as I can remember seeing at our house in all our years of hosting large gatherings of kids. In fact, I'd say, there almost seemed to be a correlation between the chaos on my dining room table and floor and the calm amongst the children. I actually left the room after a while, to pour myself a cup of coffee and read the paper, because everyone was so busy at work they didn't need me.

Around dinner time, as the valentine making slowed down, I ordered a giant pizza and set out plates and cups. Gradually the kids filtered downstairs to our playroom for ping pong and a movie. My original plan had been to spend that time clearing away the valentine mess and getting our house back in order. But I decided instead to snuggle up with the kids and watch the movie, too. Sometime close to eleven, when I tucked the children in, I confronted the mess in my dining room again. Would I clean it up? No.

The next morning, when I got up and came downstairs, one or two of Charlie's friends were back at work, making valentines. Gradually, throughout the morning, others filtered in and out of the room, taking turns with the glue gun and the stapler, the wallpaper books and the tape. Parents began swinging by to pick up their kids. By noon the population at our house was back down to the usual number.

But only briefly. Another batch of friends were due at our house for dinner that night—mostly grown-ups this time, plus a few of their children. There was a time when that fact would have meant I'd be spending my afternoon cleaning. But it was a glorious day, and I longed to go bike riding with my kids. So when Audrey suggested we leave our craft supplies out and make dinner a buffet in the living room, I didn't argue.

In the end, a lot of the adults who turned up that night ended up making valentines. And as for me—instead of scrambling frantically to make everything orderly, I knew order was an impossible goal and chose instead to do something I don't always manage at my own parties: I sat down and visited with my friends. Nobody seemed to think less of me for the bits of paper and rickrack on my floor.

Well, that was a week ago, and the mess in our dining room is with us still. Hardly a day goes by that someone—paper boy, neighbor or friend—doesn't end up sitting down and making something at the table. One whole wall of the room is covered with their creations. Now my daughter has even put up a sign that says "Gallery."

The thing about a giant mess is, once it's there it can't get much worse. The other great thing about a mess is that when you have one already, you don't have to worry about making one. And as long as you leave a mess, you don't get mad at your children for not cleaning it up. You don't get tense when a toddler walks in with her hands full of those little candy hearts that say things like "Oh, You Kid." Which means the toddler's mother doesn't get tense either. So what if candy hearts end up all over the floor?

Every day I walk through my dining room and ask myself: Is this the day we clean up the mess? And every day I conclude, no, not quite yet. Imagine, I think to myself: If I had vacuumed and dusted that first day, the dining room would already be due for vacuuming again. As it is, instead of spending all that time vacuuming, I've spent it making things. Valentine cards. Birthday cards. Cards that celebrate no special occasion whatsoever, besides the simple joy of being alive.

I have no doubt my children will find plenty of things to criticize me for, over the years. But something tells me, twenty years from now, not a one of them will be lying on some therapist's couch complaining that their mother didn't spend enough time vacuuming up glitter. More likely they'll talk about all the times I yelled at them to pick up their messes.

"This was a happy week," my daughter said to me the other day. "Oh yes?" I said to her. "Why is that?" "I don't exactly know," she said. "But I love our mess." I knew what she meant. Our mess is growing on me too, in more ways than one.

[*February 23, 1991*]

Life Is Too Precious to Spend Crying

This morning, I started my day with a cup of coffee and a letter from a reader of this column. She's a woman around my age, mother of two. In many ways, her life is rich and full. No terrible health or money problems. Her husband isn't a bad person. They have good times together.

There's nothing frivolous or selfish-sounding about this woman: She isn't looking for a perfect life. She doesn't expect every day of her marriage to feel like her honeymoon. She doesn't cry into her pillow at night because her husband didn't buy her a diamond for their anniversary, or because she found a grey hair in her brush this morning. The pain and disappointment about which she writes concern something far more basic that's missing from her life: a sense of well being in her marriage.

"I am unhappy much of the time," she writes. "My husband and I are different in ways that I am finding very hard to live with. I have not given up on my marriage, but I also know that there are ways in which my marriage is inhibiting my growth, my quest to become my best, days during which my insides scream, 'No, this isn't right! I can't live this way!' So I need to ask you: When do you know that enough is

enough? When can you say that you've done everything you could to save your marriage? When do you decide that living without your husband is ultimately better than living with him? When does your self cry out so loudly that you can't avoid its cries any longer?"

Already I can hear the voices of another set of angry readers, writing to me (and to her) to point out the number of times this reader uses the word "I." Writing to say that once you have children, it's their needs that are paramount, and not those of some spoiled, whining "self" crying out for growth. And then there will be letters—from people who have also known hard times in their marriages, but ones they managed to overcome without resorting to divorce.

I believe those people's stories—believe that a marriage is not something to be given up on without deep examination of the alternatives. I believe that many difficult marriages are salvageable. I believe that many marriages can be rescued, through counseling, through organizations such as AA and Al-Anon, through prayer, and sometimes through simple, honest communication.

But I also believe that there are marriages—and try as we did, my husband's and mine was one—which belong to another category. The marriage could continue. Nobody would die if the couple stayed together. Life would go on. The children might appear to flourish. But to the people living in those marriages, the fit would simply never be right. And when that's the way you live your life, it's more than your own self that suffers. A person who is profoundly unhappy in a marriage is also depriving his or her partner of the experience of being wholly loved and accepted, rather than endured. A person who silently cries out, as the woman who wrote me this letter does, "I can't live this way"— and then does live this way, despite her cries—is also quietly teaching her children to ignore their own inner voices, and failing to convey to them what may be the most important lessons we can teach them: to be true to one's self and to celebrate the extraordinary gift of being alive. To live one's life to the fullest. To be the best person we can be. We need to teach our children something else, too, I believe: that along with the obligation to help others in this life, our children also have the right to be happy.

Back to the question this reader asked me: When do you know that enough is enough? How can you tell the difference between a marriage of rough edges, imperfect fits, occasional pain and regular disagreement (which is to say, a marriage like virtually every marriage I know, including some very good ones) and one of "irreconcilable" differences?

Two partners in the same marriage may not necessarily agree on just where their own marriage stands. In my husband's and my case, the same marriage that had come to feel unbearably painful to me felt at least endurable to him. In the end, though, it was my husband who said "Enough." My husband told me he wouldn't stay married to me any longer—because it was not endurable to him to stay married to an unhappy woman. Fearful as I was, for our children, I'm not sure

I would have found the strength to leave, on my own. I'm deeply grateful to him for his wisdom in recognizing that fact and making the decision for me.

A year and a half later, I know it was the right one. I miss so many comforts of marriage: someone to share my coffee with in the morning, someone to sleep with at night. I miss sitting in the front passenger seat of the car and letting my head rest on his shoulder on a long drive. I miss having someone walk in the door at the end of a long day to ask me how mine went. More than anything, I miss talking about and sharing our children. But between us, right now, lies too much old pain for talk.

I said my husband was the one who recognized that enough was enough. But there was another crucial factor contributing to my recognition of that fact. It was the death of my mother, a woman who had relished and celebrated life more than anyone I've ever known. Her death taught me to recognize the preciousness of my days. The model she gave me, of a woman who had left an unhappy marriage, well into her fifties, to forge a good new life on her own (something my father ultimately did too) gave me the courage to believe that all of us—my husband, my children and I—would not only survive the pain of our family breakup, but emerge stronger and better for it.

I came to feel that life is too precious to spend crying. Too precious to spend arguing. Childhood is too precious to spend with unhappy parents. Adulthood is too precious to spend crying out, "This isn't right. I can't live this way." If you feel that way, you need to change your life. Maybe you can change your life and still stay married, and if so, that's the best of all. In the end, for me, the only way to change my old way of life was to leave. And so I did.

[*Spring 1991*]

Reaching for the Sun: A Farewell

We ran out of toilet paper again the other day. We have three flavors of Ben and Jerry's ice cream in our freezer, sixteen different teapots on our shelves, not to mention around three hundred sets of salt and pepper shakers. But no toilet paper. Not last Tuesday, anyway.

"Mothers aren't supposed to let things like that happen," said my daughter sternly. At 13, and the oldest child, Audrey is an astonishingly competent person who endures her mother's failings with a mixture of irritation and benign amusement. Mornings when I step into the shower these days, I am likely to find a Post-it note from her on the mirror. "Is this a bathroom or a shoe store?" she will have written (referring to my habit of leaving my shoes in the middle of the floor). "Call me crazy, but I'd just as soon not find gerbil droppings on my bedspread." (Her brothers were making an obstacle course for their pets.)

My daughter now reminds me regularly of all the ways in which she would do things differently from the way I do them. (She would separate the dark laundry from the light and put damp clothes in the dryer promptly, before mildew had time to develop. She would make sure her brothers took nightly showers. If she were in charge, we'd have a basement full of toilet paper. Also—another downfall of mine—trash bags.)

In fact, my daughter has been telling me since she was three or four years old what it is that mothers are and are not supposed to do. (They are also not supposed to buy rhinestone-studded cowboy boots. Pretend to be Peggy Fleming in the middle of a crowded skating rink. Allow their sons to peel off all their clothes and cover their entire bodies with mud. Mothers are not supposed to pull into a train station with their three children, after a weeklong expedition to our nation's capital, at ten minutes before midnight, with $6.00 left in their purse, to discover in the fine print on their parking stub that the garage where they have left the family station wagon closed for the night an hour earlier. And eight hours later, when they arrive at the parking garage to retrieve their vehicle at last, after spending an uncomfortable night on the floor of a friend's apartment, and they find out that the car's battery is dead, they are not supposed to burst into tears. Audrey was six at the time of the locked-garage incident, but she has never forgotten it as a prime example of the sort of thing mothers are not supposed to let happen.)

It is not just our children who bring to us their ideas of what it is mothers are supposed to be like. Mothers of my generation (and fathers too) grew up with a lot of ideas from television. A man I know—still single at the age of 43—says he has spent his whole life trying to locate Donna Reed. Join the crowd, I told him.

Then there were our own parents. My mother wore a girdle, stockings and heels just about every day of my youth, except when she was gardening. In all the years I lived at home, I only saw her cry once, although I know now (as I think I must have known then) that she inhabited a deeply unhappy marriage and carried with her enormous career frustrations too. I know now that she was lonely, angry, frustrated, and scared. But mothers back then weren't supposed to feel those things. Or show them, anyway.

I came into my own motherhood at the forefront of a revolution. The message society conveyed to my friends and me, as we entered womanhood, was that we could accomplish anything. We could have it all. Marriages and babies, and careers, too. No more bridge clubs for us. We would find career fulfillment. And then come home to bake the cookies and give the birthday parties, same as our mothers did, without ever missing a beat or dropping a stitch. We traded in the girdles and stockings for panty hose and aerobic gear, but the idea was still the same. Mothers could do anything. Mothers were perfect.

I thought I would fall in love, get married, have babies, and live happily ever after. I really did believe that. And I was right that having children was the best experience of my life. I just didn't know that in addition to providing me with the greatest riches I have ever known, it would also leave me feeling bankrupt sometimes—overspent, overdrawn, wiped out. I didn't know that I would often find myself standing in my kitchen, with this infant in my arms more precious to me than breath, whose tears I couldn't stop, feeling more loneliness and isolation and pure panic than I'd ever known before. Mothers were supposed to have all the answers. So why was I still coming up with questions?

For 13 years now, I've been trying to figure out what it is that mothers are supposed to do. And for a while there I thought it was, simply, everything. I thought it was a mother's job to be there every time a tear fell, or preferably one minute before. I thought it was a mother's job to make her children's lives as perfect as her own had failed to be. Mothers made the world safe for their children. (Also fun, exciting, and interesting.) It was a mother's job to make her children happy.

And of course, when your children are very little, they think those things, too. At three or four, my sons would say, "You made me do it" if they spilled their milk or lost their toy. Because of course, if a person makes herself responsible for her children's happiness, she must also be accountable for whatever sorrow comes their way.

I will always remember a day I found myself driving with my son Charlie, headed directly into the sun. Charlie was two years old at most. He was squinting, covering his eyes, and then he started to cry. "The sun's in your eyes," I told him.

"Take it out!" he said. He really believed I could do that.

When I left my marriage two years ago—and then again when I made the decision not to take my children with me for the remainder of that school year—a lot of people offered up their ideas to me, once again, about what mothers were and were not supposed to do. Mothers were supposed to stay married to fathers. Mothers were supposed to be home every night to tuck their children in. Mothers were supposed to meet the needs of their family first, whatever their own might be. Mothers were supposed to be strong.

What I would say now is, mothers are supposed to take care of their children, all right. And part of that job requires them to raise children who can survive without them. You can't set out to make your children happy. You make a happy life, with your children as a crucial part of it.

I was standing in my garden the other day, admiring my flowers. The iris were in bloom, and the poppies were budding. The tulips were finished, and the zinnias (my favorites) only a couple of inches tall. And I found myself thinking how wonderful it would be if all my favorite flowers could be in bloom at the same time. Lilacs and lilies, marigolds and snowdrops.

Then I thought, there I go again. Wanting everything. When part of the beauty of a garden is watching the stages it passes through. And the way the passing of every flower marks the coming of a new one.

I miss babies, and I love teenagers. Two years ago I grieved that I would not grow old with my children's father. A year ago I rejoiced at falling in love. Now I'm discovering that being alone can also be all right.

It's not only children who grow. Parents do, too. And as much as we watch to see what our children do with their lives, they are watching us to see what we do with ours. I can't tell my children to reach for the sun. All I can do is reach for it, myself.

[June 15, 1991.
This was Maynard's final column.]

MERLENE DAVIS

When Merlene Davis told *Lexington* (Kentucky) *Herald-Leader* editors that the paper didn't have the guts to hire a black columnist, she never thought she would be tapped for the job. But two hours after she made the comment in a staff meeting, she was offered a column. "There's no newspaper that moves that fast, so it was scary as all outdoors," she says. "I didn't do it for myself personally. I had no desire to do it."

Because her editors made the offer so quickly, she figured they knew she would fail; then they could say they tried a black person but it didn't work out. "I was terrified," Davis says. "It seemed to me I was either going to carry all the black people into a new future, or I was going to drop them back over the wall if I failed." There were no patterns to follow, no role models, and no guidelines. "They said go for it," she recalls. "I didn't know how to write a column—everybody else had their little set way of doing their columns, but I couldn't do them that way." Davis says she knew she would fail.

Three years later she is the only black columnist at the paper, and she has a loyal following. "She's an original," says editor Tim Kelly. "People identify with her. Whether they agree or not, they read her." Although her column is positioned on the front of the paper's Lifestyle section three times a week, Davis writes about a range of issues, mixing personal essays with opinions on community, national, and international issues and events.

Her first column was about giving a sermon to the children at her church, knowing she was likely to embarrass her daughter. As she tells it, she asked how many were going to stop lying and never lie again. When everyone raised their hands, Davis told them they were lying. "I said the choir lies, the preacher lies. It was the truth. At the end there was no applause, nothing. I didn't look at my daughter when I sat down." Davis ended her column by saying that after church, her daughter told her, "You did good, Mama. Nobody ever tells us the truth. Everybody needs to hear you."

Her fear of giving the sermon symbolized the way she felt about writing a column, she says, but both were well received, and Davis continued to write one column a week on top of her regular lifestyle beat. After two months, she demanded a raise and got it. "I remember all of a sudden it was the power of the column, the feeling that you cannot touch me now—the first time I've ever experienced empowerment," Davis says in a husky voice. "I could go up to these white men [her editors] who had terrified me before . . . and now I knew that if I talked back I wasn't going to suffer because [the newspaper's] readers like me." She chuckles, remembering a childhood experience: "I stood in a corner in first grade when I had talked a lot. Now I get paid for it."

Early the next year she was asked to do two columns a week, and after eight months was made a full-time columnist, which meant writing three columns every week and widening her focus. Even then she didn't have the confidence that she could do it, she says. She was afraid she wouldn't have enough to talk about. But she says life has been like that, challenging her when she gets too comfortable. "When I say, 'This I can live with for the rest of my life'—only when I have managed to get it to fit the way I want it to fit—does some wrench come into the works and throw it all out," she says. "Somebody doesn't want me to be comfortable. The Lord has a sense of humor."

Davis never expected to become a journalist, much less a columnist. She turned to journalism as a way to make money. A college drop-out, she was unemployed and had a four-year old daughter when she returned to the University of Kentucky to study English. She ended up majoring in journalism after a professor convinced her she could get a job as a reporter. "I needed a job at the end of two years. That was my pure interest," she says. She loved to write but wan't so sure about being a reporter. "I was scared of just walking up to people and asking them questions. It comes from years of being black, years of being a woman," she says. "It was aggressive, and you weren't supposed to be aggressive."

After an eleven-week summer program for minority journalists at the University of California in Berkeley, Davis got a job at the *Memphis Press Scimitar*. She was in her early thirties, but "still scared to death of reporting. People say I have an outgoing personality, and that's why I can do all this stuff. I can do it now because I have a little power behind me. Then there was no power. You know, you get brave with power."

In those days, Davis was glad just to have a job and wasn't even thinking in terms of a career. "That's lofty," she says. "I didn't see that as being possible in Memphis. There was nobody above me but white males." She encountered racism in Memphis and what she describes as a plantation mentality among many blacks, a reluctance to change the status quo. So when John Carroll, then editor of the Lexington paper, invited her to join the *Herald-Leader* staff, she came home. The first couple of years were "pure hell," she says, because she was labeled inexperienced and given story assignments that nobody else wanted.

After two years, she was assigned to the paper's Lifestyle section and began to thrive. One of her first stories was a report on the unofficial caste system in the black community, which is based on skin color—a theme filmmaker Spike Lee later explored. "All kinds of black folk jumped on me from all over the place. You're not supposed to tell our secret," she says. "I still had that idealistic crap in my heart that I was supposed to break ground, to wake people up, to challenge them, black and white. That's when I started sprouting wings. That's when I said, 'Whoah, I'm good at this.' And you know, when you get confidence, nothing can stop you. [Before], I had no self-esteem; now I had self-esteem." Despite her renewed confidence, Davis says each column presents new challenges and "some are going to come out ugly." She writes as honestly as she can about her life and the issues that affect her.

"I'm not claiming to be a high political writer. I'm not claiming to be anyone but someone who will validate that woman who is a mother, wife, churchgoer, all these other things being torn into little bitty pieces," Davis says. "I try to give her a reason to say, 'Somebody else is doing it.' Everybody's going through it, but unfortunately a lot of women tend to keep things to themselves, and then they think, 'I'm the only one.'"

"The things she writes about are universal," says Angela Duerson Tuck, assistant city editor of the *Atlanta Constitution* and Davis's former co-worker. "She tells it like it is. She doesn't mince words. It makes me proud that she's a woman, and a black woman."

Always trying to see the humor in difficult situations, Davis wants people to "lighten up, smell the roses," and realize that this is just one day of their lives. One column, written after a trying day with her toddler, explored the notion of what it would be like to hang her son from a ceiling fan and turn it on. "That made me laugh. It lightened up the situation." Her humorous columns on the details of family life have earned her the unofficial title "the black Erma Bombeck." Davis doesn't mind.

Not everyone tunes in to the humor of her columns, however, particularly when the humor hits uncomfortably close to home. Then readers let her have it. For example, a tongue-in-cheek column calling dentists "sadists" outraged some readers. Dentists wrote to say she had turned children from dentistry for life. "Come on, don't give me that much power," Davis says, laughing. "It's the pain that's going to keep them away."

Her serious columns also provoke readers. A column highly critical of the county school system for high freshman failure and dropout rates drew fire from teachers and administrators. Piqued by an unsigned letter from "concerned teachers," which suggested that she use her column to extol the positive aspects of public education, Davis responded with another column saying she did not intend to "sit back and allow the future of this country to plummet with our children's levels of education. If I can do anything to bring about a change, I will. Until that time, I will continue to scream at the top of my lungs, 'The emperor has no clothes.'"

Although she is black, Davis says she writes for harried white women with children. "I don't think white women know as much as I know. I think white women need to be slapped in the face and awakened," she says. "My job is, number one, to challenge her to do more with her life, and number two, to help her realize that, yes, you're going to be frazzled, but laugh at it."

She says she reflects the confusion that people have in their lives. From her own experience, she knows how scattered people can feel. "When you have all your body, mind, and spirit focused on one goal, I don't think there's any goal you can't achieve," she says. "But having children and trying to concentrate on the kids—and I don't want my marriage to fail, and I want to be a good neighbor, and a good church member, I want to be a good follower of God—. I see myself in bits and pieces all over."

It takes time for her to build up energy to accomplish a goal. Usually she acts when she is fed up. "I can ignore a lot of stuff for a long time, and then I can't ignore it anymore and I have to change it immediately," she says. "If I ever focus in on something, I have always gotten what I wanted. Racism hasn't stopped it, sexism hasn't stopped it, only me."

Davis had been criticized by some readers for failing to take on more black issues, but she says the criticism has stopped because "I will criticize black folk as well as white. Black folk don't know what's going to come out of my mouth now, so they leave me alone." She values the freedom that her column gives her and doesn't want to be stereotyped. "I am not just a black person, so I have avoided that. I don't write columns only on blackness because I am not only black. I am a columnist first," she says. "I don't want it to sound like I'm trying not to be black, because I'm always going to be black, and I'm always going to suffer and remember the pain of being black, but I'm a columnist first."

After writing a column criticizing President Bush for focusing on the children of the world instead of on children in the United States, Davis received a critical letter from a woman who described herself as an "African born in America." "That's pretentious," says Davis, "this woman taking me to task for not being more African. That is not my goal; I don't want to be African, I want to save America. That's where I live, that's where my kids live, that's where everybody I know lives. I don't see how we're going to be able to deal with Africa effectively if we're falling apart on the inside. Outside looks marvelous, inside is just wormy."

Davis says she is "writing what I want to write." She gets ideas from co-workers, family, things she observes and reads about or hears on television, and letters from readers. She's always been opinionated, she says, but now she writes it down. Her topics are those she feels strongly about. "I have to identify with it. If I can't identify with it, I can't write about it. I have to feel something."

With a computer at home she has the flexibility to write where she pleases. But it's a toss-up between getting enmeshed in newsroom politics and responding to the demands of two children under five. If she has an idea for a column, writing it takes her little more than an hour, including revision. "I do a fast go-through, go back and do it again," she says. If she doesn't have an idea, the process can take two days. With three columns a week, that's all the time she has.

Her columns mix political and social issues with personal reflections. One day she might take prizefighter Mike Tyson to task for abusing his position, the next she might tell a story about life with two pre-school children and a teenager. Davis adopted a son in 1988, and a year later, at thirty-nine, found out she was pregnant again. The third column of the week usually comments on local government, schools, or police.

In fact, a column about the police almost ended Davis's career as a columnist. She had written a bitter commentary on a local controversy involving the shooting of a black man by a white policewoman. Editors held the piece—not because of the subject, she says, but because of the style. "They were trying to tell me how to write a column. But I've got power," she says, anger edging her voice. "Do you understand what I'm saying? By now, I know my style. I think I know my readership. And they want to tell me after two years how to write a column." She quit.

The head of the local Urban League, Porter G. Peeples, told her that her visibility as a black woman was more important than the style of one column. "He convinced me that it was important that I get my black voice out there," Davis says. Peeples said he told Davis she had an obligation to the black community. "Central Kentucky likes to think everyone has it fine, there's no need to deal with these kinds of issues; [Davis] has a style that forces you to think about these issues." Peeples also said the column and picture of Davis were important because they give hope to young African-Americans.

Since that incident, her range has widened and her voice as a columnist continues to evolve. "When I started, I wanted white folk to look into my life and see my life was not any different from theirs—I had a husband who didn't empty the garbage; I had kids who were nasty; I went to work every day, and I got confused," she says. "I wanted white folk, and mainly women, to look at me and see a black person is not any different from them."

After a while, most readers no longer regarded her only as a black person but began to respond to her columns as stories of universal experience, she says. It's been a rough journey. When her picture ran with the first columns, she received hate mail. "People did not want to see a black person writing a column commenting about local issues," she says. "I got what I call my 'nigger letter' once a week. . . . I have several laminated at home just to keep my feet on the ground." Even though she makes light of it, Davis acknowledges that hate mail hurts.

She has a simple philosophy for dealing with her critics. "My mama told me that as long as you're on this earth, if everybody likes you, then you're not doing something right. My goal is to strike everybody's chord. If I can't be comfortable, then nobody's going to be comfortable."

What's next? "I don't know what will happen next, because the wrench is going to come. I'm getting comfortable," she says. "When the wrench stops coming, I'll realize then it's over."

Marriage Can Often Be Wild Kingdom

After talking to several wives through the years, I have discovered that husbands are made of molasses. It's not because they are sweet, but because they move so slowly.

It's fortunate that I have talked with these wives, because for a while there I thought I had married a space alien—one that nodded, but didn't completely understand English. This lack of comprehension developed only when I asked him to do something around the house.

My husband is a former high school football running back who garnered headlines in this very paper. I know this because he carries the dried yellow clips in his wallet. The trophies won't fit there.

If I'm not mistaken, it's mandatory for running backs to have speed and agility. They have to be able to think quickly, and duck and dodge to cross the goal line.

Unfortunately, I usually don't see any of these characteristics in my husband until there is a football game on TV. Then the man becomes a gazelle.

He can run to the bathroom, dart up to the kitchen for a bowl of popcorn and canned refreshments, then dash back down to the family room before a huddle breaks during a televised football game. Not a kernel is dropped; no liquid is spilled.

But if I say, "Why don't you rake the leaves today, honey?" the gazelle magically is transformed into a water buffalo.

Boyfriends are not like that.

Boyfriends are right at your side at the snap of your fingers. They hover over you trying to anticipate your every desire.

My husband used to be like that. Nothing I wanted inconvenienced him. When we were dating, I asked him to drive to Cincinnati to get me a doughnut. He did it.

When, during a blizzard, I asked him to get me an ice cream cone, he said, "What flavor?"

He doesn't do that anymore.

Now, he's a husband. There is a law against that sort of thing now. Besides, isn't that what women's lib is all about?

We have discussed this problem on several occasions, and he always says that he will do the work when the mood strikes him. He says that his body is a finely tuned machine that he alone must direct.

That may be so. My body, on the other hand, tends to be directed by necessity and the seasons, which is why I believe leaves should be raked in the fall and not in the spring. I also believe windows should be caulked while the weather is still warm and not when the mercury dips to negative numbers.

But I have learned that pointing these things out to him is of no avail. A water buffalo does not take kindly to being pushed, especially during a football game.

So what I've learned to do is this. If the windows need caulking, I gather all the necessary equipment and head for the door.

As I set out, I cheerfully yell over

my shoulder, "Watch the kids, honey. Don't let them get that plaster of Paris on the living room couch. And remember to take something out of the freezer for dinner. A chocolate layer cake would be nice for dessert. And fold up those clothes in the dryer.

"And don't forget, the girls have Scout meeting at 3 o'clock and the dogs have to be at the vet by 4. Will dinner by ready by 5?

"Oh, I forgot to tell you. I invited the Johnsons over for dinner."

Within seconds, the gazelle appears.

"I'll do that," he says, breathlessly yanking the tube of caulk from my hands. "You might hurt yourself, dear."

Maybe this speedy action has something to do with the neighbors seeing a mere woman doing "men's work." Or maybe it's the thought of blocking two little hoodlums with one hand and fielding a roasted chicken with the other. I don't know.

Things still are not perfect, but I only see water buffaloes on TV now.
[*November 29, 1987*]

Queen Got a Proper, Down-home Welcome

I'm not easily impressed, especially by people.

Last week, however, a woman I didn't know handed me a gasp and a smile with a simple hug.

Alice F. Frazier, a 67-year-old great-grandmother in Washington, D.C., welcomed Queen Elizabeth II

and first lady Barbara Bush into her home and gave each of them a hug.

To do that to Mrs. Bush was no big deal. To touch the queen, however, was apparently one of the biggest social blunders of the century.

The woman threw caution to the wind, what with all the security that surrounded those two women, and did what came naturally.

Faced with a visit from the queen and first lady, I don't think I would have had the guts to do the same.

I had to talk to Mrs. Frazier. I just had to ask for the reasons behind the hug—and to ask about something else. Mrs. Frazier had cooked up a little snack for the occasion: Southern fried chicken wings, homemade potato salad and a tossed salad for filler.

It was fare cooked for a queen, and I wanted the recipes. I am, after all, ruled by my stomach.

So I called Mrs. Frazier. Here I was, some nosy person from way down in Kentucky asking her a question, which she answered without hesitation.

"I really didn't think about it," Mrs. Frazier said of the hug. "Where I come from, that's what you do when people stop by your house."

But you don't do that, I said. You don't touch the queen unless you have special permission, I guess.

"No, I guess you don't," she said. "But she came into my house. That's what I do."

I loved it. Not even visiting royalty could change this woman.

That made me curious about Alice F. Frazier.

She was born in Mooresville, N.C., where her father worked in a mill. She was nine when her mother died, leaving her to tend her younger siblings.

Mrs. Frazier married when she was 20 and stayed in Mooresville until her father died. In 1956, she and her husband and four children followed the trail blazed by the rest of her family years before and moved to Washington. They were looking for a better life.

She worked in a hospital, "on the floor with the nurses, cleaned at the agriculture building and worked at Norge Village, washing and folding clothes."

She and her husband also worked in a drugstore. She cooked in the cafeteria, and he worked on the loading dock. He died in 1970.

Then, eight years ago, the company merged with another, and Mrs. Frazier, then 59, was let go. She was unemployed for nearly the first time since she quit school in the ninth grade.

"They didn't want old workers," she said.

But she was a cook. Great cooking comes with experience and age, doesn't it?

"Yeah. But they didn't want old workers."

And neither did anyone else. She did the best she could until she turned 60, when she started living on Social Security.

One of her four children is dead, a victim of alcoholism; another is paralyzed, a victim of an accidental shooting 20 years ago. Mrs. Frazier has nine grandchildren and 12 great-grandchildren, one of whom was born just before the queen's visit.

Life goes on.

Last summer, when Mrs. Frazier was offered the chance to buy a three-bedroom house, she took the leap, bringing along a daughter and four grandchildren.

"Renting is all right," she said. "I kept my place up just the same when I was renting. But owning is different. There's nothing like it."

It was because of that ownership, because Mrs. Frazier was the first person to take advantage of the conversion of public housing into something folks could call their own, that the queen dropped by for a visit.

Which brings us back to the food.

"I didn't know if I should cook something or not," she told me. "But I was taught that you go ahead and fix it just so you have something to offer. That's the only way I know."

Mrs. Frazier shared the recipes willingly. But it really didn't help me much.

For the fried chicken, "I like to sprinkle mine with some Lawry's seasoned salt and some garlic powder," she said. "Then I roll it in flour and put it in the deep fryer."

That wasn't good enough. I needed specific measurements.

"Well, you know, just a little," she said.

OK. She was being cagey. What about the potato salad that she's famous for?

"I use some sweet relish, some green peppers, onions, a little mustard, hard-boiled eggs and celery," Mrs. Frazier said.

Details. Give me details.

"Well, I boil the potatoes in their jackets and then peel and chop them. I chop all the rest of it up and mix it all together with a little mayonnaise."

How much?

"Just a little." This was not going well.

Mrs. Frazier said she also served a tossed salad with homemade dressing. The salad was simple: tomatoes, lettuce and cucumber. She usually adds onion, but she didn't want to offend her guests. So she served the sliced onions separately.

As for the dressing, well, it was the same story.

"I use mustard, but not too much. And I use ketchup, more than anything, with sweet relish and mayonnaise. But it comes out the color of ketchup. Then just throw it all together."

Yes, yes. But how much?

"It all depends on how much you're going to make. If you're making only a little bit, then use just a little."

Right.

It was like asking my mother or grandmother for a recipe. They didn't measure anything, either. No wonder this new generation can't cook.

To wash it all down, Mrs. Frazier had prepared iced tea and her favorite drink: Kool-Aid mixed with ginger ale.

I don't know about the queen and Mrs. Bush, but I would have asked for a plate to go.

Talking to Mrs. Frazier brought back memories of church dinners and family picnics—back before cholesterol ruled the taste buds.

I thanked her for that, and I thanked her for being herself when most others would have changed.

After hanging up the phone, I realized that if I told her I was dropping by, she would give me a big hug and serve me the same menu.

Which means either that Mrs. Frazier considers Elizabeth II to be "regular people" or that she treats everybody like a queen.

[May 31, 1991]

In Imperfect World, We Can Only Ask Why

The topic of conversation among many mothers and fathers this week was the apparent suicide of John A. Palumbo III. His death brought home to us the true fragility of life.

The 16-year-old was the son of Ruth Ann Palumbo—a friend of mine, a woman who grew up in my neck of the woods, a woman who is genuine.

I cannot possibly imagine what she's going through today. A big part of me selfishly doesn't want to.

If it were my child who thought the pressures of life were too tremendous to go on, the first thing I'd probably do is blame myself. Maybe my child would be alive if I had done this or if I hadn't done that, I would think.

That's got to be the worst thing for me, my friend or any parent to do. Kids don't come with a guarantee that they will fulfill the dreams we have for them or the dreams they have for themselves. Some of them will, and some won't, and we parents never know which of those categories our children fit into. If we did, we could intercede before it's too late.

And sadly, we parents don't receive instructions on the

horrendous responsibility of molding a young life until afterward, when everyone knows what we should have done.

We are already pulled in several directions, and we can't be all things to our children. It's not physically or mentally possible, especially if our children are teen-agers.

That's the age when they start feeling their oats, thinking they are adult when we all know they are not. We've got to give them room to try their wings while still holding fast to the perch.

As one of my friends said of being a parent, "It's the hardest job in the world." As the mother of a teen-ager, a toddler and an infant, I can testify to that. On some days, it's almost impossible.

And yet, when something goes wrong, we punish ourselves, using hindsight to try and make sense of it all.

There are few of us who wouldn't do things differently if we knew the results ahead of time. But we can't see the future. We're only human.

And so are our children.

Somehow, some way, we've got to drum it into our children's heads that nobody is perfect. We all make mistakes. None of us has a storybook life.

The difference between an adult and a child is that the adult knows tomorrow is another day.

Looking back over my life, I can't remember a more traumatic age than when I was a teen-ager. It didn't seem like I could do anything right for my mother.

My father pretty much stayed out of all the disputes, either by his having to work two jobs to support us or by allowing my mother's word to be law when it came to home life.

She demanded my best at school, at home, all the time. I didn't want to give that, didn't want to expend that much energy. I wanted to just give pieces and use the rest of my energies to focus on far more important things. I'd give examples, but now I can't remember a single one of those pressing issues.

The thought of running away fluttered through my mind, followed closely by a prayer that something bad would happen to me and make her so sorry.

I'm sure my mother would have been shocked to learn I harbored such thoughts. I don't think she understood that my world existed for only that day.

Finally, after I don't know how long, I realized that every day is at least a little different from the day before. In about a week, my entire outlook could and would change. But there were some iffy days before I realized that.

What made me survive while others didn't? If I knew that, no parent would ever suffer the grief my friend has to work through today.

Parents would not have to wonder silently or out loud whether they, too, might have to grieve.

And no more young lives would end for a lack of hope.

[*November 21, 1991*]

ANNA QUINDLEN

The picture that runs with her column shows a soft-eyed young woman with dark swinging hair and a mischievous smile. Anna Quindlen looks too young to have secured a regular place on the op-ed page of the venerable *New York Times*. "It drives me nuts," she says. "When I get in trouble, I never can figure out whether they're saying 'that stupid woman' or 'that stupid kid.'" Hers is the only regular column by a woman on one of the most influential opinion pages in the country, and it is different from other columns on the page. Quindlen's columns are not "think" pieces; they are engaging, often provocative essays filled with personal anecdotes and detailed observations—life filtered through the mind of an intelligent woman.

But Quindlen resists the notion that she's special, saying the key to her success is that she's just like her readers. "It's how average I am. I'm from the same background that millions of people are from, leading the same life that millions of women are." Although her 750-word column, "Public & Private," is distributed twice a week to some 300 papers nationwide by the *New York Times* News Service, Quindlen tries to retain a certain innocence. "As soon as I have a sense of myself as real special, then it's time for me to stop doing this, because we don't need another real special person writing," she says. "We need somebody who has a real clear sense of ordinary life and how ordinary life is impacted by events."

Not everyone agrees that Quindlen is average. Some criticism has come from feminists who say her privileged middle-class background has shaped her perspective and that she doesn't understand the circumstances of those less fortunate. Quindlen acknowledges that in looking at the world she has tended to "see the full part of the glass. I think my optimism is what some people like—and what some hate."

Feminists have also criticized Quindlen for quitting a top *Times* editorial post to stay home with her children.

Other criticism is predictable: Conservatives dislike her consistently liberal stance, and some men complain about male bashing or, worse, being ignored. She seems resigned to being loved and hated. "I suppose that what inevitably happens if you do it right is that a certain segment of readership relates to you completely; a certain segment is at least entertained by your turn of phrase, and a certain segment just hates your guts," she says. "I think that's the way it works for all of us."

In the end, Quindlen says hers is the only mind she knows well enough to write to: "Writing a column—writing anything—is an incredible act of audacity and arrogance because it assumes you have something really interesting and pivotal to say. The idea of trying to please people with that kind of audacity seems senseless. You just do it."

Although she's been writing a column of one kind or another for about ten years and was awarded the Pulitzer Prize for commentary in 1992, Quindlen says she has never gotten comfortable. Sitting in her sunny office in the *New York Times* building in midtown Manhattan, she leans forward and says intensely, "What keeps you healthy is having a job that terrifies you all the time. I'm getting less terrified now, but if you're not terrified by a job like this, then you have no business doing it. At some level, the terror is what makes you say 'Make one more call, think one more time about not what the glib answer to this is, but what the real answer is.'"

It is not her audience that scares her, but "always wanting to be at the top of your game. I know I'm supposed to feel that one out of three can be throwaway columns, but I just can't manage that. I always try to make it better." Writing two columns a week, Quindlen is always conscious of being on deadline. James Reston, her former colleague at the *Times*, wrote the description of column writing that she likes best. It's like standing under a windmill and being knocked over by the blades. "You say, 'Thank God that's over,' and you look up and there's another one coming right down at you."

Quindlen's current column is a synthesis of reporting and opinion, in which she generally focuses on a topic close to the news. Although her arguments are underscored by the emotion she expresses and by personal anecdotes and observations, the column is a departure from the intensely personal "Life in the 30s" column she wrote from 1986 to 1988. That column provided an intimate glimpse into her feelings on issues like abortion and birth control, the family and the work-place. She also wrote about the details of her own life, including her childhood and her parents, about becoming a mother, about being a Catholic and being a woman. One critic reviewing a collection of those columns called Quindlen "an astonishingly graceful writer." Another said she was "smart and funny and warm." The column had a loyal following.

"I think I reflected the confusion [of readers]," she says. "The best part about doing that column was that people would write to me and say, 'I thought I was the only person in the world who felt that way.' What they don't realize is that I wrote those columns thinking I was the only person in the world who felt that way. So it validates me at the same time they think it's validating them."

She sees this reciprocal relationship as a key to the columnist's art. "I don't think you can envision a certain kind of reader, but you've got to envision a dialogue," she says. "When you write these columns, you have to envision at the end of every paragraph someone saying, 'Well, I don't understand how you can say that. That hasn't been my experi-ence at all.' And then reading the next paragraph, and saying, 'Well, maybe if you put it that way'—that sense of being stirred and arguing back."

Drawing on her life experience is essential to Quindlen's columns, although she says it is disconcerting to have people think they know all about her. One woman, for example, told her she knew Quindlen had had an abortion because she writes so passionately about the subject. "That's a trip," says Quindlen. She has never said in a column whether she has had an abortion. "Readers want you to be who they have in mind." Readers may become so familiar with a columnist's voice that they consider her a close friend. "That's part of why readers were outraged when I wrote a column saying I wasn't going to have amnio-centesis. It's not what I would do if I was their best friend." Regular readers think they know mental, physical, and spiritual attributes of columnists. "They see me on the street and say, 'I thought you were taller.' They have a picture in their mind and they don't want it upset. It's a disconcerting aspect [of being a columnist] and it never goes away."

Although she shied from being labeled a woman's columnist when she did "Life in the 30s," she now deliberately writes with a woman's perspective, choosing issues that matter to women but may not be of as much interest to men. One column, for example, criticized New York state officials for abusing public funds while cutting library "story hour" programs for toddlers. "Would most of my male colleagues take off on that point? I'm not sure. Certainly my older male colleagues wouldn't resonate to it as much because it's been a while since they used story hour."

Quindlen lost some readers when she switched from "Life in the 30s" to "Public & Private." She said some told her they felt betrayed when she started her new column, and she understands their anger. "I know what they're trying to say—'This doesn't seem like it's just for me.'" She's aiming for a middle ground between the intimacy of the old column and what an op-ed columnist typically does. Initially, Quindlen wasn't so sure she wanted to be on the *Times* op-ed page because the mandate of those columnists seemed to be to convince readers to think the way they thought. "I'm not interested in that. I'm not interested in directly shaping public policy. I'm not interested in telling the president what he should do," Quindlen says. "What I'm interested in is sharing with people my confusion and my thought processes about certain things, and reflecting how people are feeling about those issues themselves, possibly for the edification of leaders who have lost track of that."

She doesn't pretend to have answers. "When I was a kid, I used to read all these voices-of-God columnists who were so sure they knew exactly what everybody should think. I don't feel that way. Even issues I'm relatively sure about, I'm not 100 percent sure of."

Abortion is one issue Quindlen has now resolved for herself, after years of internal debate. Although she supports a woman's right to choose whether to have a child, she can still see valid reasons for opposing abortion. Sometimes readers see her openness to both sides as a sign of weakness, but Quindlen defends herself, saying, "I feel like what is interesting is not the position but the process."

Quindlen describes herself as a liberal feminist, a term that might seem odd in light of her choice to leave a top *Times* news job to stay home with her children. But she is "a feminist with a feminist to raise," she says, a woman who wants to decide what's best for herself and best for her children. Quindlen says she still identifies with the time in which she came of age, the early 1970s, and doesn't want to lose that sense of possibilities. She sees herself in Gloria Steinem's observation that women become more radical as they get older. "The men I know who were rad guys in college are getting more and more conservative all the time," she says, "and the women I know are getting froggier."

Although Quindlen's picture does not accompany her column in the *Times*, the byline makes it clear that the author is a woman. When the column first appeared in early 1990, many readers took note of her gender, and wrote her, and the letters keep coming. Some think the subjects she writes about are insignificant; others are cynical about her position on the page with the likes of Tom Wicker, William Safire, Anthony Lewis, and Russell Baker. "People write in and say clearly I'm a token, but the proof is in the pudding," she says. "Is it clear that I'm a lame duck on our op-ed page? No. I don't think anybody reads the page week in and week out and says clearly, 'This is the person who doesn't belong here because she can't turn a phrase or she doesn't have a brain in her head.'"

The significance of having a woman's voice on the op-ed page is enormous. "Not to put too Marxist a spin on it, but you have an oppressed-class person on the page, a person who's known what it's like to enter a room and be discounted simply by virtue of physical appearance," she says. "You have a person who perceives lots of pivotal social and political issues of our day personally," such as child care and abortion. "I don't think of child care as legislation. I think of it as an omnipresent personal problem."

Another reason, close to Quindlen's heart, is "that somewhere there's a little girl running a block newspaper who can look at the *New York Times* and say, 'That's what I want to be when I grow up.' That was an impossibility for little girls when I was growing up." Quindlen's only female role model was columnist Dorothy Thompson, whom she read about when she was twelve. Growing up in Philadelphia, Quindlen wanted to write fiction but decided to go into the newspaper business so she could support herself. Once she got into it, she was hooked.

Persistence—what she calls pushiness—and talent took her rapidly up the ladder. She started working for the *New Brunswick* (New Jersey) *Home News*, just out of high school, after badgering the editor for a job. She was hired as a copy girl and clerk and got to do a few stories. After enrolling in Barnard College, she talked her way into a summer reporting job at the *New York Post* at age nineteen and worked there again following graduation for about two years.

At twenty-four, she moved to the *Times*, during a period when the paper was looking for bright writers and trying to hire more women. She worked first on general assignment and women's news, then nabbed the city hall beat. When she was asked to write the *Times*'s "About New York" column, it seemed like her dream assignment.

"You could find your own stories—little perfect things you knew told you everything about life in the city," she says. "So when I got that I was as happy as a pig in shit." She loves New York, saying that when she came to college in the city, "it was like walking into a house I'd always meant to buy."

After six years, she was named deputy metropolitan editor, the highest ranking woman in the *Times* newsroom and one of the youngest. She remembers executive editor A.M. Rosenthal saying someday she would be metro editor, that the sky's the limit. Then she became pregnant. And five months after returning from maternity leave, she became pregnant again. "Ohhh," she groans, "did those guys feel blindsided? Yes." A month before her second child was born, she decided to quit. "It became clear I couldn't take another leave. I knew the center wouldn't hold," she says. "It became clear the job would have to go."

She felt torn about her decision to quit because she was afraid it would reflect badly on other women. She says she would have understood if everyone had said, "What *do* women want?" but she thought that if she could maintain the editors' good will and respect, "It would make them understand all of the things women are and want to be, and all of the things that men should want and seem not to."

She worked at home on a novel and wrote some "Hers" columns for the *Times* Sunday Magazine. On a visit to the newspaper, when Quindlen asked Rosenthal if he minded her writing a column for other newspapers, he told her to do one for the *Times*. In less than five minutes, he came up with the idea for "Life in the 30s," telling her to write about what she talked about with her friends on the telephone. Quindlen recalls thinking that he was trying to give her a break and keep her at the *Times*, and that "neither of us thought it was going to be popular." But the column was a hit, and Quindlen built a huge following. "I thought she would be terrific," says Rosenthal, "but I didn't know how rapidly she would become one of the best known columnists in the country."

Her decision to end that column was made after she became pregnant with her third child. The pregnancy coincided with her sense that it was "time to stop taking off my emotional clothes in public." She also wanted to work on the novel. But Max Frankel, who had become managing editor, persuaded her that she was a performer, telling her that the 35,000 people who buy hardcover books would never be enough of an audience for her. So she agreed to write "Public & Private" once a week for the op-ed page, later adding a second column. She also finished the novel, *Object Lessons,* published in 1992, which immediately made the *Times*'s Best-Seller List.

Quindlen writes in an upstairs study next to her bedroom in her home in Hoboken, New Jersey, twenty minutes across the river from Manhattan, mostly during the hours when her two older children are in school. The youngest is in the care of a full-time nanny and hasn't yet discovered that her mother works upstairs. Writing comes easily, but it's always agony when the computer screen is blank. "It's amazing, the difference in my mood Wednesday and Thursday morning," she says, before and after a column is written. Quindlen is something of a stop-and-start writer but considers herself "a reasonably facile writer at this stage. I tend to write a couple of paragraphs, go play with my daughter, write a couple of paragraphs, have a cup of coffee, go talk on the phone, write a couple more paragraphs, take out three of the ones I've written, and when I've finished, call up the word count, which is usually about 300 over what I can afford," Quindlen says. "Then I go back and cut and move things around a lot."

Her writing voice is her speaking voice, she says, so it's not hard to maintain, "because when I open my mouth it's what comes out." Because she reads widely, she tends to be influenced by the style of the writer she's reading at the time. Reading Faulkner, her sentences tend to be long; in the midst of a novel by Trollope, her sentences are a little clipped. Her great strengths, says Rosenthal, are her "magnificent writing ability and her empathy. She presents herself to readers totally. She is very open. She represents an entirely different point of view than we've ever had there [on the op-ed page]."

Other than editing for style and length, no one tells her what to write or not to write. "I work for the publisher," she says. "Our relationship consists of a warm greeting, the certainty of my hiring, and the possibility of my firing." Her ideas generally come off the top of the news. She also gets ideas from readers' letters and from friends and colleagues. "I plan twenty-four hours ahead," she says, laughing. "I have a whole list of ideas that may or may not come together. It's pretty seat of the pants." Reporting is the backbone of her column. She tells of writing a column about condoms, "and I realized it was me pontificating about how condoms are not going to work." So she went and spent some time in a birth control clinic so she could pump up her column with real-life observations.

Her style typically is to engage readers with a concrete example or personal anecdote, then move to the larger issue. To begin a column about the deterioration of America, for example, she described what she saw in New York's Port Authority Bus Terminal—where the building itself had been cleaned up but was filled with panhandlers, con artists, drunks, and angry, tired commuters trying to flee to the safety of their homes.

"I write from the heart," she says. "I'm not a cerebral writer. . . . I wish I was more of a cerebral writer. I wish I was smarter. I'm basically a very emotional writer. I write from my gut. It's how I've always been as a newspaper person—from the gut as opposed to the more cerebral think-piece school. Sometimes you read a column and you hear the clicking of the person's brain," she says, citing her colleague at the *Times* William Safire. "Others make you cry or laugh, and those are the gut columns. I'm always a little sensitive writing a gut column as a woman, that it's going to be perceived as the 'ruled by the tides effect.'" She imitates an imagined editor: "Anna's really pissed off today. It must be PMS [premenstrual syndrome]."

Once a week she comes into the city to read her mail and take care of correspondence. Her spacious office is on the tenth floor of the *Times* building with the editorial writers and other op-ed columnists; three windows afford a sweeping view of midtown. She has her own secretary, and her voice is part of the national dialogue. But when she's writing, Quindlen doesn't think of herself as somebody special. "This really blows my mind every time I walk in here," she says.

PUBLIC & PRIVATE

A Mistake

I put my notebook on the kitchen table and pointed to the top line.

"Who's that?" said my husband, looking at the name scrawled in my handwriting.

"The Central Park jogger," I said.

There were many of us who knew that name, and there were others in the financial community in New York City, her co-workers and classmates and clients, who knew it, too. I sometimes thought as many people in this big city knew that name as could populate a small one—say, Palm Beach, Fla. And we all had our reasons for not revealing it: some because they loved her, some because they respected her, some because their newspapers forbade it.

I fell into that last group, but I had another reason too. I did not use her name when I wrote about her because I thought it was the right thing to do. She lost her memory, her balance, and finally, on the witness stand, her anonymity. I thought that was enough. And I believed the reader lost nothing at all by not knowing.

Rape inspires very personal passions and this will need to be a very personal column, because it is also about The New York Times. Last week The Times made the decision to print the name of the woman who has accused William Kennedy Smith, the nephew of Senator Edward Kennedy, of raping her at the Kennedy family home in Palm Beach. Editors at The Times said the use of her name on an NBC news broadcast took the matter "out of their hands."

Her name was printed in a profile that contained the allegation by an unidentified acquaintance that she had "a little wild streak," what we in the trade call an anonymous pejorative, as well as the fact that her mother was named as the other woman in the divorce of a wealthy man she later married.

It included information about the 17 traffic tickets she has received in the last eight years, as well as an anecdote about a restaurant chef who fixed her pasta after closing time, then was "disappointed" when she went to a bar with him and struck up a conversation with other men.

I imagined one of the editors for whom I have worked asking, "How does all this advance the story?" The answer is that it does not. It is the minutiae of skepticism.

There is a serious argument to be made about whether journalists should follow society or anticipate it, whether our refusal to print the names of rape victims merely perpetuates the stigma, or whether changing the policy would merely thwart prosecutions and shatter lives.

If we were to change that policy, there could not be a worse case in which to do so than this one. For NBC to change it in a case involving one of America's most powerful families inevitably suggested that the alleged victim had lost her privacy because of its prestige. For The New York Times, a paper that has been justly proud of taking the lead on matters of journalistic moment, to announce that it was forced to follow was beneath its traditions. To do so in a story that contained not only the alleged victim's "wild streak" but the past sexual history of her mother could not help but suggest that the use of the name was not informative but punitive.

In the face of what we did in the Central Park case, the obvious conclusion was that women who graduate from Wellesley, have prestigious jobs and are raped by a gang of black teenagers will be treated fairly by the press, and women who have "below-average" high school grades, are well known at bars and dance clubs, and say that they have been raped by an acquaintance from an influential family after a night of drinking will not.

If we had any doubt about whether there is still a stigma attached to rape, it is gone for good. Any woman reading the Times profile now knows that to accuse a well-connected man of rape will invite a thorough reading not only of her own past but of her mother's, and that she had better be ready to see not only her name but her drinking habits in print. I hope that the woman in Palm Beach, whose name I will not, need not use, had some sense, however faint, of the pressures she would face. It could not have been a fully informed decision. I have been in the business of covering news for all my adult life, and even I could not have predicted this. Nor would I have wanted to.

[*April 21, 1991*]

Enough Bookshelves

The voice I assume for children's bad behavior is like a winter coat, dark and heavy. I put it on the other night when my eldest child appeared in the kitchen doorway, an hour after he had gone to bed. "What are you doing down here?" I began to say, when he interrupted, "I finished it"

The dominatrix tone went out the window and we settled down for an old-fashioned dish about the fine points of "The Phantom Tollbooth." It is the wonderful tale of a bored and discontented boy named Milo and the journey he makes one day in his toy car with the Humbug and the Spelling Bee and a slew of other fantastical characters who change his life. I read it first when I was 10. I still have the book report I wrote, which began "This is the best book ever." That was long before I read "The Sound and the Fury" or "Little Dorrit," the Lord Peter Wimsey mysteries or Elmore Leonard. I was still pretty close to the mark.

All of us have similar hopes for our children: good health, happiness, interesting and fulfilling work, financial stability. But like a model home that's different depending on who picks out the cabinets and the shutters, the fine points often vary. Some people go nuts when their children learn to walk, to throw a baseball, to pick out the "Moonlight" Sonata on the piano. The day I realized my eldest child could read was one of the happiest days of my life.

"One loses the capacity to grieve as a child grieves, or to rage as a child rages: hotly, despairingly, with tears of passion," the English novelist Anita Brookner writes in "Brief Lives," her newest book. "One grows up, one becomes civilized, one learns one's manners, and consequently can no longer manage these two functions— sorrow and anger—adequately. Attempts to recapture that primal spontaneity are doomed, for the original reactions have been overlaid, forgotten."

And yet we constantly reclaim some part of that primal spontaneity through the youngest among us, not only through their sorrow and anger but simply through everyday discoveries, life unwrapped. To see a child touch the piano keys for the first time, to watch a small body slice through the surface of the water in a clean dive, is to experience the shock, not of the new, but of the familiar revisited as though it were strange and wonderful.

Reading has always been life unwrapped to me, a way of understanding the world and understanding myself through both the unknown and the everyday. If being a parent consists often of passing along chunks of ourselves to unwitting—often unwilling—recipients, then books are, for me, one of the simplest and most sure-fire ways of doing that. I would be most content if my children grew up to be the kind of people who think decorating consists mostly of building enough bookshelves. That would give them an infinite number of worlds in which to wander, and an entry to the real world, too; in the same way two strangers can settle down for a companionable gab over baseball seasons past and present, so it is often possible to connect with someone over a passion for books.

(Or the opposite, of course: I once met a man who said he thought "War and Peace" was a big boring book, when the truth was that it was only he who was big and boring.)

I remember making summer reading lists for my sister, of her coming home one day from work with my limp and yellowed paperback copy of "Pride and Prejudice" in her bag and saying irritably, "Look, tell me if she marries Mr. Darcy, because if she doesn't I'm not going to finish the book." And the feeling of giddiness I felt as I piously said that I would never reveal an ending, while somewhere inside I was shouting, yes, yes, she will marry Mr. Darcy, over and over again, as often as you'd like.

You had only to see this boy's face when he said "I finished it!" to know that something had made an indelible mark upon him. I walked him back upstairs with a fresh book, my copy of "A Wrinkle in Time," Madeleine L'Engle's unforgettable story of children who travel through time and space to save their father from the forces of evil. Now when I leave the room, he is reading by the pinpoint of his little reading light, the ship of his mind moving through high seas with the help of my compass. Just before I close the door, I catch a glimpse of the making of my self and the making of his, sharing some of the same timber. And I am a happy woman.

[*August 7, 1991*]

Ms. President

Donna Karan, the only fashion designer who seems to recognize the existence of hips in her clientele, perhaps because she owns a pair herself, recently ran an arresting series of magazine advertisements.

In one, the woman in the pin-striped suit is standing behind a bunting-draped lectern. In another, she is sitting on the back of a convertible amid grim guys with headsets, confetti dappling her hair. In a third, she is raising her right hand, a handsome man at her side, while a judge holds the Bible. Congratulations, Ms. President.

The model looks scarcely old enough to meet the constitutional requirements and too décolleté to meet the public ones. She's accepting the tribute of a grateful nation with a black-lace bra peeking from her unbuttoned blouse, fashion's current Madonna/whore obsession. The slogan is "In Women We Trust," but there's something slightly camp about the whole thing.

Camp is how the nation still sees it as well.

You've got to wonder, approaching a new century, when America will begin to take seriously the idea of being led by a woman. The concept heretofore has always been presented as a cross between a futuristic fantasy and a sitcom premise. Cue the laugh track.

We've heard the rationales. We've heard that there are not enough terrific women in the pipeline, that with so few in the House and Senate it is inevitable that most of the major players are men.

There are about to be two problems with the pipeline excuse. One is that a record number of women are running for seats in Congress this year. The second is the dirty little secret that has suddenly become so apparent: there are not that many terrific men in the pipeline, either.

In a recently published study called "Women in Power," two psychologists talked to 25 of the country's most powerful female elected officials. They found that many of them did not run for office until after their families were well launched, foreclosing the Wunderkind status and power-base building that accrue to men like Bill Clinton or Al Gore. They found that many of them were gingerly negotiating the contradictions between traditional notions of leadership and traditional notions of femininity.

But many had been told from childhood that they could do anything, and they still believed it. Give the chance, maybe they could convince us, too.

Consider Ann Richards, who became famous for her convention speech about how good ol' George Bush was born with a silver foot in his mouth—and who, God bless her, has no dirty linen left unaired after a snake's belly of a gubernatorial challenge. Governor of Texas, a biiiig important state. Smart, can-do, and as charming as a full moon on an autumn night. Truth is that if Ms. Richards is not soon mentioned as a national candidate, it won't be because of her competence. It will be because of her chromosomes.

I've heard women wonder aloud about when the idea of a woman President will be something more than an occasion for gags about the First Man. Opportunities for women have expanded so much that those gender deserts in which change is scarce water have become more wrenching.

This month the American Catholic bishops released another draft of their pastoral letter on women's concerns. It begins well, calling sexism a sin, and then ends, sadly, with the church's continuing theology of exclusion, its reaffirmation of the priesthood as the exclusive preserve of men. "This constant practice constitutes a tradition which witnesses to the mind of Christ and is therefore normative," the letter read.

I could inveigh here against the sheer foolishness of any system that excludes at least half of its finest potential leaders. But the murmurings about a woman President (as well as women priests) are not only about expanding what seems to be a shockingly shallow applicant pool.

They are questions about how we as women are valued, and how we learn to value ourselves. Neither political nor church leaders seem to adequately appreciate that a system which, by custom or covert agreement, considers women unsuitable for its highest positions sends them a message: You are subordinate clauses in the world's history.

No rationale can obscure that message. When our daughters ask why they may never see a woman President or a woman priest, we have no good answers for them. That is because there are none.

[*April 19, 1992*]

[Quindlen's columns copyright © 1991, 1992 by The New York Times Co. Reprinted by permission.]

MOLLY IVINS

As one of the first woman journalists to cover Texas politics, Molly Ivins went out of her way to let people know that being female played no part in getting stories. Tall and athletic, Ivins was accepted as "one of the boys" by the mostly male Capitol press corps and state legislature. She even played on the press corps's basketball team. But one day she knew she had gone too far.

As Ivins tells the story, she was covering the Texas Senate, where the pages are all young women, when she was elbowed by a male colleague, who said, "Look at the ass on that girl." That was followed by a jab on the other side from another male reporter, who told Ivins, "Look at that pair of knockers." "It was at that moment," Ivins says dryly, "I decided I could not be one of the boys."

An arresting storyteller, Ivins says she perfected the art by listening to Texas politicians. Hilarious stories often spike her satiric column on Texas and national politics. And Ivins no longer worries about being one of the boys. She is accustomed to being a maverick, to maintaining a consistently liberal voice in an overwhelmingly conservative state.

"What you need—and this is [freelance writer Robert] Sherrill's great motto—is sustained outrage," Ivins says in her low, gravelly voice. "It doesn't matter how cynical you get about politics; it doesn't matter how slow or how long it takes, as long as you still have the capacity to become angry over injustice." But the trick is to stay angry over injustice without becoming cynical, she says. "You can laugh or throw up: I choose to laugh."

Ivins works at getting her readers to laugh with her while provoking them to think. People don't read newspapers because they tend to be so dull, Ivins says, and she writes her column in an effort to get people interested and involved in politics. "The best way to do that is to get them to laugh." She has mastered the barbed one-liner, which she hurls with relish at politicians from the president of the United States on down. "We all enjoy laughing at politicians," she says. "It's better than the circus. You might as well watch the show; you're paying for it anyway."

Although Ivins had written a column for ten years, she finally agreed to national syndication only in 1992, and the column took off immediately. Within three months more than a hundred newspapers had purchased it, according to Richard Newcombe, president of Creators Syndicate, which distributes the three-times-weekly essay. Newcombe says there had been some concern that Ivins's column was too regional in focus, too Texas-oriented, for national syndication, but that concern proved unfounded. "She's everything a newspaper columnist should be," he says: "witty, insightful, interesting, and she offers insights and perspective offered nowhere else."

Peter Bronson, editor of the *Cincinnati Enquirer* editorial page, agrees. He decided to buy Ivins's column because "she's a good writer and she approaches things with a spicy viewpoint." Bronson says he thinks Ohio readers can appreciate the regional flavor of Ivins's writing; his only worry is that national syndication will cause her to lose her unique Texas style and turn her into "the same bland oatmeal we get coast to coast."

The syndication of Ivins's column coincided with her transfer to the *Fort Worth Star-Telegram* after the demise of the *Dallas Times Herald*, where she had worked since 1982. Although the *Herald* had distributed Ivins's column to a dozen other Texas papers, her national audience had consisted primarily of people who read her pieces in such liberal magazines as the *Progressive* and *Mother Jones* or who had seen her on the "MacNeil-Lehrer News Hour." But after her 1991 collection of columns, *Molly Ivins Can't Say That, Can She?* made the *New York Times* Best Seller List and stayed there six months, her agent persuaded her to try syndication. "The book made her incredibly hot as a personality," says Dan Green. "People wanted to get to know her; people wanted to hear more from her," he says. "She delivers the goods." Asked if people are desperate for an honest voice, Ivins replies, "People are desperate to laugh, for God's sake."

Ken Bunting, assistant managing editor at the Fort Worth paper, put Ivins's column on the front page when she joined the paper in March. It was a radical move, which Bunting says he knew would be controversial. "It has raised some eyebrows and some ire," he says.

Readers demanded that the column be dropped. Many cancelled their subscriptions. After the column had run for four weeks, Bunting was checking the printouts and didn't see any cancellations because of Ivins's column. "I said, Molly, you're slacking off," Bunting jokes. Even after six months, some readers were still irate, but complaints had tapered off. "After a while, they get used to you," Ivins says. "It's not that the right wingers are ever going to agree with me, but they get used to the voice and are not so outraged by it."

Not much seems to faze Ivins, but the national success of her writing caught her by surprise. She said Random House editors told her they would be pleased to sell 20,000 copies of her book. But close to 100,000 hardback copies were sold, and a 100,000 copy press run was planned for the paperback edition. After appearing on national television and radio to talk about her book, Ivins found herself a celebrity. She had gotten used to being recognized in Texas and to receiving calls and letters from readers, but she wasn't prepared for the fallout following the book's publication.

"The recent phenomenon of becoming a celebrity, of becoming mildly famous, was difficult for me. I've been happy for years being a maverick and outsider," she says. "It was very disconcerting to get fed into what I consider to be this immense celebrity manufacturing machine and to get spit out the other end." Ivins's reaction to the publicity was so negative she went to a therapist to find out whether she was suffering from fear of success. "Then, fortunately, my paper died and I wound up broke and unemployed, and I felt a lot better about it all," she says, pausing before she delivers the punchline. "I've decided I don't suffer from fear of success, I suffer from fear of becoming an asshole." A friend told her, "Molly, it's okay to say you've been on the Letterman show and you're going to be on the Tonight show, but when you say 'I've done David and I'm going to do Johnny,' then you have something to worry about."

One of the stranger twists for Ivins was learning that the new central character in the television series "Designing Women" would be modeled after her. The Ivins-type character was to be "a Texas woman who doesn't move her mouth when she talks," Ivins says. "It strikes me as somewhere between ludicrous and disconcerting that a character in a television series would be based on me. . . . I thought, 'Jesus, you're not dead.'"

Ironically, Ivins had considered putting together a one-woman show based on her book. She says she thought it would be fun to try, but realized she was too busy and needed to make some choices. "I decided I am a writer and that's what I need to concentrate on." She also realized she doesn't have time to get involved in making a movie or creating a tv series from her book.

To help with the flood of requests for speaking engagements and other public appearances, Ivins hired Liz Faulk, the widow of Texas humorist and First Amendment defender John Henry Faulk, to screen her mail and phone calls and help with scheduling. Ivins answers every piece of reader mail that's signed and has a return address. "I have a system," she says with a deadpan drawl. "Now, on even numbered days I read my mail with great attention—especially if they're angry about something I've written—in hopes of learning something. Is there some piece of information that impressed this person? Was it a cheap shot I took that sent up their hackles? On odd-numbered days, I just say 'F— 'em if they can't take a joke.'"

Sometimes the mail is unsigned, and sometimes it's vicious. She shows a visitor a recent letter, oozing hate, which she says is fairly typical. The writer, who signed his name but didn't give a return address, not only attacked her political views but ripped apart Ivins's appearance, suggesting she was a lesbian feminist. All columnists get mail from fans and enemies, but what Ivins finds perturbing about missives like this is that the writer attacked the way she looks, something that is unlikely to happen to a male columnist.

It reminds her of the time she was criticized by a male columnist at another paper for a column she had written about the criminal justice system. The columnist was condescending, referring to her as "that little Molly Ivins." At six feet, Ivins was mildly amused at the reference but irked because he had attacked her on the basis of her gender, not the issues she had raised. Ivins replied in her column that "perhaps he had a hard time distinguishing between his brain and his dick." When an editor at the *Times Herald* changed "dick" to "nether organs," Ivins complained: "I said, 'The problem with that is the dumb sum-bitch is going to think I meant his feet.'"

Routinely sprinkling her conversation with four-letter words, the kind that appear in print with only the first letter followed by dashes, Ivins explains, "I have a foul mouth." But she rarely uses expletives in her columns, instead picking up on the creative, often hilarious way her sources speak. "I like strong and flavorful language and I like the fact that Texas politics is conducted in strong and flavorful language," she says, "and it seems to me a disservice to turn that into pablum." Although her political stance is consistently liberal, conservatives and others opposed to her politics read her column because of her skill in capturing a regional flavor. "I write Texas," she says. She also enjoys playing with words, and her dislike for President Bush is intensified by the way he butchers the English language.

One of the more famous anecdotes about Ivins's love of language involves a story she wrote that ended her career at the *New York Times*. She had been at the *Times* for six years and was Denver bureau chief, covering nine states, when she wrote a feature about a community chicken slaughter in a small town. She described how everyone sat around drinking beer, listening to music, and plucking chickens. Unable to resist the pun, Ivins called it a "gang pluck." Her editor was irate, and Ivins returned to Texas soon afterward and started the column.

She is known for her candor, toughness, and the ridicule she heaps on public officials; her writing has been called uninhibited. She presents an I-could-care-less public image, dressed in slacks and a t-shirt at work, driving around the state capital in a half-ton pickup truck. But Ivins also has a quieter, more reflective side. Her voice grows softer and more deliberate as she talks about her journalistic standards. For example, she says she is scrupulous about keeping her promise to a source not to print information given "off the record" or "not for attribution." She says she would never knowingly print something that wasn't true, and she isn't interested in writing about the private lives of politicians, including the dalliances of presidential candidates such as Bill Clinton or Gary Hart. "I could probably wreck many marriages with what I know," she says, "but I wouldn't do that unless it affected public business. I'm not spending my life finding out who sleeps with whom. That's not what I do."

She would have reported on former U.S. Congressman Wilbur Mills's tryst with a stripper after they fell into the Washington Tidal Basin together, because then it became part of the public record, and because Mills's alcoholism was affecting his public duties. Otherwise, the media has no business probing people's private lives, she says. "For the press to set itself up as the judge of character is sheer hypocrisy—there's no less likely group of moral stalwarts than the gang on the bus. I think we've gotten ourselves in a terrible bind."

Ivins has plenty to write about without delving into politicians' private lives, and she says as long as the Texas legislature meets, she can't help but be funny. "Look at the material. I've practiced journalism all over the country, and the material isn't as good anywhere else . . . you can't make up stuff this good." Ivins is modest about her part in shaping the material, and she says it makes her "squirmy" to talk about her writing. "It's amazing how uncomfortable it makes me to be asked, 'How do you write?' It's like being asked, 'How do you know how to walk?' If you think about it too much, you won't be able to do it."

Ivins follows in a long tradition of American writers who use humor to comment on politics. "We are entitled to laugh," she says. "There's far too much unthinking respect given to authority." But it can be tricky to write humor. "It's much easier to be funny when you're speaking, because you can, with an expression—the lift of an eyebrow or a gesture—indicate that you're just kidding. And, of course, an enormous amount of humor is in the timing, as any comedian can tell you. When you write humor, you have to write in the pauses, which is a matter of thinking, skill, and experience."

She is most concerned about the potential for aiming humor at the wrong target. "It's something that I've thought a lot about. This is one of those thundering generalizations, so brace yourself: There are two kinds of humor—a wonderful healing kind of humor that draws people together and makes us chuckle over our foibles and makes us recognize our common humanity, and the kind of humor that holds people up to ridicule and contempt." Ivins frequently uses the latter—satire—which she describes as the weapon of the powerless against the powerful, the pen against the sword.

She is disturbed by what she sees as a trend of aiming satire at powerless people, citing comedians who make fun of gays, women, cripples, and minorities. It has reestablished a climate where racism and racist jokes are accepted, she says. "It seems to me that to aim satire at powerless people is not only cruel but profoundly vulgar. It bothers me a great deal to see it misused."

In a decade of writing the column, Ivins's biggest regret is having wounded people with her humor when she didn't mean to. "I have had that experience more times than I care to remember," she says. One incident stands out: a friend who was a conspiracy theorist wrote her shortly after Grace Kelly died from an automobile accident to say that the pope was responsible for Kelly's death. That struck Ivins as funny, and she wrote a tongue-in-cheek column in which she named her friend and told what he had said. A few days later she received a letter from him saying he had never realized he was a figure of fun, that he had considered himself a serious student of history, and that her column had caused him real pain. "I have never gotten over that. To this day I still wince," she says, "and that's the reason I don't often write about civilians—people who are not in politics."

Politicians are a different story. "As far as I'm concerned, politicians are in sort of a free fire zone," she says. "I mean, nobody put a gun to their heads and forced them to run for public office." She's not worried about the fact that her column might deter anyone from running for public office, saying, "I seriously doubt that anybody who had political ambitions was deterred by the fact that somebody might write something comical about them. [Politicians] have real power; you don't."

Political reporters often wind up seeking approval from the people they're covering; they become part of the establishment. Ivins intends to remain a maverick. She has borrowed her journalistic philosophy from the late columnist I.F. Stone, who said that in order for a journalist to remain independent, "you must sit in your bathtub and not want anything." While Ivins has done a lot of drinking with politicians over the years, it hasn't kept her from writing about them. Even harder than maintaining a distance from sources, she says, is to stop wanting the esteem of one's peers.

Writing the column is relatively easy; Ivins says she likes writing as much as she likes eating. She can crank a column out in an hour, though she prefers to have at least three. "The more time I spend on a column the better it is," she says. "If I can let it marinate, then go back and look at it, I can always make it a little bit better." At the 1992 Democratic national convention, she wrote a column in twenty-four minutes when Ross Perot dropped out of the race. She writes at a computer watched over by a stuffed armadillo, and revises as she goes along. "Frequently I don't know when I start how I'm going to end up," she says. Each column is about 1,000 words, and Ivins says writing copy that length has become second nature—even letters to her mother turn out to be 1,000 words. Although her writing is only lightly edited, she gets annoyed when editors change her sentences, particularly where the editing affects the rhythm of a phrase.

The toughest part of writing her column is coming up with an idea. Ivins says she identifies with the bumbling, alcoholic columnist on the old "Lou Grant" show, who inevitably whined, "Has anybody got a good idea for a column?" Two-thirds of the time her ideas come from the newspaper; she finds she's either "laughing hysterically or absolutely furious." When she can't find something in the news to write about, she turns to the files of newspaper clippings that fill cabinets along one wall of her office. Readers also supply ideas. Her editors at both the *Herald* and the *Star Telegram* told her that if she ever came up dry she should call and tell them. She's done that twice in ten years.

"It's the smartest thing I ever heard of," she says. "It's better not to write than to write just some tedious piece."

When she started writing a column, she had a fantasy that she would work ahead, get two or three columns in the can, and be able to do some investigative reporting. "It never happens. I'm always writing on deadlines. You never get ahead, never." Like other columnists, Ivins feels the pressure of trying to produce a gem every time. The worst thing about writing a column, a columnist friend told her, is that you don't always hit a home run. You've got your doubles, triples, and singles, and sometimes you just walk. Ivins says in most cases she is fortunate to have interesting material, which enlivens her copy.

Ivins writes for her readers, "those to whom I owe my loyalty; I don't write for my peers, I don't write for politicians." Even though she's nationally syndicated, she thinks of herself primarily as a *Fort Worth Star-Telegram* columnist. Writing for readers means remembering why you're writing, she says. Politics is a fascinating game, and political writers can get caught up in the skill with which it's played. "They forget the chips on the table are people's lives," she says with intensity.

Besides writing her column, Ivins is working on a book she hopes will help readers understand and become involved in the legislative process. She has focused on the death of a bill in the Texas legislature that would have required mandatory brake inspection for trucks. A year after the bill died in committee, a truck with failed brakes rammed a school bus and killed more than thirty children. Through such stories, Ivins wants to show how legislation directly affects people's lives. She hopes to finish the book by the end of 1993. Someday she would like to write a book about Mexico.

Although Ivins had been a reporter for several years before she began writing a column, it was not difficult for her to make the transition to writing opinion. In fact, she had chafed under the requirements of objective reporting in her first reporting job at the *Minneapolis Tribune*. "I was terribly frustrated by the constraints of objectivity and traditional styles of newswriting," she says. "I felt increasingly unable to describe what I really saw, particularly in the context of the civil rights turmoil of the 60s, within an establishment daily newspaper." So she returned to Texas in 1970 to edit a small alternative paper, the *Texas Observer*, and "to help bring about the revolution." She loved working at the *Observer*, a hard-hitting weekly that has been the training ground for many well-known Texas writers, and she became accustomed to taking a point of view in her stories.

But after six years at the *Observer*, she found herself doing stories she had already done.

In 1976, she accepted an offer to join the *New York Times*, and in doing so she says she traded journalistic freedom for the clout of a mainstream national newspaper. She remembers one *Times* story in particular, a front-page exposé she wrote on the appalling conditions at government-operated uranium mines, which resulted in a congressional investigation and changes in the law regulating miners' insurance. "That one front-page story did more good than six years at the *Observer*," she says. In the end, she was forced to choose between that kind of clout and journalistic freedom. When the offer came from the Dallas paper to write a column—with the promise of total freedom—she chose the column. "I decided for who I am, freedom is worth more than clout," she says. Writing a column didn't seem that different from her *Observer* experience, and she says she was never scared, but excited by the prospect: "My reaction was 'Wow!'" She recalled what a pioneering woman pilot, Katherine Stinson, told a reporter who asked how a woman could be brave enough to fly: "My Mamma always told us not to be afraid of getting hurt. Of course, we got hurt, but we were not afraid."

Raised in a conservative Houston family and educated at private schools and at Smith College, Ivins began developing her own political ideas as a young child. She remembers thinking that adults were lying when they told her not to drink out of the "colored" fountain because it was dirty. "When you can see that the colored fountain is cleaner, you know something's not right. I grew up knowing the falseness of that." Once she realized she was being lied to about race, she began questioning everything else she was told. In high school she was a rebel who read the existential philosophers, and she was sympathetic to the civil rights movement.

As a teenager, her goal was to become the Great American Novelist, but she says she soon realized she'd better find another way to make a living. She decided to become a foreign correspondent, thinking it would be fun to roam around the world and get paid for it. In fact, that was one reason she joined the *New York Times*. "I assumed I would also get married and have five children, and do this with no difficulty at all," she says, sighing. "Ah well."

Her introduction to journalism came during two summers of work in the Complaints Department at the *Houston Chronicle*, where she says she learned what readers really care about. After graduating from Smith in 1966 with a degree in history, she earned a master's degree from Columbia Journalism School and studied for a year at the Institute of Political Science in Paris before going to work for the *Minneapolis Tribune* as a police reporter. She still reads widely, including Spanish and French newspapers and news magazines and a number of conservative journals and newspapers. "I read everything I can get my hands on," she says. "Your mind is like any other muscle— if you don't use it, it shrinks, atrophies. Just as pianists practice scales, journalists need to read."

Rejecting a comparison with "Prairie Home Companion" creator Garrison Keilor, Ivins says Keilor's humor brings people together and makes us laugh at our common foibles. "I practice something else entirely," she says: "Satire, which is holding people up to contempt because they deserve it. I believe in democracy. I relish our Texas politicians, and I want other people to relish them, too, in all their glorious folly.

"I want people to be involved. I want them to know how funny and wonderful [politics] is and how it's affecting their lives. In an age when information is power, the best I can do is be sure it's disseminated widely and appears in something that doesn't cost more than a quarter."

South Sure to Rise above Expectations of Yankee Pundits

NEW YORK. Am in the Big Apple posing as an expert on Texas politics. I'm besieged by local scribes seeking enlightenment. "Tell us," they beg, "What about Tsongas? Will Texans vote for a man with a name like Tsongas?"

I have assured them that Tsongas is a name familiar to every Texas voter. I have not explained that's because Tsongas is the fifth line of the eye chart when we go to get our drivers' licenses renewed. Some things are better left to mystery.

One always has the disconcerting impression while here, playing Professor Irwin Corey, World's Greatest Authority, that no one is really listening. If, when asked some question about Bill Clinton, you were to reply "Ishkabibble," no one would be surprised. Instead, they'd all write it down as yet another example of just how strange and quaint those bizarre Texans are.

The question inevitably occurs to the Texan in New York, "Just how dumb do these people think we are?" And the answer is, y'all don't want to know. A Southern accent still stereotypes you as a borderline moron in this part of the world. In the national consciousness, the three enduring images of the South—magnolias, moonshine and mint juleps—are balanced against a portrait of hateful rednecked bigots. But more powerful than both those stereotypes is the notion that all of us are slack-jawed, slope-browed ridge-runners.

It's impossible to exaggerate the extent of that impression: It is so deeply imbedded in American popular culture that it's a wonder we don't have a National Association for the Advancement of Southern People. In all American war movies, there are three buddies who serve together from their first day in basic to the heroic deaths of one or more of them. The hero is always a clean-cut blond kid from the Midwest with two pals: One is a fast-talking, dark-haired ethnic wiseacre from New York and the other is a Southerner too slow to tell c'mon from sic'em.

Where do they get these ideas? What to my wondering eyes should appear a couple of years ago in *The New York Times* but the headline "Old Southern Custom, Dirt-Eating, Seen On Wane." I'm a lifelong Southerner and I've never met a mud-muncher myself. Roy Blount, a distinguished son of the South, was moved to invent an entire menu based on this to-him-novel regional custom. Blackened red dirt. Red dirt and rice.

The effects of this prejudice on national elections as they move into the South is dramatic and depressing. You may recall what happened in 1988. The whole slew of candidates headed South after New Hampshire and began talking less about compassion and more about leadership. They boldly endorsed a strong national defense,

fearlessly stood up for traditional family values and courageously swore they'd never raise taxes. Jesse Jackson won seven states, including Texas.

Look what we're getting this time. The national press corps has already decided we're too dumb to vote for Paul Tsongas. The fact that he has a funny name will presumably matter more to us than whether he's talking sense. Pat Buchanan arrived in the South and promptly began running ads that claim President Bush supports pornographic and homosexual art. Look, I'm prepared to believe a great many things about George Bush that do not reflect credit upon him, from his conduct as head of the CIA to the reasons he dragged us into that war with Iraq. But there is no way in hell you can convince me that George Bush promotes and supports pornographic, homosexual art. How dumb do these people think we are? Give us a break, will you?

Our homeboy Bill Clinton we're supposed to reject because he failed to volunteer to fight in Vietnam, a war he didn't believe in, thus showing how dumb he was. And everyone knows that the mere mention of sex in relation to a politician causes all Southerners to react like Tennessee fainting goats: We promptly flop over on our backs with our legs straight up in the air, out cold from horror.

George Bush, never one to overestimate the intelligence of the voters himself, has been going around presenting us with his program for economic recovery: "The United States is the greatest country in the world," he explains. I don't know. Complex economics like that may be too much for us.

I for one can hardly wait to see what the South will do with all this condescension. I have visions of a Jerry Brown sweep from Wink to Bobo. Not a bad idea, actually. The reason Jerry Brown is having a better time than anyone else in this campaign is because he's free to tell the truth—he's the little kid yelling that the emperor has no clothes. Of course this is a corrupt political system. Of course the elections of one candidate over another, or one party instead of another, will not change squat until we change the way campaigns are financed. They'll just keep dancin' with them what brung 'em. I think we ought to amaze all these Yankees and vote for the man telling the truth. Whatthehell?

[*March 5, 1992*]

Let's Quit Chewing on Rubbergate and Tackle Real Issues

AUSTIN. Rubbergate gets funnier and funnier. The sight of Secretary of Defense Dick Cheney, surrounded by generals dripping with brass, explaining it all to us with charts and pointers was too fabulous.

Didn't you expect Gen. Schwarzkopf to show up any minute to explain, "First the check went here, then we made an end run around the bank balance, but the enemy recorded the maneuver on its high-tech satellite, so . . ."

Now, the president says that for all he knows, *he* might have bounced some checks when he was in the House—'cause the whole system was so screwed up.

This reminds one of the theme song of the John Wesley Hardin Fan Club (not to be confused with the John Dillinger Died for You Society): "*He wasn't really bad; he was just a victim of his times.*"

The excuse for misbehavior and even crime, which liberals are prone to ponder but which conservatives have always rejected with righteous indignation, is that one's environment has something to do with how one behaves.

Hey, if a 16-year-old kid whose mama was on drugs and whose daddy decamped before he was born, who grew up in the projects surrounded by drugs and crime, who gets abused by his stepfather and sent to a crummy school where he never learns to read; if that kid winds up committing a crime and it's all his fault, how come Newt Gingrich was writing bad checks? Did Tom Foley really make him do it?

Wuss of the Year Award goes to the Minnesota congressman who made his wife stand up and take the blame. He stood there with his arms crossed, like, "Boy, is she gonna get it when we get home."

The ineffable Charlie Wilson of Lufkin, who disappointed many of his fans by appearing so low on the list of the Big 24, observed, "Piety must be a terrible burden to try to bear through one of these things."

And unctuous self-righteousness even worse.

Don't you think some group of Capitol Merry Pranksters ought to at least short-sheet Gingrich's bed?

Your Responsible Observers—
David Broder springs to mind—are
concerned lest all this lead to some
dire loss of faith in government, a
debilitating degree of cynicism that
might even damage democracy.

Nah, let the sun shine on them
all: We've got enough sense to take
a real close look at he who casts the
first stone.

Bill Clinton, who has not yet
been accused of writing bad checks,
has been trying out an interesting
line of late: "Look, I'm not a
perfect person." As a qualification
for the presidency, it has a certain
charm.

We are now living in an oddly
confessional culture—television
chat shows from Oprah to Geraldo
to Sally Jessy to Jenny Jones are
peopled by citizens "sharing" with
the rest of us what it is like to be
married to impotent partners, or a
victim of incest, or to be a cross-
dressing dwarf. It is enough to
make one yearn for a resurgence of
that fine old New England trait,
reticence.

The trouble with this chat-show
confessional genre is that rather
than increasing genuine empathy
for those suffering life's more
outrageous slings and arrows, it
remains a shallow, titillating form
of entertainment, designed more to
appeal to our prurient interests
than to extend our understanding.
It may be true that we are all
sinners, as Jim Bakker and Jimmy
Swaggart were so fond of
reminding us, but the sad fact is
that many of us still prefer to dwell
on that comforting, self-righteous
sense that sinners and even victims
are Very Different from ourselves.
They deserved it.

What would happen if we all
grew up enough to admit that we
aren't perfect and neither is anyone
else, even granting that some of us
come a lot closer than others? I'm
not qualified to address what the
effect on our immortal souls might
be, but it sure would go a long way
toward curing the hypocrisy and
self-righteousness that mar our
politics.

Then, when we hit a Rubbergate,
instead of having to watch these
disgusting displays of either
abasement or blame-shifting, we
would find pols with the sense to
say: "There it is. It's wrong, so let's
change it."

And then we could all get back to
worrying about more important
stuff, like how to fix the economy,
make some progress toward social
justice and get rid of the
designated-hitter rule.

We so rarely get a chance to
rejoice in unmitigated good that
it behooves us not to let an
opportunity go by. On Tuesday, the
white people of South Africa voted
by 69 percent to proceed toward
democracy for all the citizens of
that country. Lord knows, it will
not be easy, but they did the right
thing. After all the tragic history
that country has endured, what a
triumph for the good.

If it does not sound
presumptuous, I would like to add
my tiny mite of congratulation to
them all.

[*March 19, 1992*]

In Texas, Attitude Makes Up for Lack of Altitude in Men

AUSTIN. A colleague from out of state called to inquire, "What *is* it about these Texas runts?" He meant the political runts with an attitude. "I'm talking about Ross Perot, Claytie Williams, John Tower, Bill Clements. What *is* it with these people?"

I explained that it is not easy to be a short, male Texan. If you can't be a long, tall Texan, our tradition calls for you to weigh in with at least 130 pounds of bad attitude to make up for it.

Nor is the phenomenon limited to Republicans and right-wingers. For example, both Jim Hightower and Sam Rayburn could be listed as runts with attitude, except that, since they're Democrats and thus politically correct, we would have to call them vertically impaired, or possibly differently abled height-wise.

Several readers have written to object to my having referred to Ross Perot as a chihuahua. Actually, this was not intended as a reference to his size, or even to the size of his ears. It was his voice I had in mind; he yaps.

Now, my readers have pointed out that Perot's physical characteristics, including his stature or lack of it, have nothing to do with his qualifications for the presidency, with which I heartily concur. I was merely attempting a descriptive analogy. He does sound like a chihuahua. Under no circumstances would I suggest that this bars him from the presidency. Harry Truman also sounded like a yapping dog, but it had no effect on his presidency.

Well, much as I have enjoyed playing with Perot, whom I actually rather like, I'm afraid it's time to point out a few of his failings beyond Bad Haircut.

Ross Perot is a liar. It's really quite striking and leaves me with a certain respect for professional politicians, who lie with such artistry, such deniability, such masterful phraseology that they can always deny their denials later on.

Perot lies the way Henry Kissinger used to lie but without Kissinger's air of grave, weighty authority. Perot just flat out lies. What's more, when he lies, he accuses everyone else of lying. He never said this; he never said that; he never said the other. They're making it all up. They're all liars.

They're all out to get him. You should check on their reputations (hint, hint).

Some bidness expert explained the other day that Perot lies like that because he's an entrepreneur, and those guys are always out on such limbs that they have to lie. It was a new theory to me.

Perot is seriously into paranoid, right-wing conspiracy theories. Actually, this is not news. We've known this about him for years. But now we have to do some serious thinking about what it means to have a president whose grip on reality is both infirm and elastic.

By now your humble servants in the ink trade have documented Perot's connections to Lyndon LaRouche-ites, Christic Institute fantasists, Ollie North at his wiggiest (Perot says Ollie is lying, Ollie made it all up, no such thing ever happened) and various oddball spinoffs of the there-are-still-POWs-in-Asia theory.

Ross Perot spies on people. Perot keeps saying he didn't know anything about instances of EDS employees being spied on. Maybe so. But he hired a P.I. to snoop on Sen. Warren Rudman of New Hampshire, a P.I. to snoop on some of the *contra* stuff, sent his own company lawyer and two pilots to check into parts of the October Surprise scenario, offered to show supposedly incriminating photos to the *Star-Telegram* publisher and to a *Washington Post* reporter.

I don't like the way the guy plays. If he can't have it all his way, he takes his ball and goes home. Whether it's the promise of a big donation to a Dallas charity or General Motors, Perot's been a bully and a quitter. And no matter whom he crosses or who crosses him, his story is always the same: He's completely in the right and the other guy's completely in the wrong.

I think it is a damned lousy idea to vote for anyone who's paying for his own campaign. You've all heard me complain for however long you might have been reading this column about the way we finance elections in this country. It's sorry, it's sleazy and it's got to stop.

But the biggest loophole in the campaign law right now is that it puts a $1,000 limit on contributions to campaigns for federal office *unless it's your own campaign.*

Well dammit, we already know this system is giving us a government of the special interests, by the special interests and for the special interests. The players in politics all have or have access to big money. That's what's wrong with the government of this country.

OK, so maybe we figured that at least Perot wouldn't owe anything to the usual chorus of special interests. I mean, if it was all his money, maybe he'd actually work for *us.*

But look, in the first place, it's bad enough the extent to which rich people and their bought lackeys already run this country. Why make it worse?

In the second place, look at Perot's proposals. He, like Bush, favors a cut in the capital gains tax: That's the move that helps rich people. He also wants to take away Congress' power to levy taxes. In a speech to the National Press Club, he proposed this startling notion and said, "You say, 'Well, that means a constitutional amendment.' Fine."

I don't like people who think it's fine, chop-chop, no big deal, to change the Constitution of this country. I think Madison and Jefferson and Adams and all those guys were wiser than Ross Perot. I think they put the right to tax in the branch of government closest to the people for good reasons. Perot says he wants to throw out the current tax system and start with a blank piece of paper. But he hasn't said what he wants to write on it. Don't you people think issues aren't important?

Ronnie Dugger has pointed out that since presidents have already ripped up one of the major constitutional powers of Congress—to declare war—and Perot wants to remove another, that would leave Congress with just one important power: to spend.

Except that Perot wants the right to veto any appropriation passed by Congress.

Let's see, that would give him war, peace, taxes, spending. Can anyone think of anything else he'd need to be our first dictator?

[*July 9, 1992*]

[Ivins's columns originally appeared in the *Fort Worth Star-Telegram*. Copyright © 1992 by Molly Ivins. Reprinted by permission.]

SELECTED BIBLIOGRAPHY

Alexander, Shana. *The Feminine Eye*. New York: McCall Publishing, 1970.

Babb, Laura Longley [of the *Washington Post* Writers Group], ed. *The Editorial Page*. Boston: Houghton Mifflin, 1977.

Beasley, Maurine H. *Eleanor Roosevelt and the Media*. Urbana: Univ. of Illinois Press, 1987.

Belenky, Mary Field, et al. *Women's Ways of Knowing: The Development of Self, Voice and Mind*. New York: Basic Books, 1986.

Belford, Barbara. *Brilliant Bylines: A Biographical Anthology of Notable Newspaperwomen in America*. New York: Columbia Univ. Press, 1986.

Bombeck, Erma. *Just Wait Till You Have Children of Your Own*. Garden City, N.Y.: Doubleday, 1971.

———. *I Lost Everything in the Post-Natal Depression*. New York: Ballantine Books, 1974.

———. *The Grass Is Always Greener over the Septic Tank*. New York: McGraw-Hill, 1976.

———. *If Life Is a Bowl of Cherries, What Am I Doing in the Pits?* New York: McGraw-Hill, 1978.

———. *Aunt Erma's Cope Book*. New York: McGraw-Hill, 1979.

———. *Erma Bombeck Giant Economy Size*. Garden City, N.Y.: Doubleday, 1983.

———. *Motherhood: The Second Oldest Profession*. Boston: G.K. Hall, 1984.

———. *Four of a Kind*. New York: McGraw-Hill, 1985.

———. *Family: The Ties That Bind . . . and Gag!* New York: McGraw-Hill, 1987.

———. *I Want to Grow Hair, I Want to Grow Up, I Want to Go to Boise*. New York: Harper & Row, 1989.

———. *When You Look Like Your Passport Photo, It's Time to Go Home*. New York: Harper Collins, 1991.

Broder, David. *Behind the Front Page*. New York: Simon & Schuster, 1987.

Brody, Jane E. *Secrets of Good Health* (with Richard Engquist). New York: Popular Library, 1970.

———. *You Can Fight Cancer and Win* (with Arthur I. Holleb). New York: Quadrangle/New York Times Book Co., 1977.

——. *Jane Brody's Nutrition Book*. New York: Norton, 1981.

——. *Jane Brody's* The New York Times *Guide to Personal Health*. New York: Times Books, 1982.

——. *Jane Brody's Good Food Book: Living the High Carbohydrate Way*. New York: W.W. Norton, 1985.

——. *Jane Brody's Good Food Gourmet*. New York: W.W. Norton, 1990.

Brown, Charlene R., Trevor R. Brown, and William L. Rivers. *The Media and the People*. New York: Holt, Rinehart and Winston, 1978.

Cohen, Richard. "The Syndicated Columnist." In *Gannett Center Journal*, Spring 1989, 9-15.

Day, Dorothy. *The Long Loneliness*. New York: Harper, 1952.

Edwards, Julia. *Women of the World: The Great Foreign Correspondents*. New York: Ivy Books, 1988.

Edwards, Verne E., Jr. *Journalism in a Free Society*. Dubuque, Iowa: Wm. C. Brown Co., 1970.

Eells, George. *Hedda and Louella*. New York: G.P. Putnam's Sons, 1972.

Ellsberg, Robert. *By Little and By Little: The Selected Writings of Dorothy Day*. New York: Alfred A. Knopf, 1984.

Emblidge, David, ed. *Eleanor Roosevelt's "My Day."* Vol. 2, *1945-52*. New York: Pharos Books, 1990.

——. *Eleanor Roosevelt's "My Day."* Vol. 3, *1953-62*. New York: Pharos Books, 1991.

Emery, Edwin, and Michael Emery. *The Press and America: An Interpretive History of the Mass Media*. 6th ed. Englewood Cliffs, N.J.: Prentice-Hall, 1988.

Flanner, Janet. *Janet Flanner's World: Uncollected Writings, 1932-75*. New York: Harcourt Brace Jovanovich, 1979.

Geyer, Georgie Anne. *Buying the Night Flight*. New York: Delacorte Press/ Seymour Lawrence, 1983.

——. *Guerrilla Prince: The Untold Story of Fidel Castro*. Boston: Little, Brown, 1991.

Gilliam, Dorothy. *Paul Robeson, All-American*. Washington, D.C.: New Republic Books, 1976.

Gilligan, Carol. *In a Different Voice*. Cambridge: Harvard Univ. Press, 1982.

Gilmer, Elizabeth Meriwether. *Dorothy Dix—Her Book*. New York: Funk & Wagnalls, 1926.

Goodman, Ellen. *Turning Points*. Garden City, N.Y.: Doubleday, 1979.

——. *Close to Home*. New York: Simon & Schuster, 1979.

——. *At Large*. New York: Summit, 1981.

——. *Keeping in Touch*. New York: Summit, 1985.

——. *Making Sense*. New York: Atlantic Monthly Press, 1989.

Grauer, Neil A. *Wits & Sages*. Baltimore: Johns Hopkins Univ. Press, 1984.

Grossvogel, David I. *Dear Ann Landers*. Chicago: Contemporary Books, 1987.

Heilbrun, Carolyn G. *Writing a Woman's Life*. New York: Ballantine Books, 1988.

Heibert, Ray Eldon, and Carol Reuss. *Impact of Mass Media: Current Issues*. 2nd ed. New York: Longman, 1988.

Janeway, Elizabeth. *Between Myth and Morning: Women Awakening*. New York: William Morrow, 1974.

Kurth, Peter. *American Cassandra: The Life of Dorothy Thompson.* Boston: Little Brown, 1990.

McCarthy, Colman. *Involvements.* Washington: Acropolis Books, 1984.

Mankiewicz, Frank. "From Lippman to Letterman: The Ten Most Powerful Voices." In *Gannett Center Journal,* Spring 1989, 81-96.

Martin, Judith. *The Name on the White House Floor and Other Anxieties of Our Time.* Coward, McCann and Geoghegan, 1972.

———. *Miss Manners' Guide to Excruciatingly Correct Behavior.* New York: Atheneum, 1982.

———. *Miss Manners' Guide to Rearing Perfect Children.* New York: Atheneum, 1984.

———. *Common Courtesy.* New York: Atheneum, 1985.

———. *Style and Substance. New York: Atheneum, 1986.*

———. *Miss Manners' Guide for the Turn-of-the-Millennium.* New York: Pharos Books, 1989.

Marzolf, Marion. *Up from the Footnote: A History of Women Journalists.* New York: Hastings House, 1977.

Maynard, Joyce. *Looking Back: A Chronicle of Growing Up Old in the Sixties.* Garden City, N.Y.: Doubleday, 1973.

———. *Domestic Affairs.* New York: Times Books, 1987.

Meyer, Karl E. *Pundits, Poets & Wits.* New York: Oxford Univ. Press, 1990.

Miller, William D. *Dorothy Day: A Biography.* New York: Harper & Row, 1982.

Mills, Kay. *A Place in the News: From the Women's Pages to the Front Page.* New York: Dodd Mead, 1988.

Newhouse, Nancy R., ed. *Hers: Through Women's Eyes.* New York: Harper & Row, 1985.

Porter, Sylvia. *Sylvia Porter's Money Book.* Garden City, N.Y.: Doubleday, 1976.

Post, Edwin. *Truly Emily Post.* New York: Funk & Wagnalls, 1961.

Pottker, Jan, and Bob Speziale. *Dear Ann, Dear Abby.* New York: Dodd, Mead, 1987.

Quindlen, Anna. *Living Out Loud.* New York: Random House, 1988.

———. *Object Lessons.* New York: Random House, 1991.

Quinn, Jane Bryant. *Everyone's Money Book.* New York: Delacorte Press, 1979.

———. *Making the Most of Your Money: Smart Ways to Create Wealth and Plan Your Finances in the 90s.* New York: Simon & Schuster, 1991.

Ricchiardi, Sherry, and Virginia Young. *Women on Deadline.* Ames: Iowa State Univ. Press, 1991.

Roberts, Nancy L. *Dorothy Day and the* Catholic Worker. Albany: State Univ. of New York Press, 1984.

Sanders, Marion K. *Dorothy Thompson: A Legend in Her Time.* Boston: Houghton Mifflin, 1973.

Schlipp, Madelon Gordon, and Sharon M. Murphy. *Great Women of the Press.* Carbondale: Southern Illinois Univ. Press, 1983.

Seldes, Gilbert. *The Seven Lively Arts.* New York: Sagamore Press, 1957.

Shaw, David. *Journalism Today: A Changing Press for a Changing America.* New York: Harper's College Press, 1977.

———. *"The Death of Punditry."* In *Gannett Center Journal,* Spring 1989, 1-8.

Sheed, Wilfrid. *Essays in Disguise*. New York: Alfred A. Knopf, 1990.

Showalter, Elaine. "Feminist Criticism in the Wilderness." In Elizabeth Abel, ed., *Writing and Sexual Difference*. Chicago: Univ. of Chicago Press, 1982.

Society for Professional Journalists. *What a Free Press Means to America*. Chicago: Society for Professional Journalists, 1984.

Steel, Ronald. *Walter Lippmann and the American Century*. New York: Vintage Books, 1981.

Stephens, Mitchell. *A History of News: From the Drum to the Satellite*. New York: Penguin Books, 1988.

Tannen, Deborah. *You Just Don't Understand: Men and Women in Conversation*. New York: William Morrow, 1990.

Warren, Joyce W., ed. *Ruth Hall & Other Writings (by) Fanny Fern*. New Brunswick, N.J.: Rutgers Univ. Press, 1986.